NATURE'S KEEPERS

NATURE'S KEEPERS

The New Science
of Nature Management

STEPHEN BUDIANSKY

THE FREE PRESS
New York   London   Toronto   Sydney   Tokyo   Singapore

The Free Press
A Division of Simon & Schuster Inc.
1230 Avenue of the Americas
New York, N.Y. 10020

Printed in the United States of America

printing number

1 2 3 4 5 6 7 8 9 10

Text design by Carla Bolte

Library of Congress Cataloging-in-Publication Data

Budiansky, Stephen.
    Nature's keepers: the new science of nature management / Stephen
Budiansky.
        p.   cm.
    Includes bibliographical references and index.
    ISBN 0-02-904915-6
    1. Nature conservation.   2. Man—Influence on nature.
3. Philosophy of nature.   4. Ecosystem management.   I. Title.
QH75.B823   1995
333.7—dc20   95-24100
                                                            CIP

To Martha

Till their own dreams at length deceive 'em
And oft repeating, they believe 'em.
—Matthew Prior

CONTENTS

PART I

Nature Myth

ONE

"Good Poetry, Bad Science"

If this were a conventional nature book in the mode of Thoreau and his countless latter-day imitators, I should begin by describing the walk I took early this morning across field and wood. How I rejoiced in the cry of the Canada geese overhead and the flash of the white tail of a fleeting deer; how the crackling of the frosted grass beneath my feet as I crossed a hollow by the wood put me in mind of the family of wild turkeys I had seen there early in the fall; how my spirit, indeed my every pore, was open to the sweet beneficence of Nature's society unfettered by the artifices of man. No worldly thoughts could intrude upon so perfect a reverie—unless it were that ever so slightly nagging doubt that even such unassailable testimony to my earnestness, sensitivity, renunciation of materialism, and oneness with creation had failed to make up for an utter lack of originality.

But this is not a conventional nature book, and so I shall begin instead by pointing out how everything I saw this morning was a fake. Everything that I might plausibly have passed off as an example of nature raw, pure, and untamed was, in truth, nothing but the work of civilized man. The very grasses in my field are aliens, for a start, timothy and bluegrass and red clover brought to America by seventeenth-century English settlers trying for a better hay crop. The sheep and horses and cattle that enrich the soil with their dung are alien imports, too. But for their constant grazing, and for the annual visit of the haying machines, the open acres that stretch from my window to the copse at the bottom of the hill would in just a few years' time be choked with brambles and red-cedars. But even that could hardly be counted a natural process; the return of woods to abandoned farm fields is not nature reclaiming her birthright but nature led only farther astray. Red-cedars readily take over abandoned pastures today only because centuries of grazing by livestock has unnaturally suppressed the hardwoods, such as oaks, that would otherwise outcompete the red-cedars; the very abundance of red-cedar today is an artifact of the dietary preferences of imported farm animals.

Along with a taste for hardwoods and an aversion to red-cedars, the settlers' livestock brought to the New World a host of plants that now fill my fields and woods. Stealing a ride in shipboard fodder or in the guts of cattle and sheep and horses came the seeds of nightshades, thistles, plantains, chickweed, dandelions, and hundreds of other now common plants.[1]

The woods down the hill are themselves every bit as much a fake, second growth on land cut over at least once, probably several times, in the last three hundred years. The Canada geese, which once migrated every spring and fall, now stay year round in great flocks, growing fat and lazy on farmers' cornfields. On local golf courses and parks their abundant droppings have become a health hazard; the state of Virginia has instituted an unprecedented upland goose hunting season in an attempt to cope with the problem; so far, the geese, exploiting their artificial niche to the utmost, are winning hands down.

The deer and turkey meanwhile thrive in an artificial patchwork of forest openings formed of cultivated and abandoned fields. Wildlife biologists in Virginia estimate the state's deer population at one million, five times the number that existed here when Europeans first arrived. But even the pre-Columbian deer population had been artificially inflated for millenniums previous by the Indians' practice of regularly setting fire to the wood. Fires cleared the forests of thick underbrush, encouraging patches of grass and shrubs to grow in the clearings and attracting deer and other game to feed and flourish.[2]

If I set forth to look beyond my artificial view across my artificial fields to the artificial wood atop the Catoctin Mountains, I would find nothing but more fakery stretching in any direction I chose to travel. On San Francisco's Angel Island State Park, western monarch butterflies congregate in groves of eucalyptus trees transplanted from Australia a century ago. In Scotland, rare alpine birds nest on heather moors created and maintained by burning and sheep grazing. In the tropical rain forests of Central America, thousands of years of slashing and burning at the hands of corn-growing agriculturists have cut deep scars across these lands, too—lands that, in popular myth, have come to be sacred monuments to biodiversity, the fragility of Spaceship Earth, and the seamless interconnected web of all life, excepting only, of course, human life. After ten thousand years of breaking the soil, after a hundred thousand years of setting fire to the forests and the plains, after a million years of chasing game, human influence is woven through even what to our eyes are the most pristine landscapes.[3]

Such observations do not go down well these days. The fashion of our times demands that nature be a setting for soul-stirring contemplation of the infinite and unknowable, a cathedral to be entered with hushed tones and reverent thoughts, a place of God's, not man's. The nature lovers of our age jealously cling to an image of nature virginal and pure; they imagine an Arcadian wilderness where balance and harmony reign, beyond the defiling touch of man. The entire modern conception of nature depends upon denying her checkered past. Those who dare to point out man's overwhelming role, and overwhelming responsibility, in shaping even the wildest parts of the natural world are usually made to feel about as welcome as an astrophysicist at a fundamentalist Bible study class that has just taken up Genesis.

Nature lovers are hardly the first to have deceived themselves about the true character of their beloved, and we all know why lovers do that. But abetting the lovers of nature in their innocent infatuations are those prolific and less forgivable writers of trash romance that one exasperated wildlife expert has called "nonpracticing ecologists."[4] Open any popular nature book, magazine, tract, or fund-raising letter, and you do not have to read far to encounter the phrase "balance of nature" or, if not those precise words, some equivalent statement of the notion that nature, if only it is left alone and freed from human influence, tends toward a state of harmony, balance, and beauty—and conversely, that wherever man treads is trouble. "The ecological perspective begins with a view of the whole, an understanding of how the various parts of nature interact in patterns that tend toward balance and persist over time," writes Vice President Al Gore in a book whose very title, *Earth in the Balance*, invokes this notion. A mailing from the Natural Resources Defense Council, an environmental lobbying and litigation organization, reprints an interview with a Cree Indian who is quoted as saying, "The earth was created in the way it was by the Creator, and changing it is unnatural and wrong." A series of educational videotapes for children that aims to promote "greater ecological awareness" offers such messages as "this ancient forest is capable of sustaining itself if not interfered with by humans" and "changes in nature upset the delicate balance for animals and man." The Massachusetts Society for the Prevention of Cruelty to Animals complains that hunting leads to a "disruption of natural ecosystems [that] imperils the lives of non-prey animals."[5] These ideas have become such an accepted part of our culture that they are now the routine stuff of advertising and commerce, good for hawking a twenty-two-dollar "All Things Are Connected" T-shirt or a multimillion-dollar Disney movie featuring ecologically conscious lions who pontificate about the "circle of life."

This picture of nature as a place of eternal order, balance, and separate purpose, a place whose very survival depends on the absence of man and his works, is one that finds little acceptance among ecologists today, if indeed it ever did. These are beliefs that predate the emergence of ecology as a science. They have persisted in spite of what ecology has taught us. They form, in the words of the ecologist Daniel Botkin, a contemporary "mythology" about nature and the environment, a mythology whose roots lie deeply buried in our culture, in "unspoken, often unrecognized" assumptions.[6] A belief in nature's inherent perfection has for more than a century been almost inseparable from a love and appreciation of nature; the love and the belief arose hand in hand in a flush of romantic revulsion against the Industrial Revolution. But great cultural reactions tend to be overreactions, and those romantics of the eighteenth and nineteenth centuries who flouted millenniums of conventional wisdom to find beauty in wild places so long despised as malevolent or evil invented an idealized nature that animates our imaginations still. They confused the inner peace they found in escaping from the tribulations of civilization with the outer reality. Nature, so long feared as the killer of men and the literal place of the devil, became the perfect and uncorrupted work of God's creation—a place perfect in itself, owing its perfection to the very absence of man and his corruptions.

Over time this conception of nature has answered a variety of aesthetic, spiritual, ideological, and even nationalistic urges. It has done so only too well. Today many nature lovers innocently believe that the "balance of nature," or the notion that every species is interconnected in a delicate "web of life" that will collapse if but a single strand is cut, or the idea that "nature knows best" how to manage itself are scientific statements of fact derived from modern ecological research. Ecologists have been trying for more than half a century to disabuse the public of these ideas, and they seem to have almost given up. "Good poetry," said one frustrated ecologist of the balance-of-nature idea, "but bad science."[7]

He might have added "bad policy." The vision of nature as a primitive wilderness of ancient, towering woods teeming with wildlife, unchanging, eternal, self-perpetuating, shaped only by forces beyond man's control or ken, underlies countless official policies. It is rarely even questioned. Federal wilderness areas in the United States are defined, by law, to be places "where the earth and community of life are untrammeled by man, where man himself is a visitor who does not remain." The official management goal for America's national parks is the re-creation of the landscape that supposedly existed before 1492, and current park policy holds that the means to achieve this is, likewise, the exclusion of all human influence.

The inescapable fact that millions of Indians lived throughout North America for several thousand years prior to that magical date is dealt with by the easy assumption that the Indians were (depending on one's political persuasions) either primitive savages incapable of altering their environment in any significant way or ecological saints whose religion of reverence for nature forbade them to do so. The fires they set on a spectacular scale and the game they killed on an equally spectacular scale are conveniently ignored. And so, having

banned the hunters and extinguished the fires, having freed nature to
return to its primeval state of balance and order, our parks today are
overrun with elk, our woods are choked with alien Norway maples,
the western ranges are trampled by feral burros, and the once vast,
open savannas are overtaken by oaks and pines. Meanwhile we passionately and reverently protect dense, unbroken "old-growth" forests
and huge populations of deer and elk that in truth never before existed in the ten-thousand-year history of postglacial North America. A
policy of "preservation" through noninterference has nearly wiped
out endangered woodland plants, has killed ancient stands of aspens
in the western parks, has led to a vast accumulation of explosive tinder
that is now waiting to erupt in fire storms of unprecedented magnitude across "wilderness" areas, and has so distorted the composition
of animal and plant life that even such projects as the restoration of
the wolf to Yellowstone National Park, so dear to the hearts of nature
lovers, may have been rendered an ecological impossibility.

Bad enough that these miscarriages of ecological management have
taken place; worse is how passionately they are defended by the faithful believers in the wilderness myth. Strict preservation through a
hands-off or "natural" management policy has destroyed many of the
very things that nature lovers claim to value the most. But perhaps it
has proved easier to concede the loss than the principle. Dense, tangled woods overrun with animals fit the mythical vision of wilderness
too well. Open savannas or scorched clearings or elk so scarce that
they are seen but once in a lucky lifetime do not.

Perhaps more to the point, excluding man has become an end in itself. What many nature lovers want, after all, is solitude; the active intrusions that it would take to purge the land of alien grasses and weeds
with tractors and herbicides, or restore the oak savannas with bulldoz-
ers and fires and chain saws, or bring back the aspen and beavers of
Yellowstone with rifles leveled at the park's elk are not part of the program they have in mind for their wilderness experience. "Space
enough to separate you from the buzz, bang, screech, ring, yammer,
and roar of the twenty-four-hour commercial you wish hard your life
would not be . . . Wilderness that is a beautiful piece of world, a place
where you can be serene, that will let you contemplate and connect
two consecutive thoughts, or that if need be can stir you up as you

were made to be stirred up, until you blend with the wind and water and earth you almost forgot you came from." Thus spake David Brower, the eminent conservationist who headed the Sierra Club and the Friends of the Earth in the 1950s, 1960s, and 1970s. The scene of blissful solitude he sets forth has been evoked with little variation by nature lovers from Henry David Thoreau's and John Muir's day to ours.[8]

Yet a more anthropocentric view of nature is hard to imagine. There are no ecological goals in this vision, only human ones; the chief end is serenity, and the chief means to it the exclusion of man— excepting only the writer of such words, of course, who is out tending to the business of stirring up his soul in solitude. And so time and again nature lovers launch earnest efforts to "save" from human depredation landscapes or wildlife populations that are nothing but the recent and unnatural creations of man's interference, while they rail against "interference" of a kind that in truth has shaped and perpetuated for millenniums the nature they love.

An example: When Ontario's Rondeau Provincial Park was established on the north shore of Lake Erie in 1894, no deer were observed within its eight thousand acres. Though quite small, the park is the largest remaining example of Carolinian forest in Canada today—a unique assemblage of vegetation that is home to the largest breeding population of prothonotary warblers in the country. The park is also one of only two remaining habitats of the nodding pogonia, a rare orchid.

In 1899, five captive deer escaped from an enclosure in the park. Their numbers quickly multiplied. For many years rangers kept the deer in check by shooting them, but the culling program finally ended in 1973 after park authorities grew weary of constantly defending themselves against protests by animal rightists and other public groups opposed to the shootings. Since then, the deer population has once again grown rapidly, reaching about five hundred in 1992. The deer have browsed clearings hundreds of yards across, virtually stripping bare the forest floor of new seedlings of white pine, red oak, black cherry, and shagbark hickory and so bringing regeneration of the forest to a halt. A new plan to cull the deer herd to about one hundred animals, the maximum number that a study concluded could be sustained without damaging the park's vegetation, has met with the inevitable and vigorous objections of the Committee to Save the Rondeau Deer.

It is assuredly "unnatural" for park rangers to shoot hundreds of deer. But what, biologists who have studied the situation ask, is there left that is "natural" about Rondeau? It is unnatural for deer even to live on this patch of land. It is unnatural for eight thousand acres of wood to be totally surrounded by land intensively managed for agriculture. It is unnatural for wolf populations to have declined, for Indian hunters to have moved off and changed their way of life, for fires to have been fought, for exotic plants to have invaded. The saviors of the deer ignore a century of passive assaults and focus only on the active assault of rifle-toting men. "Land is managed with tremendous intensity and devotion around the park, and naively we believe we can just leave [Rondeau] alone," said one biologist who has studied the Rondeau deer. "The park is too small, too different, too isolated not to be managed."[9]

The explosion of deer populations has been a worldwide phenomenon for the last half century; so too has been the slow death of even the largest parks and forests as a result of management policies based on the ideal of noninterference. A ten-year study of the forests of Pennsylvania established a clear link between the increase in deer and the resultant loss of songbirds, woodland wildflowers, and overall biotic diversity. As deer increase from ten to sixty-four per square mile, underbrush is stripped bare, nesting sites vanish, and the number of species of songbirds in the wood drops from eighteen to twelve.[10] In

Figure 1. "Natural regulation" at work: Yellowstone's northern elk herd has grown dramatically since the park stopped trying to limit its size. The herd now far exceeds both its historic size and the Park Service's own estimate of the "carrying capacity" of the range.

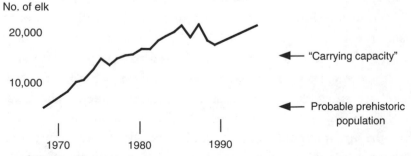

Data from Kay, "Yellowstone's Northern Elk Herd," 27–28; Yellowstone National Park, *Wolves for Yellowstone,* IV:4-35, 4-56.

Yellowstone, where elk populations have quadrupled since the park adopted a "natural regulation" policy in 1969, signs of overbrowsing are everywhere in evidence, too. One of the few places in the park where the aspens and willows are doing well is a place that park biologists, public proclaimers of the principle of natural regulation, will not point out: a plot just south of Mammoth that is ringed with an exclosure fence to keep the elk out.

Does it even matter what is natural and what is artificial anymore? The problem is too many deer and elk; the solution in Rondeau and Yellowstone and much of the rest of the world, wildlife biologists say, is simple, obvious, and straightforward—shoot more of them. "What does that tell you," complains one biologist involved in the Rondeau controversy, "when we can't even make the simple decisions?"[11]

It certainly does not bode well for making the more subtle and complex decisions. Man's long history as an agent of change in nature and nature's own perverse tendency toward disorder and complexity pose a complication that simple policies built upon the idea of nature's innate balance cannot even begin to cope with. The effects of man are often woven subtly into the very evolution of the landscape. Fires started by Indians and lightning once kept the forests of Yellowstone relatively young and suppressed insect pests and plant diseases.

Figure 2. Years of fire suppression in Yellowstone led to a huge accumulation of dead trees; the historic pattern of frequent small brush fires has been replaced with infrequent infernos.

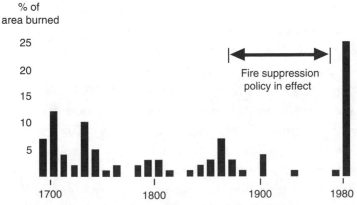

Adapted from Romme and Despain, "Yellowstone Fires of 1988," 696.

A century of fire suppression has saved the forests from burning only to make them old and decayed and ridden with pine-bark beetles and other pests now ravaging the woods in and around Yellowstone—that is, in those areas that escaped the huge 1988 fires, which were allowed to burn in the name of the new natural regulation policy but which achieved a most unnatural (or, at the least, a very rare) intensity, stoked as they were by a century's worth of accumulated deadwood that would otherwise have been burned off in smaller brush fires.[12]

The inherent instability of plant and animal populations is another subtlety that escapes the simple prescriptions of nonpracticing ecologists. The enduring belief in the balance of nature notwithstanding, catastrophes are always occurring in nature and on every scale of time and space, from a cold spring day that kills a fledgling robin to a glaciation that wipes out the species. Small, isolated populations—such as are likely to be found in protected parks and reserves—are all the more susceptible to such vicissitudes of nature. A flood, a fire, a hurricane, a blight, or a decade of cold winters can alter an area the size of New England for a millennium or more. When the hemlocks of New England were attacked by a fungus or insect pest five thousand years ago, the ensuing massive dieback persisted for two thousand years. These are not just turns about the never-ending "natural cycles" of self-regulating nature. They are *history*, events that affect the course of all that follows.[13]

Countless popular nature articles repeat the theme that predator and prey keep one another in check. "The wolf tears apart the frail and sick caribou not only to ensure its own survival but to maintain the balance of nature," a correspondent to *Harper's* magazine recently wrote, arguing that although human infliction of suffering upon animals is wrong, what happens in nature is "simply part of a larger cyclical design."[14] The story of Isle Royale, Michigan, has often been told by nature lovers eager for scientific affirmation of this belief in nature's balance. The island had been overrun with moose from the turn of the century until the cold winter of 1949 froze Lake Superior and wolves from the mainland trekked across the ice. From that point on, the story goes, the populations of predator and prey have tracked one another like two swinging pendulums joined by a spring. Wolf numbers grow, moose numbers fall; wolves fall and moose grow; and

Figure 3. Ignoring an entire generation of nature writers who extolled Isle Royale as a model of harmonious, self-regulating interaction of predator and prey, the wolves now stubbornly insist upon heading for extinction.

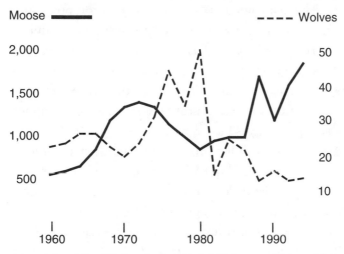

Adapted from Mlot, "Isle Royale: End of an Era?"; Peterson, *Wolves on Isle Royale.*

so on ad infinitum. Each population traces a perfect sine wave pattern through time.

The only snag with this appealing story is that since the early 1980s the moose population on Isle Royale has once again grown unchecked while wolf numbers plunge rapidly to zero, a consequence, at least in part, of the wolves' extremely narrow genetic base: DNA studies have shown that all of the island's wolves were descended from a single female. Wildlife biologists believe that extinction of the wolves is now all but certain.[15]

It is not a good bet that any isolated patch of land or life which, through accident of history, ended up as a public trust for the preservation of nature will very long escape the fate of nature through all recorded time. A lone surviving twenty-acre tract of primeval hardwood forest on Mt. Pisgah, New Hampshire, was donated to Harvard University in 1927 for preservation and study; eleven years later it was leveled by a hurricane, and so went the last stand of "virgin" forest in New England. A forty-two-acre forest of towering white pines in Cornwall, Connecticut, called "the most magnificent stand of trees in New England," was similarly reduced to a heap of fallen timber by a hurricane in 1989. The two-hundred-year-old trees, known as the Cathedral Pines, had stood 150 feet tall. After the storm, the Nature Conservancy, which had been given the forest in 1967 under the condition that the land be maintained in "a natural state," promptly issued a press release explaining that the hurricane "was just another link in the continuous chain of events that is responsible for shaping and changing this forest" and announcing that it planned to allow the forest to continue to take its "natural course." With the single exception of agreeing to clear a fifty-foot-wide firebreak around the perimeter, that is in fact what the managers have done.[16]

Yet the whole incident was full of irony. The majestic stand of towering pines was a pure artifact—not virgin forest at all, but second growth that sprung up on land cleared of hardwoods and then probably farmed for a time in the late eighteenth century by colonists. White pine stands were rare in New England before farmers began clearing fields. At the time the trees of the Cathedral Pines were seedlings—sprouting, most likely, in the grass of an abandoned cow pasture—Timothy Dwight, the president of Yale College, wrote that all the pinewoods of New England could fit into a single county.[17] White pines grew only on rocky hilltops and burnt-over patches where hardwoods fared poorly; everywhere else, the hardwood canopy would shade out the sun-loving pine seedlings, which could never compete against the shade-tolerant hardwoods.

But on the cleared ground of old fields, the wind-blown pine seeds found their moment waiting. By the turn of the twentieth century, when farming in New England had long passed its high water mark with the nation's westward expansion and hundreds of thousands of acres of fields lay abandoned, white pines were so predominant in central New England that early foresters who studied the region believed such forests were the natural, predominant vegetation type for the area; they actually designated it the White Pine Region.[18]

So the "continuous chain" of events that had made the Cathedral Pines an object of admiration and the impassioned focus of more than a century of efforts to protect and preserve it were from the start artificial.[19] The woods were not in "a natural state" to begin with when they were handed over to the Nature Conservancy with the injunction to maintain them as such. Yet when a number of local officials, as well as local admirers of the site, suggested it might make sense to clear the fallen timbers and perhaps even replant the wood, environmental purists redoubled their calls to let nature take her course, denouncing the advocates of tampering with nature's sublime plans as guilty of the crime of anthropocentrism or worse. One scientist at the Yale School of Forestry told reporters, "If you are going to clean it up, you might as well put condos on it."[20]

But why? Cleaning it up would have been no worse an ecological sin than its very existence in the first place. Before the hurricane struck, no one ever suggested that such a pure artifact as an unbroken stand of white pines in central New England might just as well be replaced with condos.

Scientists at the California Department of Parks and Recreation actually did on one occasion try to apply this sort of logic; they advocated ripping out the eucalyptus trees from the state's public parks on the grounds that they are exotic, non-native species. The nature lovers screamed again. They liked these big trees. So, it turned out, did the butterflies and birds, who were far less doctrinaire about it all than the parks' environmental scientists. For whatever reasons, 57 percent of the bird species in Angel Island State Park were found to frequent the eucalyptus groves, and 8 percent were found exclusively there. The western population of the monarch butterfly seems particularly partial to the trees, too, probably because they provide both shelter and food (in the form of nectar from the trees' flowers). Researchers who surveyed sites in coastal California where the butterflies overwinter found that 75 percent of the 112 sites contained eucalyptus trees. The other sites contained mainly native conifers, but even these native stands were not "natural"—the trees had been planted, by humans, outside of their natural range.

Of course, monarch butterflies did once manage to get along very well without trees imported from Australia. Given the history of the last one hundred years, that is now, however, beside the point. The question that matters now is what will happen if those trees are removed. As one scientist noted, it is not as if a mature forest of fifty-to-one-hundred-year-old trees can be quickly replaced with native species of the same size. Even if the eucalyptus trees were removed, the return to the presumed natural state of vegetation at the parks is by no means assured. Of the 416 plant species identified on Angel Island, 53 are non-native; many are widely dispersed throughout California, spread by their abundant, wind-borne seeds. Maintaining the natural order is at the very minimum a full-time weeding job.[21]

The invasion of exotic plants and animals is comparatively well known. America's environmental purists have learned to take no pleasure in the sweet smell of honeysuckle, they remark disapprovingly of English sparrows, and kudzu, the catastrophically lush vine that was imported to control erosion on hillsides but has now taken over vast stretches of the South, is a national joke. Less well appreciated is the equally sweeping transformation of the landscape brought about by the suppression of fire over the last three centuries. In the American Midwest, suppression of fire has let pines and oaks form dense stands on what were once open savannas. Where, in the mid-nineteenth century, as few as four trees per acre stood amid prairies of tall grasses and forbs, a hundred years later stand dense forests with unbroken canopies. To let nature literally take her course is not one of the options any longer; as the biologist Jared Diamond remarked in reference to a prairie restoration project outside of Madison, Wisconsin, "the city of Madison obstinately and disgracefully refuses to let fires in the city just follow their natural course."[22] The more usual interpretation of letting nature follow her course in this case would be to exclude any overt acts by people—which means to have oak and pine forests, not prairies. The irony is that to have nature be "natural" requires constant human intrusion. Restoration projects have been remarkably successful in reconstructing and maintaining native savannas and prairies through the use of clear-cutting followed by regular, deliberate burning. The artificial is more natural than the natural.[23]

"Nonpracticing ecologists" justify their preference for a wilderness devoid of man and his traces in a variety of ways, from the supposedly scientific to the frankly pragmatic to the outright mystical.

The claim that nature exists as a delicate structure woven of deep, even impenetrable interconnections that humans tamper with at their peril is often attributed to modern ecological research. "We must not disturb the hierarchical balance of nature and the food chain," writes the physician and former antinuclear crusader Helen Caldicott in a book that champions her new cause of saving the planet from environmental disaster. "The earth has a natural system of interacting homeostatic mechanisms similar to the human body's. If one system is diseased . . . then other systems develop abnormalities in function."

The historian Donald Worster, an influential and oft-quoted writer on environmental philosophy, asserts that "the idea that nature is orderly, that its order is rational and effective, that it is for the most part a stable, self-equilibrating order, is the most precious idea modern science has given us."[24]

And Vice President Gore claims, "We are unlikely to know enough about the effects of what we are doing to predict the consequences for other parts of the system—precisely because all its parts exist in a delicate balance of interdependency."[25]

Worster frequently invokes the ecological theory of succession and "climax" as scientific proof of this inherent order and purpose in undisturbed nature. According to this turn-of-the-century theory, a community of plants—a forest, a meadow, a prairie—exists as a "superorganic whole." It matures through a series of life stages in predetermined order, arriving at last at a mature, stable, and enduring "climax" community. Thus, one of the primary lessons of ecology, Worster argues, is that nature has a purpose of its own that man must bow to.

But to attribute such ideas to ecology is to draw a crude caricature of ecology, one that drives practicing ecologists to distraction. Climax theory has not been taken seriously by ecologists for more than half a century. The idea that communities of plants form a superorganism with properties greater than the sum of their parts, or that groups of organisms somehow interact with a common, higher purpose, is treated by most contemporary ecologists as quaint at best, mumbo jumbo at worst. "Of course some will argue that natural ecological systems have holist properties that represent more than the sum of their parts plus their interactions," one researcher dryly notes. "If this is so, the study of these systems should perhaps be carried out by theologians rather than scientists."[26]

The persistent enthusiasm for such ideas among contemporary nature lovers and their readiness to attribute them to the word of science is revealing. Even some environmental advocates who surely know better cling to these long-discredited ideas, testimony both to the power of the myth and to its practical utility. Donald Worster, for one, goes so far as to concede that climax theory has its problems, but he's not ready to let go of the idea. The reason, it seems, is that it is simply too effective a political tool to lose. He explains:

> One of the most important ethical issues raised anywhere in the past few decades has been whether nature has an order, a pattern, that we humans are bound to understand and protect and preserve. It is the essential question prompting the environmentalist movement in many countries. Generally, those who have answered "yes" to the question have also believed that such an order has an intrinsic value . . . on the other hand, those who have answered "no" have tended to be in the instrumentalist camp: They look on nature as a storehouse of "resources" to be organized and used by people. . . . This is as fundamental a moral cleavage as one can find these days.[27]

For Worster, the political value of climax theory—he calls it a "threat to the legitimacy of human empire"—is apparently more important than such a hairsplitting detail as its having been long discredited by scientific research (as we shall see in chapters 4 and 5). To abandon "climax ecology," Worster fears, "would be to remove ecology as a scientific check on man's aggrandizing growth."[28]

Worster is walking a fine line here between science and politics, and he knows it. Many environmental activists do not try to finesse the point so nicely but simply argue that conceding the acceptability of human intrusion, even for the best of reasons, will open the door to exploitation for the worst of reasons. This is the fear that nature management will, as one Canadian environmentalist put it, become a "fig leaf behind which business hides." The only way to insure that the condos don't go up is to maintain, almost as a kind of cultural taboo, an absolute stricture on human interference in lands set aside for nature conservation.[29]

Putting aside any philosophical ruminations over nature's inherent order and purpose, activists will often argue, too, that nature can't possibly do a worse job than people have done in managing things. An insistence on "hands off" is thus often an expression of skepticism, and it is a view that cannot be dismissed out of hand. The success rate of those who have claimed to be able to manage nature does not inspire confidence. The whole history of wildlife and forest management is one of arrogance, naïveté, and unintended consequences. Shooting thousands of wolves, coyotes, and bobcats, part of a program vigorously pursued early in the century to "improve" the National Forests, does not in retrospect seem like a very good idea. Attempts at managing ocean fish stocks have led to the collapse of entire fisheries. Planting of forest monocultures has set off huge disease outbreaks. Straightening rivers and draining wetlands has imperiled entire ecosystems. An engineering mentality, an attempt to impose one-dimensional and definitive solutions on a complex and changing reality, a naive enthusiasm for simplistic and even rather silly mathematical models, has long characterized the entire profession. Nature is indeed very good at making scientists look ridiculous. Thus, the skeptics will say, and with some justification, if we have to take our pick between letting nature call the shots henceforth or turning things back over to the same people who messed things up, we would just as soon take our chances with nature. "Our track record is of one failure heaped on top of another," one environmentalist says; "judging by our past record," says another, "any attempt to change ecological systems on a large scale is going to do far more harm than good."[30]

But many of these oft-cited failures, while certainly fair illustrations of the complexity of nature and of human shortsightedness, are hardly fair measures of the state of modern ecology and its ability to offer intelligent guidance. The Dust Bowl of the 1930s showed what happens when ignorance, greed, erodible soil, and a drought are combined; it may be a bit much, however, to claim, as many have since, that it is proof that man can never meddle with nature without making things worse.[31] As we shall see in part III, computer modeling, aided both by an influx to ecology of mathematicians with a much more sophisticated and realistic approach to the mathematical understanding of ecosystems and by field experiments that put these ideas to the practical test in reconstructing and restoring ecosystems, has vastly improved the state of applied ecological knowledge in recent years. The search for patterns and processes in nature has certainly affirmed the truth that there are no simple answers; indeed one lesson is that any answers must take into account the inescapable uncertainties that chance and complexity impose. But, especially in cases where the goal is to maintain primitive landscapes whose very features reflect centuries of shaping by human forces or to protect endangered species in preserves that are unavoidably subject to human influence from beyond their boundaries, to do nothing is to make a "management" decision by default. No matter what we choose to do, nature is being shaped by man. We can recognize the fact and try to deal with it, or we can ignore it and accept the consequences. The one thing we cannot do is remove human influence simply by closing our eyes to it.

Perhaps precisely because science has failed to back up their vision of nature, environmentalists have, with growing frequency in recent years, taken to invoking arguments that might at best be called outside the realm of science. Even some quite mainstream environmental advocates can be heard these days mumbling about vibrations or psychic connections or "deep" ecology. "It seems to me that a collective biological consciousness must exist," writes Farley Mowat, a prominent Canadian environmentalist best known for the book (and later the movie), *Never Cry Wolf.* "All life forms are inter-connected in physical ways; it makes no sense to deny a psychic connection," Mowat insists. He even gives an indulgent nod to the far-out ideas of "ecofeminism," quoting with approval an ecofeminist author who explains that "[women] are biologically and spiritually connected to the cosmos, its planetary shifts, the earth's tides and the phases of the moon." In his book Vice President Gore does not mention ecofeminism by name, but he too buys into some of the odder ecofeminist contentions, in particular the claim that mankind once worshiped a great earth goddess—a "religious heritage," Gore calls it, marked by "a reverence for the sacredness of the earth—and a belief in the need for harmony among all living things."[32]

The mystical expression of the belief in the "natural balance" is also found in a growing number of statements to the effect that everything from the industrial accidents at Bhopal and Chernobyl to topsoil loss, deforestation, and extinctions is a result of the human race having fallen "out of balance," not only with nature but with our inner selves. "I began to feel . . . that something was wrong with our entire world view," is a typical formulation; this author then goes on to blame the spiritual paucity of our "mechanistic world view" not only for environmental problems but for just about everything else in the world that bugs him, including "stupefying" jobs, the "absurd" arena of politics, violence, mental illness, suicide, alcoholism, overuse of Valium, and the fact that relationships are "vapid and transient." Another author in this vein writes: "A crucial dimension of this imbalance in the West is the stunted growth of our mystical awareness and the underdevelopment of our mystical brain." He adds, by the way, that this insight came to him in a dream.

It would be easy to dismiss this as a bit of fringe nonsense. Nonsense it may be, but fringe it is not; this particular book, written by Matthew Fox, a theologian at the Institute in Culture and Creation Spirituality at Holy Name College in Oakland, California, is frequently cited in the large and growing academic literature on the ethical and moral dimensions of environmentalism. The Vice President has his contribution to offer on this subject, too: "The more deeply I search for the roots of the global environmental crisis, the more I am convinced that it is an outer manifestation of an inner crisis that is, for lack of a better word, spiritual. . . . I have come to believe in the value of a kind of inner ecology that relies on the same principles of balance and holism that characterize a healthy environment."[33]

The quasireligious belief that nature has its own plan that always works for the best even when we mere humans might be tempted to think otherwise is in one sense no different from other great ideas that have seized the imagination of men over the eons; the overpopulation of elk in Yellowstone no more disturbs a believer in the balance of nature than does a massacre in Cambodia shake the belief of the devout in a loving God or a stock market crash the libertarian's faith in laissez-faire.

Like all such powerful ideas, the idea of nature as wilderness—as something separate, eternal, pristine, and harmonious—has in many ways become more important than the reality it purports to describe. Like one of Evelyn Waugh's world-weary, cynical, and doubting Catholics who still find comfort and beauty in the idea of faith, so nature lovers who concede the delusion of wilderness still cling to that delusion; indeed, it is the delusion that really matters to them. Their objection to overt meddling with nature is not so much that man will screw things up, but that the very knowledge it has been meddled with shatters the beautiful dream. Thus the writer Bill McKibben's extended complaint titled "The End of Nature," in which he laments, "The world outdoors will mean the same thing as the world indoors, the hill the same thing as the house. An idea can become extinct, just like an animal or a plant. The idea in this case is 'nature'—the wild province, the world apart from man." Having declared nature thus defined dead, he concludes:

> We have deprived nature of its independence, and that is fatal to its meaning. Nature's independence is its meaning. . . . Having lost its separateness, nature loses its special power. Instead of being a category like God—something beyond our control—it is now a category like the defense budget or the minimum wage, a problem we must work out.[34]

It is on these grounds that some lovers of the idea of nature object even to restoration projects that aim to undo man's undeniable damage. Some couch it in aesthetic terms; to alter nature for aesthetic ends destroys its very aesthetic, which consists in the idea that it has not been altered. "I argue that value exists in nature to the extent that it avoids the domination of human technological practice," states one critic. "A restored nature is a fake nature; it is an artificial human creation, not the product of a historical natural process." Leaving nature alone, on the other hand, "lays the seeds for the subversion of the imperial domination of technology." This critic admits that the closest contact he has with wildness, the deer he encounters near his home on Fire Island, are rather pathetic specimens of the "wild"—they are artificial in their abundance, he knows, they are tame, even rather grubby, coming up to the backyard for handouts all the time. But still he wants to keep them: not because they are an essential part of a functioning ecosystem, not because they are a vignette of the primeval landscape, not because they are part of the seamless interconnected web of life, but because they satisfy—an idea. "My commitment to the preservation of the deer in my community," he explains, "is part of my resistance to the total domination of the technological world." The deer aren't even the point. They are simply serving a larger purpose, as a sort of ideological manifesto.[35]

There are a lot of fancies jumbled together here: nostalgia, dissatisfaction with civilization and technology, a longing for solitude, a wish to be overawed and spiritually exalted, all topped with a generous dollop of self-indulgence. McKibben is revealing when he speaks wistful-ly of Thoreau being able to list the five white men who had climbed Mt. Katahdin before him; or when he wishes that his neighbors in the Adirondacks, who unreasonably insist on spoiling his sense of solitude by erecting things like a street light a half mile from his house, would go away, and allow him to experience "the nature that matters," includ-ing raccoons rattling about his garbage cans. *His* garbage cans, that is, but presumably no one else's. Nature isn't for the developers, but it's not really for the raccoons, either: It's for me. And so we are back to nature as a place where man is to be excluded because we *want* man to be excluded and not for any reason beyond that.[36]

There is a terrible confusion of goals and means in all of this. "Hands off" ought to be looked upon as merely one possible management tool for achieving a desired end. Its suitability ought to be judged sole-ly according to whether it can achieve that end—whether that goal is protecting a beautiful landscape or an endangered species, maximiz-ing biodiversity, or ensuring a sustainable supply of fish or lumber. In-stead it has come to be seen as an end in itself, justified after the fact by hand-waving arguments that assert it can also deliver the goods. It rarely can. The ideal of nature as a wilderness where man's influence is to be expunged has had an effect on our modern relationship with the natural world that cannot be overestimated. It has brought us to a point of crisis in conservation as we approach the end of the twentieth century. To a great extent, the policies that govern our parks, forests, endangered species—everything from town deer-hunting ordinances to international treaties—reflect the wishful ideal that nature is self-regulating and that the preservation of whatever we find desirable in nature can be achieved by eliminating humans from the scene.

This crisis is quite apart from the policy debates that have raged since the 1970s over endangered species versus economic develop-ment, trees versus jobs, backpackers versus RV enthusiasts, "preserva-tion" versus "sustainable development" or "multiple use" or "wise use." Whether it's more important to use our forests as a source of lumber or as a source of inspiration is a question about which science offers no answers. Indeed, much of the tenor of these debates has only served to further obscure the essential part that man must play in nature, no matter what. People have tended to line up on the question of whether humans should manage natural systems according to the purpose to which they would have nature put. Interventionists have usually supported their stance by arguing the benefits of civilization: Preservation is a waste of valuable resources; management, on the other hand, has tamed inhospitable nature, making it a suitable habitat for man while simultaneously supplying the necessities of a good life—lumber, electric power, food, and jobs. Anti-interventionists have argued the human need to experience a landscape free of clear-cuts, hydroelectric dams, and cattle ranches or have pointed to the utilitarian benefits of wetlands as pollution filters or tropical rain forests as reservoirs of genetic diversity.[37] Both have missed the point. Regardless of what kind of nature we would have, it is up to us to make it happen. The choice is not materialistic intervention or reverential preservation; it is a choice of success or failure, whatever end we have in mind. A researcher for the U.S. Forest Service put the situation well: "Human activities dominate the landscape; we are 'managing' vegetation and wildlife whether we are aware of it or not. . . . Nature is what we make of it."[38]

Science can help us better understand how nature works. It can help us choose the strategies and tools best suited to the goals we hope to achieve. It may on occasion tell us that certain laudable goals, such as preserving every species now endangered, are not realistically achievable within the constraints we now face and that we had better concentrate our efforts where the best chances for success remain rather than risk losing all in a fruitless struggle to do everything. Science may show how some of these seemingly irreconcilable goals can be harmonized, how a ranch or a forest can be made to grow both a crop and a habitat for wildlife—all the more important given the tiny percentage of the world's lands set aside for parks and reserves compared with the area devoted to farming and forestry. But science cannot in the end dictate those goals for us. Whether we should grow timber or spotted owls on a tract of woodland, whether we should grow cattle or bison on a prairie, or for that matter whether a hundred acres should be a farm or a forest or a lake or a field in the first place, is a value judgment. Nature has no set plan for that bit of ground or for any other.

Those who would try to understand and even manage nature always run the risk of being branded philistines or worse. Those who revere nature as the antithesis of technological civilization resent the intrusion of "mechanistic" science into this spiritual sphere, and even ecologists have some of the theoretician's—and the aesthete's—disdain for the practical. The contemplative study of the behavior of ants in a lush tropical forest is one thing; bulldozing out a firebreak or chainsawing a clearing is altogether something else again.

But does it really destroy nature's beauty if we recognize that the time has come to cease being overawed admirers from afar and take her hand? McKibben's dichotomy—that nature must either be God or be dross, that we can worship her or make her a filing clerk—ignores the beauty of insight that is the very essence of scientific inquiry. And it ignores the vast realms of human endeavor that fill the human spirit and engage our passions and our intellects both, without evoking feelings of religious devotion at all. If nature is not a cathedral, then perhaps it is a town meeting, and none the worse for it—a place of intellectual inquiry, give and take, and above all, human responsibility, a place where people seek the truth, bound only by the constraints of common sense and common decency, a place where people make decisions and learn from the consequences.

It has become common to deride modern science as mechanistic and soulless and "reductionist," destroying meaning and beauty as it reduces the world to an equation. But to a scientist a mathematical description of the natural world is the soul of insight and truth; it is the first step to seeing—*truly* seeing and grasping—the larger patterns and structures that course through the universe. The pioneering conservationist and nature writer Aldo Leopold, so often quoted out of context by those who would worship nature, wrote that "wild things" only came to have meaning when "science disclosed the drama of where they came from and how they live." The mechanistic and mathematical approach that humanist critics of science mistake for an ideology of valueless exploitation and dominance is, to scientists themselves, nothing more than a tool; it makes as much sense to denounce a scientist's use of mathematics to build up a picture of nature as it would to criticize Beethoven for having composed a symphony out of individual musical notes. "There is no future in loving nature,"

McKibben sighs, having just come from hearing the shocking news of her checkered past and wondering why he never noticed before that her nose is a bit crooked and her calves a trifle on the heavy side. Yet I somehow doubt he's quite ready to throw her over. Most of us admit there are more choices in life than headlong infatuation or the monastery. There is no end of beauty to be found in nature by those who have learned to look deeper than the surface. And frankly we'd better start behaving toward her like grown-ups before we lose her forever.[39]

TWO

The Cult of the Wild

How have we come to believe things about nature that are so untrue?

Young love always has a dash of infatuation, and our love for nature is young indeed.

In 1653 the English historian Edward Johnson took pen in hand to tell the world of the untamed forests of North America, so unlike anything that European settlers and travelers had known from the Old World. A "remote, rocky, barren, bushy, wild-woody wilderness," he called it. He did not mean it as a compliment.[1]

The modern-day admiration of nature is so nearly universal that it comes as a shock to discover of what recent vintage these feelings are. For all but the last two hundred years of civilization, anyone expressing a conviction that wilderness contained anything admirable, much less that it was the embodiment of perfection, would have been considered eccentric, if not insane. Before the end of the eighteenth century, mountains were universally disliked. They were "warts," "wens," "the rubbish of creation," places of desolation suitable only, as in Dante's *Divine Comedy,* to guard the gates of hell. Dr. Johnson, in 1738, expressed the opinion that the Scottish hills "had been dismissed by nature from her care." Other seventeenth- and early eigh-

27

teenth-century writers were no less contemptuous of the wild. The Alps were "high and hideous," "monstrous excrescences of nature," the place where nature had "swept up the rubbish of the earth to clear the plains of Lombardy." An early visitor to Pike's Peak wrote, "The dreariness of the desolate peak itself scarcely dissipates the dismal spell, for you stand in a confusion of dull stones piled upon each other in odious ugliness."[2]

What we today admire as "wetlands" were once "swamps," or even, in the words of the eighteenth-century naturalist Georges Leclerc, the Comte de Buffon, "putrid and stagnating waters." Buffon had no use for wild forests, either. "View those melancholy deserts where man has never resided," Buffon exclaimed, "overrun with briars, thorns, and trees which are deformed, broken, and corrupted . . . nothing but a disordered mass of gross herbage, and of trees loaded with parasitical plants." Landing at Plymouth, William Bradford beheld the New World—and called it "a hideous & desolate wilderness, full of wild beasts & wild men." The forests of New England were a "howling" and "dismal" place, gloomy and sinister, full of evils real and spiritual. The Indians, Cotton Mather declared, were literal devil worshipers, who conversed with demons in the black darkness of the deep wood. The woods were a place of temptation, the dark venue of man's fall where the unwary might revert to a primitive and sinful state, unchecked by the laws of civilization. Only by energetic application of the axe would "the cleare sunshine of the Gospell" come to dispel the forest's sinister gloom.[3] The very word *wilderness* was a term of unambiguous disapprobation. It meant an unimproved wasteland, a place devoid of value, a place to be shunned and hurried through.

What explains the great change of heart between then and now? How did nature change from a place of chaos, ugliness, and evil to one of order, harmony, and beauty?

Rarely has there been such an abrupt and sweeping transformation in social attitudes. And in its very abruptness lies the explanation for how the belief in nature as perfect, orderly, harmonious, and separate came to be virtually synonymous with a love for nature and why even today this special vision of the natural world holds such a grip upon us. Nature—or at least the Arcadian vision of nature as a place of towering ancient woods, wild beasts, and timeless hills, a place where man may enter only as an intruder, observer, or worshiper—was an invention of the imagination of man. To love nature, man first had to invent a nature worth loving. And in inventing nature he perhaps inevitably consulted the romantic yearnings of his soul, not the miserable experience of thousands of years of grim reality.

For the wilderness had long been viewed by most people with hostility for perfectly good reason. Mountains were places of wolves, bears, bandits, bad roads, and violent and unpredictable weather. The North American forests harbored wild animals and hostile Indians. To a farmer who needed to clear fields to feed his family and graze his livestock, the woods were a backbreaking obstacle; felling trees and pulling stumps was the most arduous job a settler faced. It was only "the literary gentleman wielding a pen, not the pioneer with an axe" who could think otherwise. To this day, farmers are not conspicuous among the backpacking set.[4]

Thus the early nature appreciation movement was both self-conscious and self-consciously elitist. Those eighteenth-century aristocrats—for aristocrats they exclusively were—who suddenly and unexpectedly began to express an admiration of mountains and other natural scenery were explicit in their belief that the ability to appreciate such beauty was not innate but acquired. Nature was something that only the cultivated, trained through an appreciation of fine painting and landscape gardening, could truly understand and value. It was a sort of connoisseurship; one could no more expect a ploughman to properly appreciate the Alps than one could expect him to appreciate a glass of fine old port. As late as 1844, the poet William Wordsworth was complaining in a letter to an English newspaper about a proposed railroad that was to be built to the Lake District. His concern was not, as a modern-day preservationist might expect, that the railroad itself would mar the countryside; the problem was rather that it would bring trainloads of untutored sightseers who were not equipped to value what they were seeing. "The perception of what has acquired the name of picturesque and romantic scenery," he sniffed, "is so far from being intuitive that it can be produced only by a slow and gradual process of culture."[5]

Such an attitude all but guaranteed that this love of the natural would be shot through with contrivance, artifice, even sensation and make-believe. The aristocratic nature lovers of the eighteenth and nineteenth centuries knew little about the natural world and nothing whatever of modern ecological science, but they knew what they liked. Their tastes were perfectly revealed in the English landscape movement, which rejected the tame, artificial symmetry and formality of traditional gardens in favor of the wild and "natural." But the flowing landscapes that replaced the rigid lines of trees in pots and clipped hedges were an invented nature, an aesthete's nature. Every curve and vista were calculated to offer "insights" and "subjects of meditation"; streams were dammed to form poetic lakes, trees were set in artful clumps, and garden buildings were pressed into service as moral or philosophical allegories. There was a great truck in classical and Gothic ruins, real and synthetic. "English landscape was invented by gardeners imitating foreign painters who were invoking classical authors," mocks the character Hannah in Tom Stoppard's play *Arcadia,* and she has it about right.

The carefully crafted landscapes of ruined abbeys, jagged cliffs, unkempt trees—"everything but vampires," Hannah says—betrayed a motive that beclouds our thoughts about nature to this day. The natural world's ability to stir the soul, even fill it with terror, was the prime attraction. This was nature as escapism. (The place that "can stir you up as you were made to be stirred up," as the Sierra Club's David Brower would still describe it two centuries later.) Much the same taste accounted for the popularity of the Gothic novel; indeed, the English landscape garden was almost a Gothic novel come to life, in crags and unkempt trees and "druidical" huts. The eighteenth-century English landscape architect William Kent went so far as to plant dead trees in Kensington Gardens "to give a greater air of truth to the scene." The idea was to create a garden that looked old, as if it had been neglected for centuries. In a few particularly memorable instances the Gothic touches went completely over the top. The owner of Pain's Hill in Surrey had a hermitage, complete with resident hermit, installed on his redone grounds. The hermit signed a seven-year contract at £700; he was supplied food, hassock, and hourglass and undertook not to cut his hair, beard, or nails and to eschew speech. Perhaps it was inevitable that he was caught sneaking down to the pub after just three weeks on the job.[6]

The feelings come first; we create a landscape to correspond. Eighteenth-century landowners could do it literally, hiring architects to throw up ruins and dig ravines about their grounds; most of us today create our romantic wilderness in the landscape of our minds. The mischief comes when we demand that prosaic agencies like the National Park Service conform to our poetic visions of how nature should look and behave.

By the end of the eighteenth century, the well-to-do English seekers of soul-stirring experience were beginning to venture forth from their libraries and gardens into the genuine "wilderness," too. They were doing what seems perfectly commonplace now but was an exceptional departure then. People simply had never visited mountains before. The first English tourists began appearing in Scotland only around 1810; it was in 1818 that the first English-language guidebook to Switzerland was published. The motive of these pioneering nature tourists was virtually indistiguishable from that of the landscape gardeners. In expressing a love of the natural world, both were expressing a hunger for heightened experience, and it was only a very particular and idealized conception of nature that could fit that bill—a nature vast, ancient, eternal, separate, and awe inspiring, a nature that at least presented the illusion of being beyond the touch of man. Such a wilderness proved the "ideal stage for the Romantic individual to exercise the cult that he frequently made of his own soul," as the historian Roderick Nash put it. But it is telling that these connoisseurs of the "sublime"—an odd word that came to be used at the time to express the contradictory emotion of fear and thrill (the notion also crops up in a predilection for deliberately contradictory phrases such as "delightful horror," "terrible joy")—were as apt to visit coal mines and quarries as mountains to satisfy this penchant.[7]

Many modern-day nature lovers, unwilling to acknowledge such a dubious parentage to their deepest feelings, have tried hard to establish a more ancient and noble ancestry to their beliefs. Ancient hunter-gatherers, who lived in a state of "balanced and harmonious" existence, altering "neither the natural firmament nor the animals and plants that share the land with them," were the original lovers and worshipers of nature, writes the environmental historian and philoso-

pher Max Oelschlaeger;[8] Western civilization has forgotten these ancient truths in its ten-thousand-year pursuit of material progress. Or
if it was not materialistic capitalism that destroyed humankind's pri-
mordial reverence for the wild, then perhaps it was Christianity, individualism, agriculturalism, Jews, the Iron Age, rationalism, or
possibly "phallotechnic society." All have been fingered at one time or
another in this century by various environmentalist thinkers of various political stripes.[9]

The particular choice of villain obviously has much to do with
one's political persuasions and motives. But the common thread that
ties all of these environmental conspiracy theories together is the
search for an ancient affirmation of a modern credo. It is reassuring to
trace one's beliefs back to American Indians or Druids or goddess
worshipers or, better yet, to show that they are instinctive, the expression of a "biophilia" etched deeply into our genes. The assertion of a
golden age is both a claim for precedence in the war of ideas and a
stirring call for revolution against a social order that destroyed it.

This may explain the credulity with which many environmentalists
(Vice President Gore among them) have accepted and propagated the
now-famous speech of Chief Seattle, a nineteenth-century American
Indian whose prophetic warnings of the coming ecological crisis first
came to wide public attention when they were used to narrate a 1972
television movie about pollution, called *Home.* "This we know—the
earth does not belong to man, man belongs to the earth," the chief declares in one of the many versions of the speech that were subsequently reprinted. "All things are connected like the blood which
unites one family. Whatever befalls the earth befalls the sons of the
earth. Man did not weave the web of life; he is merely a strand in it.
Whatever he does to the web, he does to himself."

To a few experts on American Indians, this all smelled a bit fishy.
The real Chief Seattle was a rather scraping convert to Christianity
who ceded land to white settlers and refused to join a subsequent uprising by his people. He did make a speech, around 1855, that was re-
counted thirty years later in a newspaper article by an American who
had been in the audience; but according to this account, Seattle merely praised the generosity of the "great white chief" for buying his
lands and offered not a word of ecological insight. Seattle was also

known to historians for his dignified refusal to allow the grateful white settlers to name their town after him; he objected that his eternal sleep would be interrupted each time a mortal uttered his name. The objection promptly vanished when the whites proposed levying a small tax on themselves to provide the chief with some advance compensation for his troubles in the hereafter. Nowhere was there any record of Seattle as a prophet of environmentalism.

A little research eventually cleared up the mystery. The reason Chief Seattle's speech sounded remarkably like the words of a twentieth-century, white, middle-class environmentalist was that they *were* the words of a twentieth-century, white, middle-class environmentalist. Ted Perry, a professor of film at the University of Texas at Austin, had written the script for the movie and had never claimed that the words he put in Chief Seattle's mouth were anything but fiction. But the truth has never quite managed to catch up. Seattle's anachronistic warnings about the fragile balance of nature were immediately taken as the real thing by affirmation-seeking environmentalists. They continue to be reprinted and quoted in environmental magazines, sermons from the pulpit, textbooks, classroom study kits, posters, and bumper stickers. They appear in a best-selling children's book, *Brother Eagle, Sister Sky,* which has gone through more than a dozen printings. As a seemingly far-seeing anticipation of the central credo of modern environmentalism by a representative of an ancient way of life, Chief Seattle's speech has attained the status of what one admiring environmentalist thinker, Theodore Roszak, a professor of history at California State University, has called "a piece of folklore in the making, a literary artifact mingling traditional culture with contemporary aspiration." Roszak breaks the mold of the chief's contemporary admirers in one respect; he is actually aware that the speech is a twentieth-century concoction and admits that he "initially had some scholarly qualms about citing the chief." The struggle with his scholarly conscience doesn't seem to have detained him very long, however. Seattle's "semilegendary" words, Roszak rushes on to explain, "have become precious to the environmental movement." Perhaps even more telling is what Susan Jeffers, the children's book author who reprinted the spurious speech, told a reporter when asked why, in the face of incontrovertible evidence, she still refused to acknowledge that the speech was not authentic. "When you say someone is Native American," she explained, "you can make certain assumptions about what he felt to be important." If Chief Seattle didn't say it, he should have.[10]

The real irony in all of this, of course, is that the noble savage was himself one of the inventions of the eighteenth-century romantics; he was no more real than the idealized nature the romantics invented for him to inhabit.

Perhaps the most enduring conspiracy theory put forth by modern-day environmentalists who seek to explain the loss of an ancient, nature-worshiping tradition is the one that blames Western thought in general and Western religion in particular. The ancient Hebrews, says Max Oelschlaeger, overthrew the nature gods of the Egyptians and Babylonians for a god that, for the first time, existed outside of nature, beyond nature. Gone was the need to propitiate animal or earth gods for the killing of game or other acts of exploitation; exploitation was now not only guilt free but positively encouraged. Oelschlaeger calls the Pentateuch "the grandest rationalization of an agriculturist mode of existence ever conceived." The Christian belief that the world was but "a sojourner's way station," and a sinful one at that, took the idea a step further. As the historian Lynn White argued in a much-cited essay on the historical and philosophical roots of the environmental crisis, "Christianity is the most anthropocentric religion the world has ever seen."[11]

The Christian view did allow that the earth was to be improved through man's work as an expression of God's will. But ultimately, as the Spanish philosopher José Ortega y Gasset explained, the physical life on earth is not what matters at all:

> What had seemed real—nature and ourselves as part of it—now turns out to be unreal, pure phantasmagoria; and that which had seemed unreal—our concern with the absolute or God—that is the true reality. This paradox, this complete inversion of perspective, is the basis of Christianity. The problems of natural man have no solution; to live, to be in the world, is perdition . . . man must be saved by the supernatural.[12]

Nature was at best an allegory, a message from God to be decoded. The white snow stood for the virgin's purity; the red rose, Christ's blood; the ant was a sermon on industry and laziness; the rising flames, a symbol of the soul's aspiration. Any more literal interest in the natur-

al world was suspect. When Petrarch, in 1336, climbed Mount Ven-
toux and found himself taking "delight" in being "free and alone,
among the mountains, forests, and streams," he immediately became
alarmed and proceeded to chastise himself with a few passages from St.
Augustine's *Confessions,* which he had prudently packed along. He pro-
fessed himself "abashed . . . angry with myself that I should still be admiring earthly things . . . nothing is wonderful but the soul." At times
in the Middle Ages such admonitions to eschew the earthly led to
more direct action, as when axe-wielding monks leveled forests to ex-
tirpate sacred groves or other sites of pagan nature worship.[13]

Clearing the forests was on the one hand a literal interpretation of
the commandment of the Old Testament God to subdue the earth; it
was also a more figurative fulfillment of the Christian duty to extend
Christ's spiritual dominion. "O let old England rejoice in this," wrote
one seventeenth-century contemporary of the Puritans, "that our
brethren who with extream difficulties and expences have Planted
themselves in the Indian Wilderness, have also laboured night and day
with prayers and tears and Exhortations to Plant the Indians as a spiritu-
all Garden, into which Christ might come and eat his pleasant fruits."[14]

But historians and environmentalists who seek to lay the blame for
all the old attitudes about nature which they so deplore at the feet of
Western religion are surely oversimplifying matters. It is too easy a
scapegoat. For most of history, religion was teaching nothing about
nature that the mass of men were not already well prepared to accept
from their own experience. The desert of the ancient Hebrews was a
place where less than four inches of rain fell a year and life was gen-
uinely perilous; it was the most natural thing in the world to view
such lands as cursed, the home of demons and evil spirits. Even the
Christian inversion of the real and the unreal was in one sense a perfectly rational response of people whose life upon the physical earth
was one of misery, disease, hunger, and poverty—all too often inflict-
ed by a seemingly malevolent nature.[15]

Religious sanction was nonetheless part of the formidable bulwark
of hostility to nature that the aesthetic nature admirers of the late
eighteenth century were up against. And in facing this obstacle, they
loosed one of those simple and powerful ideas that totally capture the
imagination of man. If it was a sin to take pleasure in a nature without

God, move God. Nature, thus declared the American theologian Jonathan Edwards, was "God speaking to us." The feelings of sublime terror inspired by wilderness were a reminder of God's power and wrath. Even the dirt that covers everything and "which tends to defile the feet of the traveler" is a salutary moral lesson from God, a reminder that "the world is full of that which tends to defile the soul."

Others were less explicit about the precise moral lessons of nature and began to suggest simply that sublime landscapes were suitable objects of contemplation as stirring reminders of God's magnificence and grandeur. This was a total change. The wild and terrible in nature was no longer the rubbish left over from the creation or the unenlightened province of the devil. It was a testimonial to the greatness of God. Climbing a mountain was no longer an act of sacrilege but an act of moral instruction.[16]

It was not yet an act of worship; that was still to come. Putting God in nature opened the door to more than just aesthetic appreciation. It bears repeating that the motives of those who began to express interest, appreciation, and later reverence for nature had nothing whatsoever to do with modern ecological concerns. When Henry David Thoreau wrote, "in wilderness is the preservation of the world" he was not talking about the role of tropical biodiversity in maintaining the life-support processes of the planet. By "the world," he meant the world of man—specifically the spiritual world of man. Nature mattered, not for its own sake, but for what it could do for man's soul. "I derive more of my subsistence from the swamps which surround my native town than from the cultivated gardens in the village," he went on to explain. "My spirits infallibly rise in proportion to the outward dreariness. . . . When I would recreate myself, I seek the darkest wood, the thickest and most interminable and, to the citizen, most dismal swamp. I enter a swamp as a sacred place,—a sanctum sanctorum." His motive was a "desire to bathe my head in atmospheres unknown to my feet."[17]

Here is where so much of the mischief begins. Thoreau's declaration that "in wilderness is the preservation of the world" is one of the most quoted in modern environmental writing. It is always interpreted as a precocious ecological insight, anticipating by a century the modern recognition of the environmental damage that pollution and development are wreaking. Few people recognize the fundamentally religious motivation that Thoreau's words gave voice to.

For Thoreau, nature's chief value was that it was not the town. The woods were an escape from social corruption, or, more to the point, people. "Society is always diseased, and the best is the most so," he wrote in *The Natural History of Massachusetts.* The conventions of social intercourse were stultifying. "Politics . . . are but as the cigar-smoke of a man." Commerce was frivolous. Labor was degrading, farming no better than serfdom. Even man's amusements were nothing but a sign of the depths of his despair. "The greater part of what my neighbors call good I believe in my soul to be bad." The word *village,* he said, comes from the same Latin root as *vile* and *villain,* which "suggests what kind of degeneracy villagers are liable to." Thoreau wanted to "shake off the village," where men spent empty, monotonous, vacuous, and spiritually impoverished lives. "I confess that I am astonished at the power of endurance, to say nothing of the moral insensibility, of my neighbors who confine themselves to shops and offices the whole day for weeks and months, aye, and years almost together," he wrote. It was the freedom that nature had to offer that was its chief attraction. Thoreau went to live at Walden Pond, he said, "to transact some private business with the fewest obstacles."

If nature's value rested upon its being a refuge from the evils of society, then nature, by definition, meant separation, the absence of man. It was the very fact that man and all his follies were not to be found there that made nature estimable. What Thoreau disliked about man's presence was not that it would interfere with or degrade critical biological processes; what he disliked about man's presence was its presence. Thoreau disapproved of wealth, church, rules, voting, dinner parties, and young men not as smart as he who sought to join him on his walks. He would tell the last that he "had no walks to throw away on company." The link between environmentalism and escapism is an enduring one, and Thoreau's admiration of the wild as a place to turn one's back on the town can be heard in the words of David Brower, Bill McKibben, and other nature writers of our day.[18]

Thoreau's aversion to society (and to holding down a regular job) readily explains some of the appeal that the woods held for him. But nature's stock was rising at this time for other reasons, too—all just as far removed from anything to do with ecological science, wildlife conservation, biodiversity, or the other concerns that modern environmentalists try to graft upon the woodsy philosophy of Thoreau and his fellow travelers. Many of the early American nature worshipers, including Thoreau's fellow townsmen in Concord, Ralph Waldo Emerson and Asa Bronson Alcott, were deeply involved in a whole laundry list of reform-minded causes that all shared an antipathy to the corrupt social status quo. Temperance, the abolition of slavery, dietary reform, and alternative medicine may not seem at first glance to have much in common, but all were a rejection of evils that man appeared to have brought upon himself—and all saw salvation, spiritual and physical, in a return to nature. Just as "natural law" had shown the falseness of monarchy, slavery, and other political systems that denied men their God-given rights, so natural foods and natural healing would show the falseness of alcohol and artificial medicines that denied men their God-given health.

This was an age of revivalism, millenarianism, and utopianism, brimming with enthusiastic schemes for remaking the world. One scheme that managed to roll together several of these enthusiasms in one, with virtuous and uncorrupted nature at its core, was the "cold water" movement. Publications extolling the multiple virtues of cold water flourished in the early and mid-nineteenth century. *Water-Cure World; Water-Cure Journal; The Magnetic and Cold Water Guide* were but a few of many. The Hutchinson Family Singers, a musical family from New Hampshire whom one historian has called America's first pop singing group, took to the road in the 1840s with a homespun message blending denunciations of slavery, war, alcohol, doctors, tobacco, and the usurpation of Indian lands with paeans of praise to water:

> Oh! If you would preserve your health
> And trouble never borrow,
> Just take the morning shower bath,
> 'Twill drive away all sorrow.
> And then instead of drinking rum,
> As doth the poor besotter;
> For health, long life, and happiness,
> Drink nothing but cold water.

Yes, water'll cure most every ill,
'Tis proved without assumption;
Dyspepsia, gout, and fevers, too,
And sometimes old consumption.
Your head-aches, side-aches, and *heart*-aches too,
Which often cause great slaughter;
Can all be cured by drinking oft
And bathing in cold water.[19]

It was only later that temperance became the special domain of lit-tle old ladies and busybodies; in the early nineteenth century exces-sive alcohol consumption was a major social ill in America, and the temperance cause attracted broad support from the reform-minded intelligentsia. Skepticism about the cures offered by contemporary medical science was equally well founded in reality; it was not until the very end of the nineteenth century that a patient seeking the assis-tance of a medical doctor was more likely to be improved than harmed by the treatment prescribed. Most of the cures consisted of violent purging and vomiting, bleeding, blistering, and the liberal ap-plication of remedies containing opium and alcohol or, with an alarm-ing frequency, slow-acting poisons such as mercury and arsenic. A particularly favored cure-all was calomel, or mercurous chloride, a powerful purgative—as well as a central nervous system poison. It al-most certainly hastened the demise of many in those days, including, in 1799, George Washington, who fell ill with a cold, was thoroughly dosed by his attending physicians, and promptly dropped dead. (Calomel was singled out for special excoriation in another of the Hutchinson Family's songs: "And when I must resign my breath, / Pray let me die a natural death, / And bid the world a long farewell, / Without one dose of Calomel.")[20]

But the urge to look to nature for the answer went much further. Cold water was not just a wholesome substitute for intoxicating liquors; it was God's answer to man's ills. "The God of nature has never made—at least for the globe we inhabit—any other drink but water," extolled William Alcott, the physician cousin of Bronson. "Let us . . . abandon Satan's system of poisoning . . . and adopt God's sys-tem, based on truth—on the harmonies and congenialities of nature," wrote another water enthusiast. "Wash, and be healed," said yet another. This was more than a temperance campaign. This was the stirring of a new religion. Illness was the result of violating nature's laws. Good health could be obtained only by restoring harmony and balance. Spiritual health and physical health were inseparable, and both were linked to obedience to the lessons that nature taught, as a reflection of God's plan. Rather than try to rise above nature and the "brute" or "animal" instincts, as Christianity had so long seemed to urge, the message of these "Christian physiologists" was that man must give up the sinful luxuries and excesses of civilization and return to nature. Nature was not the fallen world of fleshly and unclean desires; it was the pure and uncorrupted creation of God. "Alas! the beast that roams the forest . . . may boast of greater consistency, of a more implicit obedience to the laws of Nature, and Nature's God, than proud Man!" declared an article in one of the many publications devoted to the ideas of Samuel Thomson, a nineteenth-century herbalist whose *New Guide to Health* had sold one hundred thousand copies. "Those who live in the nearest state of nature, also approach the nearest state of perfect health."[21] (Another reformer of this era who achieved contemporary fame marching an army of followers back to nature was Sylvester Graham, mostly remembered today only for the cracker that bears his name. Graham was an immensely popular preacher of the new gospel of salvation through hygiene; he blamed "crowded cities" for the ruin of the human family, and urged a return to that state of primeval simplicity "when man was free from disease, and a perfect stranger to vice." Graham preached a regimen that eschewed all "artificial stimuli" in favor of cold baths, fresh air, exercise, loose-fitting clothing, and a diet of nothing but coarse rye or wheat meal, hominy, and pure water.)[22]

The new doctrine of dietary salvation that Graham and Thomson were offering up to their mainly Yankee audiences struck many familiar chords, with its emphasis on self-denial and Puritanism as the pathway to the kingdom of heaven. The Graham system of living was, like Christianity itself, a means to a higher spiritual end. True to the evangelical spirit of Graham's message, followers of the Graham diet offered up testimonials telling of the "flood of light" they experienced once they began eating coarse bread and taking icy baths. Indeed, some of the health-cure preachers who came to fame in the mid-nineteenth century ventured to suggest that eating right would not only unstop the bowels but bring the millennium.

In worshiping nature as God's creation, these nineteenth century nature enthusiasts forged another link between the love of nature and the beliefs in its perfection and its possession of an innate purpose apart from man's. Thoreau was surely speaking tongue in cheek when he and a few fellow dropouts from Concord society formed the Walden Pond Society as an alternative church for Sunday morning meetings and proposed plucking and eating wild huckleberries as a substitute for the more conventional sacrament of communion. But there was no hint of irony in Emerson's transcendental conviction that nature was the literal dwelling place of God: "The aspect of nature is devout. Like the figure of Jesus, she stands with bended head, and hands folded upon the breast. The happiest man is he who learns from nature the lesson of worship." Emerson believed that nature was both a source of moral instruction and discipline and the holy of holies where man would become "part or particle of God" himself.[23]

This was but a prelude to the nature worship of John Muir, who was to become far and away the most successful popularizer of the cult of the wild. The son of a stern Scottish Presbyterian turned Disciple of Christ, Muir brought the full force of his evangelical upbringing to his devotion to nature. His father was a thoroughgoing disciplinarian who discouraged any reading but the Bible and ordered the family to bed promptly after 8 P.M. prayers. He once set John to work for months on end digging a ninety-foot-deep well with nothing but hammer and chisel; he would be lowered in a basket in the morning and hauled up in the evening. Finally, at the age of thirty, Muir had had enough and, abandoning the family's Wisconsin farmstead, set out to walk to the Gulf of Mexico by "the leafiest and least trodden way" he could find.[24]

Yet even as he rebelled, he could not shake his evangelical roots. Feeling the beauty of nature, he said, was to experience "a glorious conversion." Discovering Twenty Hill Hollow near Yosemite was "a resurrection day." The forests were "temples," trees were "psalm-singing," natural objects were "sparks of the Divine Soul." In the wild, indeed only in the wild, could one "touch naked God" and "be filled with the Holy Ghost." Once, climbing a mountain, he slipped and nearly fell but was touched by a "blessed light" and saved; "had I been borne aloft upon wings, my deliverance could not have been more complete." Such a nature religion was incomplete without nature evangelism: "Heaven knows that John the Baptist was not more eager to get all his fellow sinners into the Jordan than I to baptize all of mine in the beauty of God's mountains," he wrote in his journals.[25]

Unlike Thoreau, Muir does not in the least appear to be joking about his version of the communion sacrament:

> Do behold the King in his glory, King Sequoia. Behold! Behold! seems all I can say. Some time ago I left all for Sequoia: have been & am at his feet fasting & praying for light, for is he not the greatest light in the woods; in the world. I'm in the woods woods woods, & they are in me-ee-ee. The King tree & me have sworn eternal love—sworn it without swearing & I've taken the sacrament with Douglass Squirrell drank Sequoia wine Sequoia blood, & with its rosy purple drops I am writing this woody gospel letter. . . . I wish I was so drunk & Sequoical that I could preach the green brown woods to all the juiceless world, descending from his divine wilderness like a John the Baptist eating Douglass Squirrels & wild honey or wild anything, crying, Repent for the Kingdom of Sequoia is at hand. . . . Come Suck Sequoia & be saved.[26]

Even in his arguably more sober moments Muir's religion was unwavering. Nature was a place to find God; nature *was* God. As God was perfect and pure, so nature was perfect and pure. There is "perfect harmony in all things here," he wrote; nature is the "pure and sure and universal," the "Song of God, sounding on forever."[27]

This sentiment survives virtually unchanged among the nature lovers of our day. Asked by the Canadian environmentalist Farley Mowat how they came to devote their lives to environmental protection, one activist after another described a "conversion" experience. Mowat himself told how he "glimpsed another and quite magical world—a world of Oneness." All the more so because it did not include people: "When I came back from the Second World War, I was so appalled by the behaviour of modern man that I fled to the Arctic to escape him," Mowat wrote. "The world of non-human life became for me a sanctuary."[28]

Such feelings toward nature are real and earnest and genuine. Thoreau and Muir struck a deep chord that resonates yet. Those who fight for more wilderness areas these days will speak of experiencing a sense of connection with something greater than themselves, something "primeval, threatening, and free of jarring reminders of civilization"; the defenders of the deer talk of feeling "close to nature" when they come across one of these wild animals in an urban park; even Harvard biologist and environmental advocate Edward O. Wilson punctuates 350 pages on biodiversity with the argument that it should be preserved because "wilderness settles peace on the soul."[29] But none of this is a very good measure of what constitutes ecologically sound, or even ecologically feasible, policy. Religion answers a genuine human emotion, but it is not science. And even the most ascetic religion of salvation is not very far removed from self-indulgence, with all of the attendant dangers of that emotion. It is just too easy to mistake one's personal feelings of exaltation for some universal truth. Virtuous self-indulgence has been a foible of those who have been seeking salvation in nature from Thoreau's day to ours.

There are fewer true ascetics about these days; today's nature lover is more likely to try to save the rain forests by buying the correct brand of chocolate-and-nut-covered ice-cream bar than he is to try to save his soul by eating nothing but coarse flour for two years. But attitudes toward conservation practice remain entangled in a web of introspective human sensations—the aesthetic love for nature's beauty, the spiritual search for solitude and peace and personal health, the nostalgic yearnings for a golden age. And rather than tear away those strands of confusion, the science of ecology that arose at the end of the nineteenth century was to find itself caught in them.

THREE

Nazis, Planners, Eugenicists, and Other Ecologists

If it was Romanticism that gave birth to the love and idealization of nature, if it was religious fervor that enshrined nature's perfection, it was politics that swept that message headlong into the twentieth century.

By the 1860s and 1870s, the wilderness had secured a wide and enthusiastic following. Though to his great disappointment Muir failed to persuade the aging Emerson to camp out in Yosemite with him during the philosopher's visit to California in 1871, thousands of others had answered the call and were taking to the mountains with all the ardor of a new-found love. By the 1880s, hundreds of "rambling clubs" had been formed in England; their members, more than one hundred thousand, were regularly sallying forth into the countryside to study natural history and archaeology and generally improve themselves. In America a small stampede to the Adirondacks was set off in the summer of 1869 by William H. H. Murray, a Congregationalist preacher who had written a small book praising the virtues of that bit of wilderness in New York State. Newspapers reported that three thousand of Murray's Fools, as the wilderness-seeking vacationers were dubbed, flooded into the region, overwhelming the few small hotels, fighting and squabbling with one another (and scheming and bribing) to secure boats and guides.[1]

It was also during the latter part of the nineteenth century that the first organized political movements devoted to nature preservation began to appear—the Appalachian Mountain Club (1876), the National Association of Audubon Societies (1886), the Sierra Club (1892). But the motives of these politically active groups were often curiously mixed with other political and social agendas. The nature that could be exploited to stir—or save—souls was also a nature that could be exploited to advance a political cause, not always its own. With the coming of nature politics, the nature myths that had been the special provenance of mystics, hermits, and aesthetic snobs were carried forth to a world that, for many complex reasons of ideology and nationalism, was ready to receive them with an enthusiasm that went well beyond the nature evangelism of Muir and his fellow preachers of the wilderness gospel.

This same period saw the establishment of many quite similar societies and clubs dedicated to the preservation of buildings, archaeological ruins, villages, even roads and bridges. It was no coincidence; many were founded by precisely the same people. Francis Parkman, Jr., Boston Brahmin and champion of the wilderness, was just as likely to rise to the defense of the buffalo, the Indian, and the life of the mountain trapper. He described his fight not as one for endangered species, but rather for the endangered "charm" and "poetry" of the American West. The wild had been "disenchanted," he complained; "the dullest plainest prose has fixed its home in America." It was the romance of discovery that he mourned and that encompassed a lot more than just nature per se.[2]

In England, especially, the same names kept popping up on the rolls of all sorts of preservationist societies. All of these groups described their mission in remarkably similar language whether the particular objects they were trying to save were natural or man-made. Churches and forests alike were "relics" or "monuments," part of a national heritage that was in danger of being sacrificed to mercenary industrialists or the vulgar tastes of the petit bourgeoisie. The natural, the historic, and the prehistoric were jumbled together almost indiscriminately; for example, Britain's first such group, founded in 1865, was the Commons, Open Spaces and Footpaths Preservation Society. Proposing the establishment of a Council for the Preservation of Rural England in 1926, one advocate of the cause declared that "the greatest historical monument that we possess, the most essential thing which is England, is the Countryside, the Market Town, the Village, the Hedgerow Trees, the Lanes, the Copses, the Streams and the Farmsteads." That might seem to have covered all the bases, though he was arguably outdone by another supporter of the back-to-the-land movement in that period in England, who included on his list of English national monuments "simple housekeeping in the country, with tea in the garden; boy-scouting and tennis in flannels." The preservationists were not so much interested in preserving the land as in preserving a myth about the land. And that myth in turn implied a land that never was.[3]

Some of this, of course, was simple nostalgia. The Reverend Murray, who was minister at Boston's venerable Park Street Church, exhorted his flock to break free from the grind of modern life and the sordid business of money making, return to "the old ancestral farm where you toiled when young," and there "revive sweet and sacred memories of your earlier days. . . . Go to the sea-shore, to the mountains, to the wilderness; go anywhere you can; forget your cares, and cast aside your burdens. Eat, sleep, and play like boys. Let the old, old nurse, Nature,—the one mother of us all . . . the dear old mother that never sickens, and never dies,—take you to her bosom again."[4]

Nostalgia for the old farm, for one's humble roots, for those simple boyhood days—nostalgia was a rising tide, swept by the winds of industrialization and urbanization. "Surely the spread of the factory system, and the consequent growth of huge towns, has rather strengthened than weakened this love of all things rural," observed one English naturalist in 1893. "We pine for pure air, for the sight of growing grass, for the foot-path across the meadow, for the stile that invites you to rest before you drop into the deep lane under the hazels."[5]

Nostalgia remains an animating force of environmentalists to this day, and there is nothing wrong with that per se. But much of what the nineteenth-century nature preservationists were fighting to keep was nothing more than the cultural artifacts of the previous generation. Hedgerows, the object of a long and impassioned preservation campaign in Britain that has increased in intensity since the Second World War, were for the most part planted in the late eighteenth and early nineteenth centuries in obedience to Parliamentary acts requiring the enclosure of fields. Before manufactured galvanized wire became widely available in the 1840s, hedges were simply the cheapest form of fencing there was, especially where stone was scarce. (Timber had been virtually unavailable in Britain since Elizabethan times.) Even the oldest hedges, which date back to late medieval times, were artificial and utilitarian in origin; they were planted to control livestock after the plague wiped out the manpower and childpower that had previously performed that task. Today's preservationists look with alarm as farmers pull up their hedges to make way for tractor-drawn cultivation equipment; less well known are the complaints of nineteenth-century nature lovers (or perhaps "landscape lovers" would be a better term) that the planting of hedges was marring the beauty of England's open fields—which were in turn a medieval artifact, created by the clearing of forests.[6]

But many of those who began to organize politically on behalf of nature had much more calculating motives than innocent nostalgia. Their enthusiasm for preservation, as well as their idealization of nature as a place that owed its perfection to the absence of man and his modern ways, was part of a much broader social agenda. The agitation for public parks and open spaces, for example, came overwhelmingly from social reformers who saw them primarily as a public hygiene measure. "The past hundred years have supplied civilized mankind with a complete demonstration that the evils which attend the growth of modern cities and the factory system are too great for the human body to endure," Charles Eliot, the president of Harvard University, wrote in an article in *National Geographic* in 1914, urging the creation of garden cities and urban parks. "The sources of the evils which afflict the population massed in cities are partly physical and partly mental or moral." If one could not literally return to the old ancestral farm, as the Reverend Murray had urged, then one could at least bring a bit of the old farm—and the old farm's values—to the city. Eliot argued that creating parks would provide fresh air, sunshine, and physical recreation; they would also stimulate "healthy tastes and interests" that would lift the masses from the squalor and moral degradation of their existence.

Significantly, Eliot saw in such endeavors a return to the solid communal values of an earlier America, which had received such rough handling by nineteenth century industrialism and "individualism." It was to address a social and political ill that he became an enthusiast in the cause of nature.[7]

In Britain, where the preservationist cause was even more closely tied to social reform, the movement began to take on utopian, socialist, and even racial and nationalistic political overtones. John Stuart Mill, John Ruskin, William Morris, and other social philosophers who helped to found a number of the British preservation societies were unabashedly political in their hopes for where the movement would lead; they linked preservation and a return to the past explicitly to their dissatisfaction with the existing political and economic structures. The idealized nature and the idealized past that they extolled were to serve as models for the utopian future to come. Medieval cathedrals and common lands were symbols of how the collective good could triumph over selfish individualism. The countryside, its ancient ruins, and its native species were the embodiment of the nation's true character at a time when industrialism, rapid communications, a new and unlanded plutocracy, and "cosmopolitanism" were sweeping away national distinctions. The Commons Preservation Society declared that its aim was "to restore to the Commons something of the attributes of the ancient Saxon Folk-land." Other political movements would see in the myth of ancient folk lands the stuff of more inflammatory political exhortation.[8]

For cosmopolitanism was also a code word for Jews, and in Britain and Germany in particular the cry of back-to-the-land was quickly taken up by ultranationalists and anti-Semites, who found in the mythical nature of a lost golden age an effective call to political action. An essay read at a 1913 camp meeting of the Free German Youth combined nature preservation, folk myth, and social agitation in a mix that chillingly foreshadowed the Nazi ideology of primitive, pagan nationalism: Judeo-Christian civilization was artificial, destructive, and exploitive; it had separated Germans from the life force of nature and the Bronze Age paganism that was the soul of the German *Volk;* the false and alien Judeo-Christian religion was to be replaced with a true and native German one, with the Rhine the holy river and Wart-

burg the holy mountain. During the interwar years the National Socialist League in Britain denounced Jews as the source not only of
capitalism but also of the urbanism and mechanistic and exploitive
technology that had displaced peasants from the land. (Its publication,
The New Pioneer, was also full of paeans to healthy soil and food:
"Without a healthy and productive soil we cannot have physical
health, we cannot have economic security and we cannot have the
sense of reality and real values that will give us spiritual health.") The
"Blood and Soil" patriotism of central European Fascist movements,
especially in Romania and Bulgaria, echoed the same themes. Capitalism and Jews had pushed the true people of the nation off the land;
returning to nature was a return to "the birthplace" of the nation. In a
time of bewildering economic and political dislocation, the soil of ancient and never-changing nature was one constant to cling to, the
place where the uncorrupted roots of the race and the nation were to
be found.[9]

Even the Boy Scout movement, which was to prove a hugely influential force in building a social and political constituency in behalf of
nature, was increasingly propelled by a racial and nationalistic agenda
as it was transported to Europe. As originally proposed in 1902 by
Ernest Thompson Seton, who later headed the committee that established the Boy Scouts in the United States, scouting was heavy on
nostalgia and social hygiene; it emphasized the vanishing knowledge
of woods lore as the frontier closed, the degenerative effects of modern life and the resulting high rates of juvenile delinquency, and the
wholesomeness of fresh air and self-reliance. But in a number of
breakaway groups that soon appeared—and even in the mainstream
British Boy Scouts under Baden-Powell—political and racial motives
soon began to appear. British eugenicists were among the most enthusiastic supporters of the Boy Scouts, seeing in it an antidote to
racial "degeneracy." A breakaway outfit called the Kibbo Kift Kindred
was founded by John Hargrave, an English Quaker who likewise believed that urban life and World War I had produced a "deficient race."
Hargrave's ideas were a mix of socialist egalitarianism and a Niet-
zschean doctrine of the triumph of the individual, with a good dose of
personal authoritarianism thrown in as well. (Hargrave was given to
terminating discussions with the words, "I have spoken.") By 1931,

the group had become an avowedly political movement with a new name: the Green Shirts.[10]

The political power and political exploitation of the nature myth reached its awful climax in Nazi Germany, which not coincidentally was the first European nation to establish nature reserves, order the protection of hedgerows, copses, and other wildlife habitats, and adopt stringent antivivisection laws.[11] It was the ideological, national-istic, and racialistic power of these ideas about nature that carried the day. What had begun as an effete aesthetic vision shared by a few aris-tocrats had grown into a mass movement appealing to the most basic, and not always the most attractive, human impulses. At neither its be-ginning nor its end did this vision of nature touch reality. The nature that the preservationists were politically roused to fight for and pre-serve was one that had never in truth existed. It was the nature of Gothic romance, wild and abandoned; the nature of unexplored wilderness, still unmarred by the scars of industrialization; the nature of ancient warriors and community-spirited peasants, uncorrupted by thrusting laissez-faire capitalists and the artificialities of modern civi-lization. It was the place man had not yet ruined.

America had had its own eruption of nature-nationalism. This, too, was an idealized nature, a nature invented in support of a political cause. Stung by the European condescension toward all things Ameri-can, defenders of the new nation early on began to promote the conti-nent's wilderness as a source of national pride. Buffon, the European naturalist, had in 1749 dismissed American wildlife as unprolific, im-maturely developed, and lacking in vigor, a result of the less hos-pitable climate of the New World. The native Indians were likewise evidence of the raw and undeveloped state of the continent; they were lazy and less virile than Europeans. No good American patriot could take that lying down. Thomas Jefferson insisted that American mam-mals were, too, just as big as European ones; Philip Freneau, a young naturalist writing at the time of the Revolution, called the Mississippi the "the prince of rivers in comparison of which the Nile is but a rivulet, and the Danube is a ditch."

Others, going more to the heart of the controversy, insisted that the American wilderness, far from being an evil social influence—which after all was what the European critics were really getting at—was the invigorating inspiration for a new race of free men. Thus Samuel Williams wrote in his *Natural and Civil History of Vermont* in 1809, "While the ministers of kings were looking into their laws and records, to decide what should be the rights of men in the colonies, nature was establishing a system of freedom in America." And in the first recorded exhortation to see America first, Washington Irving complained, "We send our youth abroad to grow luxurious and effeminate in Europe; it appears to me, that a previous tour on the prairies would be more likely to produce that manliness, simplicity and self-dependence most in unison with our political institutions."[12]

By the end of the nineteenth century a very different political force was at work promoting public interest in nature in America. The progressive movement would prove to be the closest scrape that any nineteenth-century nature proponents actually had with science. Yet even here the hand at the tiller was an ideological one.

Some of the themes of progressivism were the familiar ones of European socialism of the same period. The economic depression of 1873 had been a disillusioning blow that led many to question the promise of the industrial revolution and to seek an answer in the sturdy values of the past. Poverty, which many Americans had sincerely believed would be vanquished forever by the nation's growing wealth and technological progress, cast a pall over cities and farms alike. Bitter and violent strikes wracked every large city in America; gangs of unemployed men scoured the countryside looking for work or trouble. For farmers, the depression dragged on well into the 1880s. The price a farmer could get for his produce was often less than what it cost to harvest. Hayfields were burned over, milk fed to the hogs, corncobs used as fuel for the kitchen stove.

If the English countryside was, to social reformers in that country, a symbol of medieval communitarianism, then the American wilderness was to progressives a symbol of the New World's traditional promise of freedom and opportunity. The Homestead Act, which had offered settlers 160 acres of land on the frontier, had been a "safety valve." As the American reformer Henry George wrote in 1879 in *Progress and Poverty* (a book that made the ex-newspaper man an instant national hero to millions of struggling farmers and mechanics), America's once vast public domain "has given a consciousness of freedom even to the dweller of crowded cities, and has been a well-spring of hope even to those who have never thought of taking refuge upon it."[13] But now the public domain was being gobbled up by the railroads and land speculators and loggers; the concentration of natural resources in the hands of a few was but one example of a much more sweeping concentration of wealth—in banks, in railroads, in "trusts"—that threatened the very foundations of democratic government. It was to strike a blow against this dangerous concentration of wealth that the Interstate Commerce Commission was created in 1887 to regulate the railroads, the Sherman Anti-Trust Act enacted in 1890 to break up the monopolies, and the national forest reserves established in 1891 to "save the title" to public lands against further plundering by the special interests. "Any great evil eventually gives rise to protest," explained Gifford Pinchot, who would become the first chief of the U.S. Forest Service. "Slavery did; the liquor trade did; the concentration of political power in the hands of the overrich did. . . ."[14]

Pinchot was a rarity in his day, if not unique. Trained in France as a forester at a time when forestry did not exist as a profession in the United States, he had a scientific understanding of natural forest processes as sophisticated as that of anyone of his time. As a scientist, he recognized the wastefulness of the then nearly universal American logging practice of "cut out and get out"; lumber companies simply cut everything to the ground and moved on. Loggers dismissed as nonsense the idea of managing forests for a sustained yield over the long run, or replanting, or even logging second growth on once-cut land. Pinchot was also aware of studies, or at least theories and thought, that were beginning to bring what would later be called an ecological perspective to bear on such practices. The most rigorous and forward looking was George Perkins Marsh's famous 1864 treatise, *Man and Nature,* which had identified long-term deleterious consequences of these logging practices on soils and rivers.

But Pinchot was also a true-blue reformer in the best Yankee tradition, and his brief for nature never strayed very far from his larger political purpose. Pinchot's emphasis—indeed it was almost an obsession—was on the need to manage forests and other public lands for the public good. He saw the profession of forestry, and more generally the entire cause of conservation, as both a scientific and a moral calling. Conservation, he believed, was a matter of right and wrong, "a moral issue" that "involves the rights and duties of our people—their rights to prosperity and happiness, and their duties to themselves, to their descendants, and to the whole future progress and welfare of this Nation."

These days, Pinchot—and for that matter the whole modern profession of forestry that he was so influential in founding—is looked on with considerable suspicion by orthodox environmentalists. Pinchot's emphasis on "sustained yield" and on the *use* of resources—indeed his unabashedly anthropocentric tendency to look upon nature as a "resource" at all rather than as something possessing intrinsic value—smacks too much of utilitarianism. There is no denying the charge. The progressive movement unquestionably saw conservation in economic and utilitarian terms. Water and timber and soil were the wealth of the nation, and they could either be managed wisely to provide the greatest good to the greatest number or be plundered in the name of quick profit by a few selfish plutocrats. The protection of forests, progressive President Theodore Roosevelt stated in 1901, is "not an end in itself; it is a means to increase and sustain the resources of our country and the industries which depend upon them." Pinchot himself steadfastly described forestry as an applied science, a branch of agriculture, and in fact waged a prolonged bureaucratic battle to have the new Forest Service established within the Department of Agriculture rather than the Department of the Interior.[15]

In this sense, the conservation movement (Pinchot himself coined the term to describe the progressive policies of resource management for the public good) actually tended to counter some of the idealistic myths of nature, myths that were strongly echoed and amplified by the politically active nature preservation movements of Europe and America. There was no pristine wilderness to be fenced off and left undisturbed in Pinchot's vision, no ancient folk land to be venerated, no psalm-singing woods to be sanctified, no rough and untamed frontier to be kept under glass to satisfy our nostalgic longings or national pride. Conservation saw man's presence on the land as a given. Pinchot said that the "friends of the forest" were naive to think that they could simply bring to a halt the third largest industry in America:

"The job was not to stop the axe, but to regulate its use." When wisely regulated, man's presence was more than just a necessity; it was a positive good. The agricultural analogy suggested that wise management could actually improve the forest, boosting its productivity and worth. Replanting trees, controlling fires, and eliminating destructive predators were investments that would reward the public with a continuing bounty of timber, grazing, and game far into the future. Taking charge of the new Forest Service in 1904, Pinchot immediately produced a manual that he significantly titled the "Use Book"; a preface, entitled "To the Public," declared that the forest reserves "are for the use of the people." The job of the Forest Service was to help the public properly use the forests and to fight fires.

But conservationism, even in those early days, often had trouble competing with the idealized vision of nature that had already attained such a hold on the imaginations of the "friends of the forest." In his autobiography Pinchot repeatedly complained of efforts, often successful, to banish all human activity from the land that was being rescued from private plunder. The original 1891 forest reserves act had in fact barred any use, making it illegal for a private citizen even to set foot on the reserves; it took a decade of fighting to change that. A constitutional amendment adopted by New York State in the same year forbade the cutting of any tree in the Adirondack State Forest Preserve. Pinchot complained that the proponents of such measures were right in their purpose but wrong in their method. "They hated to see a tree cut down. So do I," he said, "but you cannot practice forestry without it."[16]

Despite its political clout and bureaucratic victories, the official conservation movement in fact never really succeeded in supplanting the quasireligious ideas about nature of Muir and his followers; Pinchot and Muir would later split on this very issue of "wise use" versus "preservation." The split has only deepened since. Pinchot's scientific brand of conservation, with its emphasis on active, hands-on management, has increasingly been scorned by most organized environmental groups, who see it as nothing but a sellout to timber, ranching, and mining interests. "Without permanent and inviolate reserves, ecosystem management is a timber industry strategy," states a column in *Wild Forest Review,* a publication edited by environmental activist Jeffrey St. Clair.[17] Perhaps it was inevitable that Pinchot's ambitious vision would backfire. The overconfidence and the overreaching of the early progressive forest and range managers is still frequently cited by environmentalists who disparage the idea of active management; if "scientific" management means shooting bobcats and wolves or spraying herbicides on forests or planting monocultures of Douglas firs, then so much for scientific management. Muir was right because Pinchot was wrong.

But in the end Muir's followers would have been disappointed in Pinchot's vision of the wild no matter what. They were seeking something in nature that was not to be found in the hardheaded realism of Pinchot.

That is not to say that the environmental movement has today entirely forsaken Pinchot's approach to conservation. There is an enduring tradition of scientific and legal environmental activism that owes much to Pinchot and the early conservation movement. Yet its attentions have shifted largely to the narrower and more technical issues of air and water pollution, pesticide regulation, and the like. On the great issue of man's role in managing the wild, it is the friends of the forest who today prevail.

In the year 1891, most of the friends of the forest had probably never heard the term *ecology*. The great upsurge in preservationist sentiment occurred before the science of ecology even existed. Indeed, the professional botanists of the period noted the "fad" and expressed a hope that the popular enthusiasm for nature and "nature study" might be harnessed to introduce more serious scientific study of botany into high school curriculums.[18] Sentiment led; science followed.

The word *ecology* had in fact been coined in 1866 by a German biologist and philosopher, Ernst Haeckel, but it did not achieve widespread currency immediately; in America, the first scientific journal devoted specifically to ecology did not appear until fifty years later.

As Haeckel defined it, and the definition is still a good one, ecology is the study of the relationships between organisms and their environment. Haeckel's own scientific pursuits, however, were confined largely to zoology—his specialty was amoebas—and he made few if any scientific contributions to the field that he founded. His enduring influence was rather in the philosophical ideas that he saw as inseparable from this new science. Rarely, if ever, has a scientific discipline been so completely defined from its very birth not by what it had discovered but by how it wished to conceive of the universe. An early editor of the journal *Ecology* admitted that ecology was more a "point of view" than a scientific specialty.[19]

Haeckel's ideas about what that point of view should be were shared by many early ecologists. Part transcendentalist, part utopian socialist, they eagerly embraced the ideas about balance and perfection in nature that were already a central tenet of those doctrines. The harmony that Haeckel claimed to find in nature was nothing less than a manifestation of a deeper order in the universe. Nature behaved in an orderly way because it was not just a hodgepodge of competing species; it was itself a balanced and unified organism, Haeckel said, one that encompassed not only the physical but (in terms reminiscent of Emerson and the Christian physiologists) the spiritual: nature was "mind and embodiment . . . energy and matter . . . God and the world."

Whatever this was, it was not science. Haeckel's political ideas about nature went even further than his spiritual ones. If nature reflected the deep balance and order of the cosmos, then it was a nothing less than a handbook for the total restructuring of human society. Just as a biological organism was controlled by its brain and central nervous system, so the ideal state would be strongly centralized for the greatest efficiency. Human altruism, love, and sense of duty were all to be found in laws of nature; so too were arguments in favor of "racial hygiene" (i.e., eugenics) and euthanasia. If human institutions could be brought into conformity with the plan that nature had provided, a peaceful, humane, and efficient society would result.

Haeckel was politically influential in his lifetime through the Monist League, which he had founded; many of his pupils were prominent reformers and political agitators. His ideas about holism and social reform enjoyed a wide appeal, not so much for anything they might say about how plant species interact in a forest clearing but for what they said about the human condition. The late nineteenth and early twentieth centuries were a time when many people were looking for "scientific" laws that would explain and guide human society. Darwin's works had been enthusiastically read by social reformers of both the left and the right in search of biological authority for their particular vision of the world of tomorrow. Interest in eugenics was widespread in intellectual circles; it seemed to be biology's scientific answer to the social problems of poverty, criminality, and mental illness, which were looming ever larger. In Boston and Newport, Julia Ward Howe and others of the genteel Yankee reform tradition held salons where the leading naturalists of the day were summoned to hold forth on natural history—and its implications for life, the universe, and everything. "Where, indeed, with the disintegration of traditional religion and ethics, can we hope to find the means of correcting our mental, moral and physical maladjustments, except in a biologically renovated ethics . . . ?" asked the Harvard biologist William Morton Wheeler.[20]

Where indeed. Haeckel's works were translated into English and widely read in Britain and America. His ideas especially appealed to "a generation of republican, socialist atheists, who were anxious to believe what was in effect a new religion."[21] They found in Haeckel's pantheism and his ideal of a society structured in scientific accordance with the laws of nature confirmation of the Marxist and Fabian view of an efficient modern state managed by experts for the good of all. The disapproval of "individualism" and the emphasis on the properties of the whole were very much of a piece.

Science has always been vulnerable to superficial mischaracterization by the cocktail-party chatter of nonscientists, akin to the contemporary enthusiasm for quantum mechanics or chaos theory as supposed insights into the meaning of life. Yet Haeckel's cosmological and political ideas were more than just a superficial philosophical gloss layered atop ecological research. They penetrated to the core of ecology itself, to how many ecologists interpreted their data and formulated their theories about the behavior of organisms. In a significant article that appeared in the journal *Ecology* in 1935, Arthur G. Tansley, a prominent British ecologist, complained that ecologists had allowed their thinking about order and structure in nature to be carried away by the appeal of such political beliefs. "It is difficult to resist the impression," he wrote, that the "enthusiastic advocacy of holism is not wholly derived from an objective contemplation of the facts of nature, but is at least partly motivated by an imagined future 'whole' to be realized in an ideal human society."[22]

Tansley was reacting specifically to an earlier article in the journal by a South African grasslands scientist who, in a mixture of science and philosophy, had warmly embraced the concept that natural communities of organisms were in truth a "superorganism" with "holist" properties—that is, characteristics that were greater than the sum of the individuals that made up the community. But more generally, Tansley's article was a broadside against Frederic Clements, the pioneering turn-of-the-century American ecologist whose ideas about stability and rigid order in nature had proved enormously influential—and indeed remain so to this day among "nonpracticing ecologists," decades after real ecologists have ceased to take them seriously.

Clements's actual research was very much in the mold of the new science of ecology. Traditional botany and zoology meant collecting specimens, dissecting them, identifying and measuring anatomical structures, and compiling taxonomies. Ecologists looked instead at the dynamics of nature: how species interacted, competed, and parasitized one another. Clements's method was rigorously quantitative. He did not study the plants themselves; he studied data *about* plants, particularly their spatial distribution and their environment. When he set out to study an ecological community, he simply measured and plotted the location of every single plant within a "quadrat," or grid area, along with every environmental factor that he could think of that might have a bearing on the distribution and makeup of the community: the type of soil, its water content, wind, precipitation, light intensity, air humidity. The work, he said, no doubt with a certain pride, was "drudgery to the mere dabbler" in nature study. This was no genteel botanizing or bird-watching.

But when it came to interpreting this mass of data he had accumulated on all different types of plant communities—when it came time to produce a grand theory to explain it all—it was the organismic ideas of Haeckel that inspired this dogged number cruncher. Clements concluded that the plants that made up an identifiable type of vegetation—a hardwood forest or a prairie or a savanna—were not just casual neighbors. They were literally the organically bound parts of a single complex organism. Each "formation," as Clements termed these superorganisms, "arises, grows, matures, and dies," just like any other living thing. If a forest is cut or burned, first weedy plants and brush appear; these are succeeded by pine trees; then finally, as the formation reaches adulthood, the original hardwood forest is reproduced. The adult or "climax" formation is the inescapable end result of this reproductive process; succession "can no more fail to terminate in the adult form of vegetation than it can in the case of an individual plant," Clements stated.[23]

Clements argued that the climax stage of a particular area was rigidly determined by natural geological facts—climate and soil. Given those, succession marched along with unbreakable purpose. Succession always begins with a denuded area and ends in a stable climax formation, period. Although the process might be interrupted, just as growth of an individual organism might be arrested, it cannot fail ultimately to reach adulthood in the end. Moreover, each stage of development is part of a purposeful plan, preparing the way for the next: The pines shade out the brushy weeds, clearing the ground for the hardwood seedlings that will follow.

Clements and his many disciples were not shy about pressing home what they saw as the inescapable political consequences of these ideas. Succession acknowledged that nature was not immutable; change did occur. But that change was always purposeful, orderly, directed. Succession was a process of stabilization, of nature righting itself. The obvious conclusion was that land-use management, whenever possible, should have as its aim the preservation of the "natural ideal"—the climax formation. Any disturbance of the climax by man would be fighting against the inexorable forces of nature. During the great Dust Bowl of the 1930s, ecologists of Clements's school argued that problems of pest outbreaks, desertification, and the like were in fact all a consequence of human disturbance having disrupted the climax formation. Clements himself proposed a Haeckelian political solution: Place all farms and ranches under the benevolent guidance of government ecologists who would coordinate regional land-use planning. Shortsighted individualism and petty politics would give way to scientific management for the good of the whole. "Within such a huge organism," Clements wrote—and he was actually referring here to the *nation*—"the whole is much greater than the mere sum of its parts . . . it is here that cooperation will meet its supreme test, and it can emerge from this successfully only as the ecological ideal of 'wholeness,' of organs working in unison within a great organism, prevails over partial and partisan viewpoints."[24]

A similar idea was advanced, but on a global scale, by another prominent plant biologist, Sir George Stapledon, in Britain. Stapledon thought that agriculture, forestry, parks, and reclamation should all be placed under a global planning authority, which "he thought could be run by the same type of man who had run the Indian Civil Service."[25] Clements's equation of society with an organism is a common theme among such reform-minded ecologists. Members of the "Ecology Group" at the University of Chicago were explicit in their claim that society was not just *like* an organism; it *was* an organism. The "higher levels of integration" that existed in nature had demonstrated that, just as the parts of the body cannot function alone, neither can individual organisms and neither can individual nation states. "Isolationism is a biological anachronism," they concluded triumphantly.

Another major school of ecologists, which emphasized the study of energy flows through ecological systems, reached similar conclusions about the need for world government for a slightly different reason. Only photosynthetic plants produce energy. All other organisms are consumers. Thus, except for the input of energy from the sun, life on earth constitutes a closed system that will inevitably decay unless drastic measures are taken to prevent the leakage or loss of energy. In an uncanny anticipation of Dr. Strangelove, these ecologists argued that the only hope for the survival of humanity lay in a total reorganization of society, with compulsory labor and selective breeding directed by wise scientists. A 1923 science fiction novel written by one of these wise scientists, a professor of chemistry named A. J. Stewart, laid out the program. In the story, *Nordington's Million,* the potential collapse of society owing to its precarious dependence on energy flows is hastened when a man-made grass-eating bacteria escapes from the laboratory. The earth's vegetation is destroyed, except for a small area around Glasgow, where a millionaire has managed to establish a bacteria-free refuge. He recruits a million healthy people, ruthlessly refusing to allow any more people to come in once the carrying capacity of his city is reached. Strikes are put down mercilessly. After the rest of the world collapses, the perfect social order he has created can expand and take over the world.[26]

Even as practiced by ecologists—much less as it was read by amateur nature lovers—ecology was thoroughly saturated in politics. Ecological ideas were embraced or scorned according as they bolstered or undermined political agendas. Some of the politics was internal as well. The organismic view of nature offered some scientists a justification for their own, increasingly anachronistic, research styles. The Harvard biologist William Morton Wheeler, who studied ants while he wasn't promoting eugenics and other bits of his "biologically renovated" ethics, was obviously distraught (if not bewildered) by the changes taking place in biology; cell biology and genetics were rapidly taking over the field—and turning it into a hard science. It was all rather ungentlemanly. Wheeler said the old-style naturalist's desire to appreciate rather than explain "may account for his somewhat unsympathetic attitude toward the bright high school boys now bombinating in the biological laboratories of our universities. He feels that not a few of these neophytes manifest a somewhat gangster attitude towards Nature, so eager are they to assault, scalp or rape her." In the context of Harvard in the 1920s, of course, "high school boys" was not an incidental choice of words; boys from the right families went to prep schools, not high schools. Ecology was an affirmation of the old, decent way of studying nature.[27]

The counterattack against Clements's ideas by Tansley and others was, nonetheless, waged largely on narrow scientific grounds. From almost the start, a number of botanists and ecologists pointed out that however rigorous his underlying data were, the conclusions that Clements drew from that data simply did not comport with biological reality. Continental scientists were largely dismissive, calling the ideas of climax and of the plant community as an organism "fairy tales" and "fantasies." Tansley was at first willing to accept the concepts as a "heuristic device"; they were not a literal description of reality but were nonetheless a useful tool to study and learn about landscape types and how they change. But by 1935, he had come to reject the legitimacy of the ideas even as a device. One of the major problems Tansley saw was that Clements's scheme failed to acknowledge the role of man in nature. If humans acted only to "disturb" the climax, then how was one to make sense of the natural part that at least primitive human tribes surely played in "biotic communities"? A more direct objection had been voiced several years earlier by an American botanist, Henry Gleason. His main point was that succession is simply not a rigidly deterministic process that always marches in but one direction. It starts, stops, reverses, and changes course. Even the supposedly stable climaxes themselves are short-lived. Clements had denied that "retrogressive successions" could occur. Gleason rattled off example after example where they indisputably *did* occur. A slight increase in rainfall along the western boundary of the grassland region at the foot of Rockies would push succession one way as ponderosa pines rapidly replaced the grass-covered plains; a slight decrease another year would kill off the pine seedlings or leave them standing in isolated groups as the grasses reasserted themselves. On the prairies of Illinois, the boundaries between forest and prairie also regularly shifted back and forth, sometimes moving in both directions simultaneously in different places. Gleason noted that naturally caused fires, which gave the shade-intolerant prairie plants a chance to compete against the trees, were continually disrupting what was the presumed climax formation for that area's climate and soil. Clements had insisted that only the slowest geologic changes could lead to a new climax formation for a given area. Gleason pointed out that to the extent there even was such a thing as a climax, it was being totally redefined from year to year as rainfall and fire went through their natural fluctuations. Clements insisted that change in nature was a directional process; yet others who had looked at the same data could find no reason to conclude that change was anything but change. "There is every reason for believing that succession actually proceeds in both directions indiscriminately," Gleason noted. He concluded: "Viewed from this standpoint, the climax loses much of its artificial halo with which we have invested it."

Gleason had other damning evidence. Groups of plants found together in the same natural landscapes did not behave as "assemblages" or organic entities; they were just groups of plants. The makeup of each of these supposedly unique and well-defined assemblages changed continuously over time and space; any properties of the landscape as a whole were nothing more than the "mass-effect of the action or behavior of individual plants."[28]

Further blows to the idea of succession and climax came during the droughts of the 1930s; again, something that fell far short of a major climatic change over geologic time played havoc with successional sequences as supposedly preclimax formations took over on the prairies. Even devout followers of Clements's theories admitted that what was nothing more than a short-term change in weather patterns had had lasting, perhaps even long-term consequences for the landscape. By the 1940s, the idea of climax and superorganism was vanishing rapidly from the ecological literature, and it was essentially gone by the 1950s. A careful analysis by one science historian of the doctoral dissertations of a prominent group of grasslands scientists found that even "archival" citations of Clements's work ceases altogether after 1945. The idea of discrete vegetational zones determined by climate and soil type also makes its exit at this time.[29]

Yet Clements's ideas live on with a vengeance today in popular ecology writing, both in their specifics (climax, succession) and in their broader implications (nature is orderly and purposeful and, if left undisturbed, will tend toward stability). Ecologists who dare to point out the fallacies of these ideas have been subjected to ferocious attacks by outraged environmentalists, who seem to be almost astonished at such sacrilege. Environmentalists are so certain that Clements's ideas are the proven theories of ecological science that the only possible explanation they can come up with for such heresy is a sinister one. The environmental historian Donald Worster claims that in denying that nature has a set order and purpose, these heretical ecologists are guilty of a "new permissiveness" toward nature; it is all, he says, a Reagan-era apologia for "modern industrialism" and its "entrepreneurial ideology." As Worster writes, "Revisionism and relativism in ecological science is motivated, at least in part, by a desire to be less disapproving of economic development than environmentalists were in the 1960s and '70s." Worster sees sinister hints of Reaganomics everywhere in modern ecological science—in the repudiation of the superorganismic nature of ecosystems; in the new emphasis on the behavior of individual, competing species; in studies that stress the role of disturbance and discontinuity in nature over harmony and unity; even in the use of economic metaphors in ecological research papers. Science, he suggests, is nothing but culture and politics by another name.[30]

The assertion that science is but an exercise in cultural relativism, that science is what its political implications are rather than what its experimental findings are, that the truth is revealed in the rhetoric and metaphors used by its practitioners rather than in their mathematical equations, is of course a convenient one for academic humanists and others who may be ill equipped to understand those experimental findings or mathematical equations. No one denies that culture influences scientific thought. But some things hold whether one believes in God, the Enlightenment, or Ronald Reagan. People who spend their lives combing literary texts for hidden meanings think they're on to something big when they find an ecologist writing a popular essay that describes plants "earning their livings." People who understand science are less impressed by this game of deconstructing metaphors.

The real problem is that "ecology," to many environmentalists, is not a science at all. It is not something to be evaluated and tested on scientific terms. It is rather an ideology to be measured against a moral and political yardstick. What Worster is really denouncing is not bad science, but rather sacrilege—sacrilege against the system of moral values he has erected upon a few scientifically dubious but philosophically appealing ideals. Or, to update the metaphor, perhaps the correct term is not sacrilege but sellout. The opposition to urbanization, industrialization, and technological progress that has been a central theme of environmentalism from the time it became an identifiable political movement in the late nineteenth century has made the movement a catchall for anti-status-quo social sentiment. As such, environmentalism became a natural successor to the sixties protest movements as a way to off the establishment, with the added benefit that one was no longer required to mix with the proletariat but instead could do it by living in the country and going backpacking. The philosopher Peter Singer, for instance, tells how his student radicalism and opposition to the Vietnam War led to his taking up the cause of animal rights and environmentalism: "Once you are against the military/industrial complex in general, well, it doesn't take much to see its effect on the environment and the rest of the world."[31]

Thus, to many contemporary environmental writers, the appeal of ecology as a science is that it is supposed, in an oft-quoted phrase, to be a "subversive science," one that perfectly mirrors the "subversive," antiprogress politics of environmentalism. "Intuitive" ecology has un-

dermined the "mechanistic straitjacket" of traditional science, rejecting the Western, linear, mathematical, reductionist formalism that
sustains our technological and exploitive society.

> Ecology speaks of a natural world of deeply humane characteristics. . . .
> In this world, cooperation, interconnectedness, even "mutual aid" have
> been discovered in abundance . . . in the natural balance, the ecological
> worldview finds an answer to some of the most destructive values and
> beliefs in the West. . . . [I]t exerts a persuasive influence over minds
> which are ready to turn away from the one-sided, human-centered, tech-
> nologically bewitched and polluted life of modern industrial culture.

So states one writer. Says another: "Ecology does not systematize by
mathematical generalization or materialist reductionism, but by the
almost sensuous intuiting of natural harmonies on the largest scale. Its
patterns are not those of numbers, but of unity in process; its psychol-
ogy borrows from Gestalt and is an awakening awareness of wholes
greater than the sum of their parts." Or a third: "By pointing up the
essential role of every part of an ecosystem, that if one part is removed
the system is weakened and loses stability, ecology has moved in the
direction of the leveling of value hierarchies."[32] It would appear that
even those who dismiss science as subjective, relative, ideological, and
culturally biased still want to claim that science is on their side, which
is perhaps the next best thing to having God on one's side. But, as we
shall see, ecological science really has something very different to say
about the nature of the natural world, and about man's place in it,
from what any of these wishful caricatures suggest.

PART II

Nature Reality

FOUR

Disorderly Conduct

In the mountains of southern Chile grow great forests dominated by trees of the genus *Nothofagus,* the false beech. With a lifespan of up to five hundred years, some of these magnificent trees that today form the dense forest canopy were seedlings when Christopher Columbus set foot upon the New World.

The first botanists who entered these remote and towering woods believed they had discovered a classic example of a forest climax community. The sun-loving shrubs and trees that had first invaded this land had long ago been shaded out by the slow-growing giants that came to dominate the forest. According to the classical scheme of forest succession, the dominants were, by definition, those species able to reproduce under the dense canopy of shade that they themselves cast over the forest floor. Once established, the dominants would reproduce indefinitely, a stable, self-perpetuating equilibrium that would hold for millenniums—so long as it was left undisturbed by man.

It took a long time for botanists to admit it, but there was something terribly wrong with this explanation. *Nothofagus* seedlings are virtually absent from the forest floor. Other trees are present in all sizes and ages; the false beeches appear only in the narrow age-band of the oldest trees that form the canopy. It is these other trees that by rights ought to dominate; they are the ones that can reproduce under the shade of the mature forest. *Nothofagus* seedlings are incapable of growing under the conditions that *Nothofagus* itself creates.

What keeps these other species from ousting the false beeches and claiming their birthright? The mountains of southern Chile are among the most seismically active places on earth; that should have been a clue. For it is nothing short of repeated disaster that is responsible for the illusion of stability that these old-growth forests present. *Nothofagus* are adapted not to stability but to chaos. The mountains are regularly shaken by powerful earthquakes, which trigger landslides and avalanches of debris. The volcanic soil that covers the steep mountainsides turns to a greasy soup when wet; layers of porous, gravel-sized ash alternate with very fine powdery ash that lubricates the soil like wax on a linoleum floor. Mile-long mud slides are not uncommon. At other times erupting volcanoes set huge fires. Catastrophe strikes on average several times during the half-millennium lifetime of a *Nothofagus* tree. The soil beneath the old-growth stands that exist today have been found to contain several-yard thick deposits of ash or debris or other evidence of deep scarring.

When the hillsides are laid bare by these upheavals, *Nothofagus* seedlings grow in abundance, outcompeting shrubs and herbs. By the time that shade-tolerant competitor species have invaded one of these denuded hillsides, the false beeches have gained a substantial head start. And before the false beeches can die and be replaced in the canopy by their natural successors, disaster will usually have opportunely struck again. Simply put, *Nothofagus* cannot reproduce without outside intervention—intervention of the most drastic kind, intervention which does nothing less than level the forest as surely as the most environmentally ignominious clear-clutter, and which leaves a pretty bad erosion problem to boot.[1]

Rather than an intrusion that upsets nature's timeless balance and equilibrium, disturbance is a necessity for much of the life on this planet. The false beeches of southern Chile are just one example of the countless species that are unable to complete their life cycle in the absence of disturbance. Disturbance occurs across all scales of time and space. Waves strike the shore every few seconds, tossing small boulders across the sea floor, scraping loose barnacles and sea plants. Lightning strikes the earth two hundred million times a year; only perhaps 1 percent starts fires, and most of those are quickly extinguished by rain that accompanies the storm, but still the cumulative effect is enormous. Charcoal layers discovered in the soil testify to the fact that 95 percent of the forests in the north central United States and southern Canada have burned at one time or another. Fire-history studies of the western United States indicate that once every couple of hundred years lightning sets off a major inferno. Years of drought or high winds or an insect outbreak that has left piles of dead wood conspire to carry the sparks to the crowns of the trees, spreading the flames in a firestorm that does not stop before hundreds of thousands or even millions of acres are consumed.[2]

The largest hurricanes strike with roughly the same frequency. Tremendously destructive hurricanes blew through New England in 1635, 1815, and 1938, flattening forests and leaving heaps of debris scattered across the countryside. The 1938 storm destroyed the last remaining tracts of uncut old-growth timber in the region. (Hurricane Andrew, which struck the Everglades in 1992, was considerably less destructive but nonetheless leveled seventy thousand acres of mangrove forests and uprooted somewhere between 25 and 40 percent of the region's pines.) Disease outbreaks and insect invasions also leave their mark, sometimes for thousands of years, as in the case of the infestation that nearly destroyed New England's hemlocks five thousand years ago. It is only a matter of time before the next hurricane or epidemic will once again change the course of the landscape's history. Meanwhile, not a year passes without ice storms, flash floods, droughts, or mud slides. Not a season passes without disturbance of the landscape by beaver dams, gopher burrows, even moose footprints—all of which create patches that one species or another owes its very existence to.[3] The "normal" state of nature is not one of balance and repose; the "normal" state is to be recovering from the last disaster. In most ecosystems the interval between disturbances—fire, frost, flood, windstorm—is almost always less than the life span of an individual member of the dominant species. So much for balance.[4]

The simple picture of forest succession leading to a climax community does not even begin to do justice to the richness and complexity of life. The temperate forests of North America have always been a mosaic, formed by a never-ending succession of disturbances, from the toppling of a single tall tree in a high wind to a fire that clears a hundred square miles. To portray the story of this forest as a succession that marches unwaveringly from weedy annuals to shrubs to shade-intolerant pines to a climax of old-growth shade-tolerant hardwoods is at best a gross caricature. All of these stages had to have coexisted, simultaneously, throughout the modern history of this landscape. Both shade-tolerant and shade-intolerant trees regularly reached the canopy. Small gaps—a single tree that falls over, creating a chink in the canopy but not altering the amount of light reaching the forest floor to any great extent—might be filled by shade-tolerant species such as hemlock, sugar maple, and beech. Major disturbances—hurricanes or forest fires—favored shade-intolerant species: white pine, tulip tree, red oak, black cherry.

Forestry methods that seek to minimize disturbance, and which have on that count been considered environmentally preferable to clear-cutting entire stands, have the ironic effect of vastly narrowing the diversity of the forests. In an experiment in New Hampshire, selection cutting was practiced exclusively; single, marketable trees were removed one at a time with minimal disturbance to the surrounding wood. The result was that the canopy eventually contained 92 percent shade-tolerant species. The researchers concluded that the only way to restore the original mix of species would be to introduce a mix of selection and clear cutting in a way that more closely mimics the natural disturbance processes. Nature clear-cuts; so should we.[5]

Indeed, the principal consequence of the swirling patterns of constant change found in nature is a vastly richer diversity of life than would exist if the classical—or mystical—notions of timeless stability and equilibrium in nature were really true. A continually disturbed landscape contains many more microhabitats than does a landscape where uniformity and stability reign. On the prairies of western Nebraska, pocket gophers heap up acres of bare soil and litter around their burrows, creating a continually renewed seedbed for short-lived annuals that are usually outcompeted by the more tenacious perennial prairie plants. Much the same phenomenon occurs on the mounds dug up by badgers in tallgrass prairie.[6] Along the California shoreline the jostling of waves stirs up sediments rich in the microscopic algae that limpets feed upon and jars loose from small boulders the larger plants that crowd out limpets on less disturbed surfaces. On the Washington coast mussel beds heavily disturbed by waves contain empty patches colonized by the plant known as sea palm; the plant is absent from beds where strong waves are infrequent.[7] It is a truism of ecology that no two species can occupy the same niche. Disturbance acts to greatly increase the number of niches that a given landscape supports.

Or to consider it from the point of view of the occupant of the niche, disturbance is what makes life possible. The niche created by fire, for example, has been intensively exploited by a host of plants that could hardly exist otherwise. Poised to take advantage of the flood of sunlight and open soils following a forest fire, these plants have evolved mechanisms to quickly colonize disturbed ground and to grow and reproduce while the window remains open. Many of these fire-adapted plants have light, windblown seeds that spread rapidly over open ground, much more rapidly than the heavy acorns or nuts of hardwoods that depend upon squirrels or other mammals for their dissemination. The first plants to colonize fire-scarred ground are often annuals, which invest all of their energy in rapid growth and the production of huge quantities of seed. They are in it for the short haul, out to milk the precious sunlight for the quickest return. But it is a strategy that only disturbance makes possible. Like all speculators, they are exploiters of the market's volatility.

Fire-adapted trees and woody shrubs cannot indulge in the same rampant speculation that weedy annuals can; producing woody growth that must last for years to come means less energy available for seed production. But they have evolved a number of strategies that similarly aim to insure that they will be ready to reproduce when fire has cleared the ground. White pine seedlings send out shallow roots that can take hold quickly but only in light, burned humus that is clear of surface litter, lichens, and dense grass; they fare poorly in the heavy humus of an unburned forest floor. Some scrubland species flower and produce seed only when they are stimulated by the flood of light and extra soil nutrients that follow a fire. Others have developed ways to bank the seeds themselves until they are needed. Some seeds contain a light-sensitive pigment known as phytochrome, which triggers germination only when struck by sunlight. Chaparral shrubs of the genus *Rhus* produce dormant seeds that germinate only after the heat of a fire melts their waxy seed coat. The seeds of the jack pine remain sealed within tightly closed pinecones until a fire melts a resinous substance that keeps the cones glued shut; twenty-year-old cones have yielded viable seeds. All of these strategies are simply ways to avoid wasting seeds by casting them on unprepared and unsuitable ground.

Even the supposed climax species hedge their bets. They have to have some way to exploit gaps that do open up; these solid citizens of the forest must have what botanists aptly call a "fugitive" aspect, a way to take it on the lam when the looting starts. Oak and hickory and other "sprout hardwoods," for example, can regenerate after a fire by resprouting from their roots. Though this is not their principal mode of propagation, it constitutes clear evolutionary recognition that even species well adapted to stability must be prepared to face upheavals.[8]

The vegetation that flourishes after a fire sweeps through is home to many birds and mammals; they, too, are creatures of disturbance. Moose are the annuals of the animal kingdom—annual weeds with antlers. They follow fire to browse on the flush of green shoots that sprout through the charred ground. In good years moose disperse quickly and crank up their birthrate to make the best of the new habitat that chance has presented them. Beaver, hare, black bear, cougar, wild turkey, prairie chicken, bobwhite, grouse, and ptarmigan are all adapted to the conditions created by fire. On the prairies, fire encourages food plants such as chokeberry and blackberry; it destroys cover for predators to hide in ambush; it makes seeds and insects easier to spot; it even inhibits many parasites of birds and mammals by eliminating the intermediate insect hosts that the parasites need to complete their life cycles or, by warming and drying the ground, denying the parasites the moist conditions that their larval stages often require to develop. (Fire exposes the soil directly to sunlight and drying winds; indirectly, the blackened soil absorbs heat more readily and thus warms faster.) Destruction for some means life for others.[9]

Confined to the experiences of a human lifetime, man has had a hard time grasping the essential part that destructive forces play in nature. It defies our intuition, our sense of aesthetics, our sense of the value of material things; it certainly defies the centuries of belief in the balance and perfection of nature that have animated the environmental movement. The woods, John Muir said, are a cathedral. Our normal reaction to such a statement is not to run out and cheer an act of arson. Indeed, it is hard to find a word in the English language that adequately captures the idea of repeated, extensive change that is for the good. "Damage," "destruction," "perturbation"—all the words that ecologists find themselves using to describe the disturbance processes in nature (even "disturbance"!) bear distinctly unfavorable connotations. These are the things that human civilization has sought to combat, not celebrate. Ecologists have been forced into ungainly coinages such as "patch dynamics" and "nonequilibrium determinants" in an attempt to find a neutral way of expressing the notion that nature is continually remaking itself. It is all uncomfortably reminiscent, perhaps, of too many famously ironic testimonies to human hypocrisy ("we destroyed the village to save it"). How much simpler (and safely virtuous) it is to believe that nature is a timeless edifice.

A few turn-of-the-century foresters who were able to overcome these cultural and cognitive barriers recognized the value of carefully planned burning as a forest-management tool, but they ran smack into another obstacle: The idea was political poison. Gifford Pinchot's Forest Service had waged a massive propaganda campaign to reverse the age-old attitudes of the American pioneer, in whose eyes there was no grander sight than a good rip-roaring wildfire, which could accomplish in one day what it would otherwise take an army of axemen a whole summer. In the best inquisitorial tradition the Forest Service disdained to show mercy in its war on forest fires lest mercy be mistaken for weakness. Government managers feared that allowing even small, controlled burns on national forests would set a bad and inconsistent example that would only encourage the backsliders. And Pinchot, in any case, was eager to do much more than just set examples. He wanted to extend government jurisdiction to private forest lands, which he and other professional foresters believed were being grossly mismanaged, and fire prevention was his most powerful political argument in favor of such an expansion of government authority. The sloppy practices of commercial loggers—huge piles of logging debris, or "slash," were routinely left lying on the forest floor—and a general carelessness with fire were regularly torching off huge infernos, probably of an intensity far greater than any natural disturbance processes. A 1911 law authorized the use of federal funds for fire protection along the watersheds of navigable streams, and subsequent acts and the Depression-era Civilian Conservation Corps greatly expanded the reach of the federal firefighters. (The Forest Service even hired a psychologist in 1939 to try to figure out why southerners insisted on burning their woods; the psychologist, John Shea, not surprisingly concluded that the practice reflected deep and irrational psychological impulses. Setting fires was, he said, a "folk custom"; the explanations that the woodsmen themselves gave for the practice—that burning kept down the snakes, ticks, and weevils—were merely the "defensive beliefs of a disadvantaged cultural group.")[10] If the settlers declined the Forest Service's psychotherapeutic prescription, the wildfires nonetheless succumbed to the political and fiscal clout that the federal government brought to bear. From 1926 to 1930, more than four hundred thousand acres burned each year in the Northeast; by the 1970s the average was down to eighty thousand a year.[11]

A great success, no doubt, and one repeated all across the country. But it came with a terrible price. As forests age, year after year, safe from the ravages of fire, ecological diversity in many areas has plummeted. Old trees fall victim to disease and insect pests, such as the spruce budworm, that were historically kept in check by fire. Huge quantities of dead wood accumulate on the forest floors, threatening to trigger a vast holocaust prevented in the past by frequent low-intensity ground fires that regularly consumed accumulated fuel loads before they ever reached such dangerous levels. The massive campaign of forest fire suppression in this century has greatly reduced the number of fires but greatly increased the intensity of the few that do occur. And those intense fires, far from promoting landscape and species diversity the way light burns do, can reach such an intense heat that they sterilize the soil and leave only a uniform, and barren, landscape.[12]

The early grasslands ecologists agreed with the powers that be that fire was detrimental or, at best, insignificant. In truth, fire was what had kept their prairie a prairie, by suppressing competing forest trees. The subsequent control of fire, and the loss of prairie that ensued, is now generally recognized as having contributed to the extinction of the heath hen, a chicken-like bird originally found on the scrub-oak plains of Massachusetts, Connecticut, New York, New Jersey, and Pennsylvania. Initially, forest clearing by the New England settlers led to an increase and spread of the birds. But the suppression of fire, which had maintained its native habitat, and the subsequent reforestation of the Northeast in the nineteenth century sent populations into a nosedive. By 1840 the bird had vanished from mainland Massachusetts and Connecticut; by 1880 it was confined to Martha's Vineyard; by 1931 only a single individual was left.

Other species not driven to extinction were driven into the encroaching woodlands. Many birds and mammals long considered by biologists to be woodland species—including deer, turkey, and ruffed grouse—now appear to be more properly classified as forest-edge or grassland animals. They have simply been forced by circumstance to eke out an existence in a less than ideal habitat.[13]

If scientists have not always been quick to pick up on such facts, it is in part because the adaptations in nature to disturbance are often subtle. The California condor, an endangered species, has the peculiar habit of gorging itself to the point that it needs a long, clear runway in order to get airborne after feeding. Regular burning of the chaparral can maintain these open spaces. But absent these strip-clearing fires, the birds have to digest overnight before they can again struggle into the air; these prolonged absences from the nest, during which time unattended nestlings go hungry, appear to have hastened the demise of the species. Ruffed grouse are quite sensitive to the fire stage of the forests they nest in; the low brush in eight-to-twenty-year-old forests offers cover for breeding, with the density of grouse dropping almost to zero in older forests. Kirtland's warbler, another endangered species, is even more finicky. It nests exclusively in homogeneous stands of five-to-fifteen-foot-tall jack pines. Only those trees, which are typically ten to fifteen years old, have low branches which, in mass, form a dense thicket that covers the ground and allows the birds to enter and leave their nests without being observed by predators. After fifteen years the jack pines drop their lower branches; after another decade or so, competing shade-tolerant species begin to take over the forest altogether. Without a fire every fifteen years that destroys at least a sizable chunk of forest within the Kirtland's limited habitat in northern

Figure 4. The virtues of forest fires: A profusion of aspen stems regrows following a fire or clear-cut, providing both food and cover for breeding ruffed grouse. In mature hardwood forests an understory of hazel offers an inferior substitute.

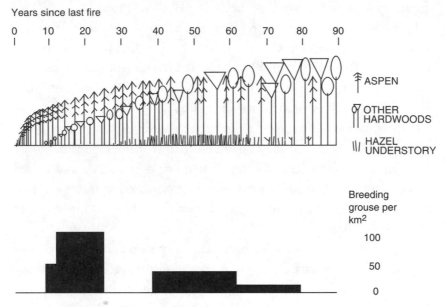

Adapted from Bendell, "Effects of Fire on Birds and Mammals," 88.

Michigan, the species simply cannot survive. Smokey Bear notwith-standing, ecologists were in this case able to persuade the authorities that they had no choice. A dozen 320-acre blocks of jack pine forest were set aside; they are burned in rotation, one every five years, thus ensuring that at any given time at least one block will always be within the ten-to-fifteen-year window.[14]

The recognition that individual birds and mammals are rarely harmed in forest fires was also slow in coming. It is not intuitively or scientifically obvious. Only through animal tracking studies, physical measurements of soil temperature during blazes, and postfire surveys have scientists established that birds and mammals in fire-prone re-gions are seldom killed in forest fires. Despite what we all remember from *Bambi,* most animals react calmly to a blaze, either going into burrows or simply moving away. Rodents that were confined during a burn by cages placed over their burrows survived, as long as the bur-rows had two openings to prevent suffocation; measurements showed that soil temperatures drop dramatically even a fraction of inch below the hottest part of a blaze. In one chaparral fire surface temperatures were over a thousand degrees Fahrenheit; a half inch below the surface it never got above sixty degrees. Biologists intensively searched a 640-acre spruce-aspen forest in Alberta following a severe wildfire and found no dead grouse or hares and only three dead voles.[15]

The problem we face in coming to grips with change in nature is by no means entirely ideological or political; some of it is just human nature. Many of the dynamic forces in nature operate on time scales longer than the life of a single researcher and certainly longer than the life of a single research grant. But more important may be the human instinct to seek out patterns and form generalizations. One recent ecological paper noted that researchers have a natural tendency always to look upon averages as typical and variations about the average as nothing more than noise or sampling errors. The search for order and regularity is our way of organizing information. But the old saying that a man can drown in a stream whose average depth is three feet is the warning to be heeded here. It is variation about the average that tells much of the story of ecology; it is variation that lets the moose survive and the false beech regenerate and the white pine reach the forest canopy. None of those things could ever happen in an "average" forest.[16]

Popularizers of ecology canny enough to have dropped the line that nature is eternal and never changing have usually come to terms with its dynamic character simply by cramming this new brief into their old satchel; when it comes time to address the jury, they are sure to use that tried and true speech about the balance of nature. Fire is thus part of a "natural cycle" that repeats over and over—as long as it is not interfered with by man, of course. It is nature's way of maintaining its balance, always returning to its starting point; it is proof again that if only man will not intrude, nature can take care of itself in the long run.

The reality is much more chaotic, much chancier. The outcomes are not preordained; but for that hurricane or this fire, the world we see around us might well have turned out very different. Those species that have adapted to disturbance are making a bet, no more. When ecologists speak of natural disturbance "cycles," they are being unintentionally misleading. Most are cycles in name only. They are random, shifting, wobbling, never twice the same. As a species, the white pine has evolved to exploit disturbance. Still, it is the lucky white pine seedling that ends up growing on the spot where a fire has passed through the season before. It is a lottery; it is actually worse than a lottery. The officials can at any time decide that maybe they won't hold a drawing after all and just keep the money instead.

The only environmental cycles on the planet even modestly constant are those dictated by geophysical facts: at one extreme, the daily rotation of the earth about its axis and the annual revolution about the sun that are responsible for the alternation of night and day and the procession of the seasons; at the other extreme, the once-a-hundred-millennium variation in the ellipticity of the earth's orbit and the precession of the equinoxes—the month of the year during which the planet passes closest to the sun—which drive the Milankovitch cycle, the alternation between glacial and interglacial periods. (Even the Milankovitch cycle is far from regular, however; the peaks are never exactly the same height, and the interval between peaks is sometimes more than a hundred thousand years, sometimes less.) Between those two time scales, the most honest description of environmental change is that it is just change. On the scale of time that matters for life, the environment is never in a steady state or even in a steady-state fluctuation about an average; it is constantly changing in a way that defies both human prediction and biological adaptation.[17] Since the end of the last ice age fifteen thousand years ago, temperatures have risen and fallen repeatedly, at different times in different places. Some seven thousand years ago the Great Plains were experiencing warmer and drier summers than they do today; ragweed, sagebrush, and pigweed had begun to replace prairie grasses, creating dust bowls much like those of the 1930s. At the very same time Quebec still lay under a sheet of glacial ice hundreds of yards deep. When the warming of the postglacial "climatic optimum" finally penetrated the area around Hudson Bay thousands of years later, white pines grew hundreds of miles north of the present-day tree line.

Fossil pollen, preserved in lake bottoms or peat bogs over the centuries, has provided us a record of these vegetational changes. The enormous variety in the shape and size of pollen grains allows experts to identify the plant that produced them, often down to the genus

*Figure 5. Life on earth is continually buffeted by climatic change that is both errat-
ic and violent. Only on time scales of 100,000 years or longer do regular patterns
begin to show up. (Top, temperatures inferred from fluctuations in oxygen isotope
concentrations measured in ocean sediments from the equatorial Pacific; middle,
temperature at Vostok station, Antarctica, derived from carbon dioxide concentrations in ice cores; bottom, global mean temperatures from direct measurement.)*

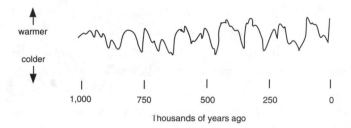

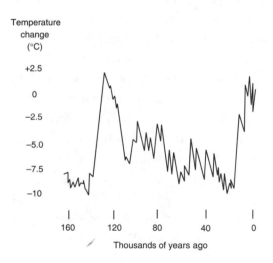

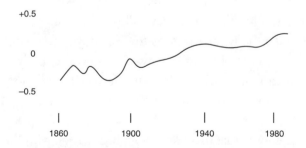

Adapted from *Encyclopaedia Britannica,* "Climate and Weather."

level; the proportion of different types of pollen gives a rough measure of the relative abundance of the various plants on the ancient landscape; and radiocarbon dating of the sediment layer that each sample is taken from gives its age. The pollen record of North America tells a story of continual change on a time scale, very roughly speaking, of a thousand years. A Minnesota forest 10,000 years ago was tundra; 9,200 years ago it was jack pine and red pine; 8,300 years ago it was paper birch and alder; 7,000 years ago it was white pine.

The changes continue unbroken to the present day. Following the climatic optimum, global temperatures fell, the glaciers advanced and retreated twice, most recently in the "little ice age" of 1350 to 1870; bogs spread, prairies retreated, jack pine forests grew. Ponds and lakes in southern New England left by the scouring of glacial ice began to disappear as soon as they were formed; the process continues today as reeds, cattails, and bulrushes along shallow shores die and decay, slowly turning lake-bottom mud to rich soil that is then invaded by swamp shrubs that draw out the remaining moisture, paving the way for forest trees.[18]

Can life ever settle down in this ever-changing environment? The traditional argument that ecologists of the old school made was that as great as these environmental changes have been, they are exceptional and transitory. Having passed through the recent climatic upheavals that marked the end of the Ice Age, nature will once again regain its equilibrium. Predator and prey will settle back into a stable balance with one another; niches will be tidily filled in a web of mutual dependency; forests will resume their stately march toward their eternal climax state. Because it was believed that "normal" interglacial periods last for hundreds of thousands of years, any disequilibrium we see in nature today—predator and prey populations out of balance with one another, forests whose mix of species keeps changing—were simply chalked up to the unusually short time that had passed since the last glacial age subsided. Like the reverberations that continue after a bell is struck, they will soon settle out and die away. Given time, life will make the normal adjustments, species will settle into stable relationships with one another, populations will cease to fluctuate, forests will stabilize in form and structure.

Recent research has shown that there are two things wrong with this argument. One, as we have already seen, is that major environmental upheaval is the rule, not the exception. Great progress has been made in the last three decades in developing techniques to study glacial history, and on closer examination it turns out that there were far more glaciations throughout the two-million-year-old Quaternary period than earlier researchers realized. Interglacials were usually extremely brief—not a hundred thousand years, but no more than ten to twenty thousand years. In other words, no more than the time that has already passed since our last glaciation. Thus, the current state of biological disequilibrium we see in the world today, far from being some transitory exception, must be wholly typical of the last two million years. There is *never* enough time for nature to equilibrate between glacial upheavals.[19]

Some ecologists have tried to take heart in the fact that in some areas, such as northern New England, it takes only four hundred years or so for a "climax" forest to attain maturity; the interval between major glacial disturbances (ten millenniums) or even catastrophic fires and hurricanes (about one millennium in northern New England) is much longer. Thus, the argument goes, there is plenty of time for stability to assert itself between disturbances.[20]

What this ignores, however, is that by the time stability can reassert itself, it is already a *new* stability. Slowly shifting changes in climate can lead to the complete replacement of vegetation during these quiet intervals of a thousand years or so. The forests may be safe from a frontal assault by fire or ice, only to be undermined by more gradual climate change.

The second problem with the just-give-him-time-and-he'll-settle-down argument is that many of the geologic accidents that came in the wake of the last glaciation had demonstrably irreversible consequences. They were one-way ecological doors, with no way back. In other words, nature is the product of history. It reflects not some immutable cosmic cycles but rather the accumulation of countless accidents. It might all have turned out very different.

Just within the geologically brief period since the last ice age—a period that represents one one-hundred-thousandth of the time that life has existed on the planet—the number and magnitude of irreversible accidents that have shaped the landscape and the life within it ought to be a sobering splash of cold water in the face of those who still dream of harmony and stability in nature. Twelve thousand years ago a vast inland salt sea was formed in the St. Lawrence valley as the earth's crust, warped downward by the pressure of the mile-thick glaciers that had rested on its surface for thousands of years, sank below sea level. Then, when the ice blocking the valley suddenly melted, the sea rushed in. Humpback whales, seals, and codfish flourished. Two thousand years later they were gone: The crust rebounded, sealing off the lake from the sea, and freshwater from melting snow diluted the saltwater. In the west, floods on a scale scarcely imaginable ripped through the Columbia River basin every twenty to sixty years—as many as forty times altogether—as a glacial lake in what is now western Montana alternately filled and drained as the ice dam on its western end gave way. Such floods, known by the Icelandic word *jokulhlaup,* or glacial outburst, sent five hundred cubic miles of water cascading across the land; the entire lake, with a volume equal to that of modern-day Lake Ontario, was emptied over two weeks. The local ecological consequences would have been devastating. Small lakes in the path of the floods, and all of the life within them, were repeatedly destroyed. Land was stripped bare of trees, plants, and soil. The effects are readily apparent even today, thousands of years later. The channels that the waters coursed through are today covered with a thin soil over basalt bedrock, supporting only sparse vegetation.[21]

Again and again, quirks of fate and chance dictated the course that life would follow. Birds stopping by newly formed lakes carried microbes, seeds of water plants, and eggs of snails in the mud on their feet. Many species of aquatic insects, such as mayflies and stoneflies, are today found in both the southeast United States and southern Canada, in the basins of the Saskatchewan and Mississippi rivers. The juvenile insects are confined to water; the adults are poor flyers; high ground separates the two river basins today. There is thus no way that these insects could today migrate between these two isolated parts of their modern-day range. The answer to this mystery is found eleven thousand years ago. As the glaciers retreated, a chain of glacial lakes that stretched from the vicinity of modern Lake Superior and northward and westward briefly linked the basins of the modern-day Mississippi and Saskatchewan rivers. A geologic accident that dumped a pile of ice in the right place dictated the course of life on the planet for millenniums to come.[22]

Even the predictable disturbances that are continually turning over new patches of habitat have unpredictable consequences. Pure chance often dictates which particular species happen to move into the new terrain, creating new history in the process. The pool of potential recruits that occupy surrounding patches, their migration rates, and the luck of the draw is what in the end determines the fate of nature.[23]

There is a more subtle argument sometimes advanced by proponents of equilibrium. It goes like this: Though the environment may be continually changing, though the vegetation at any given spot on earth may be in a state of flux, still the organisms that make up any given ecological community have a history and identity, *as a community,* that has remained intact at least as far back as the last glaciation—and perhaps even further back, to previous interglacials. A boreal forest may shift north or it may shift south as climate fluctuates; it may be crowded into a tiny refugium at the peak of the glacial advance; but it's still a boreal forest. The long, shared evolutionary history of each of the plants and animals that make up this forest—no matter how briefly they may have come to rest at any given place—ensures that an equilibrium was long ago established among them.

In effect, this argument is a revival of Frederic Clements's ideas about plant associations. The members of a plant community are bound together by a web of mutual associations; each association has a unique identity; the bonds that tie the individual species together to form that identity are so strong that the total assemblage can be considered a single coherent organism. As noted earlier, this idea was immediately and forcefully rejected by many botanists who could find no evidence that plants actually exhibited any group behavior. Henry Gleason complained that the idea was suspect on theoretical grounds, because every plant is separately, and without cease, trying to expand its domain, exercising reproductive powers far in excess of its needs— all good Darwinian competitors in the struggle for survival against its fellows. Botanists who studied plant communities found no sharp edges from one to the other. And rather than maintaining a single, unique, unvarying identity, these "plant associations" showed conspicuous differences in their composition from one end to the other of their geographical range.[24]

It was not until the 1950s, though, that Gleason's "individualistic" concept of vegetation was vindicated by unequivocal evidence from the field. Grabbing the bull by the horns, or rather the plant by the stem, botanist Robert Whittaker began taking an exhaustive running census of plants as he ascended mountainsides in Tennessee, Oregon, and Arizona. Climbing the mountains, he passed through a gradient of environmental conditions, warm to cold, wet to dry. If plants really did form tightly knit communities—"nation states of trees," is the ecologist Paul Colinvaux's felicitous and facetious phrase—then their distribution should fall into clusters (see figure 6). Instead, Whittaker found, each species behaved totally independently. Rather than link up into communities with unique biological identities, species tended to maximize their ecological distance from one another. Each species had its own preferred niche, with no two exactly alike in their distribution. The result was practical proof of the basic ecological theory which says that species evolve so as to avoid competition, dispersing themselves across environmental gradients. Those individuals within

Figure 6. Plants as individualists: If ecosystems were truly "superorganisms" of interdependent species, plants would distribute themselves across environmental gradients as shown at the top. Actual measurements reveal that it's every plant for itself, with the abundance of each varying independently of others. (Santa Catalina Mountains, Arizona; a = ponderosa pine; b = silverleaf oak; c = manzanita.)

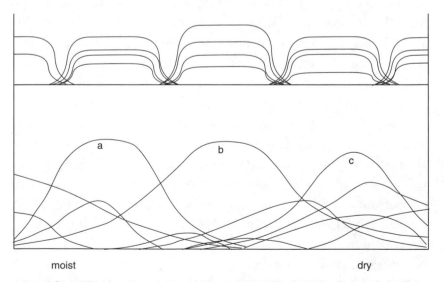

moist   dry

Adapted from Whittaker, *Communities and Ecosystems,* 36; Whittaker, "Gradient Analysis of Vegetation," 229.

a population that will flourish and pass on their traits to succeeding generations are those positioned along the environmental gradient in such a way as to minimize overlap with other, competing species.

Nor did Whittaker's data reveal any sharp boundaries separating one vegetational zone from another. Each plant's distribution smoothly graded into the next. Whittaker found that, in effect, the very existence of vegetational zones was an optical illusion. Humans tend to focus on the most predominant species in the landscape, seeing a band where pines predominate, or beeches or oaks. What we do not notice is the continually changing makeup of less predominant species. Moreover, the human eye and brain, always working to find patterns, try to resolve a smooth, continuous gradient into discrete chunks. In reality there is no sharp line where the pines stop and the oaks start. But where the mix shifts from 51–49 percent pines to 51–49 percent oaks, human perception draws a line. Whittaker points to an apt analogy in the colors of the spectrum: The change of colors in a rainbow is smooth and continuous, yet the human eye resolves this infinite number of colors into comprehensible if arbitrary chunks of red, yellow, orange, and so on.[25]

What all of this means is that there is no such thing, really, as a pine forest, or a mixed-hardwood forest or a tall-grass prairie or a tundra. These are human categories, not biological ones. They are simply names that we have applied in a rough attempt to impose intellectual order on the infinite diversity of landscapes that exist.

Within the last twenty years or so, further studies have hammered the final nails in the coffin of the idea that though climates may come and go, a boreal forest is still a boreal forest. Pollen analyses have proved that forests do not simply pick up and migrate en masse. As the glaciers retreated, bands of vegetation did not simply shift northward, keeping their character unchanged. Rather, individual species responded at radically different rates to a changing climate. A boreal forest ten thousand years ago had a composition very different from that of a boreal forest today.

Some species can respond almost instantaneously to new climatic conditions. Where two similar species coexist, competing for the same resources, the response to a shifting environment can take place in situ, without any delay for migration: The better-adapted resident species simply overwhelms the other. The one degree-Fahrenheit rise in average global temperatures since 1900 has provided many examples. In a mere fifteen-year interval from the 1930s to the 1950s, the southern barnacle *Chthamalus* replaced the more cold-adapted northern barnacle *Balanus* over a wide stretch of the British and Irish coasts, for example.

But generally there is a much greater, and widely variable, time lag for biological responses. Animals can disperse and extend their range as much as hundreds of miles a year. For plants the average is several hundred yards a year—though again there is great variation from one type of plant to another. The light, wind-blown seeds of poplars disperse much faster than the heavy acorns of the oak that are carried by squirrels, for example. Time lags may be stretched out even further by the tendency of plants already established in a site to tenaciously hold their ground against even better-adapted newcomers; it takes a catastrophic event, such as fire or a climatic change so severe that the residents are actually killed off, to clear the ground and allow a fair competition to take place.[26]

The different migration rates of different species ensures that climate change stirs up a kaleidoscopic pattern of new ecosystems. No two are ever exactly duplicated at different times and different places. In the central Appalachians, the so-called chestnut-oak-hickory forests had chestnuts five thousand years ago. In the "same" forests of Connecticut, the chestnuts did not arrive until two thousand years ago. The hemlock and beech forests of Massachusetts must have looked very different in the past from how they do today; for one thing, they didn't have any beeches. The hemlocks beat them by a good two thousand years. Today, the range of the beech is *still* expanding; in upper Michigan it has moved forty miles west in the last five hundred years.[27]

Life on earth is continually trying to catch up with the planet's changing climate and never quite succeeding. It is as if everyone is trying to play a game where the rules change every year. Adding considerably to the confusion is the fact that some players are slower learners than others; they haven't even caught up with last year's rule book. The ensuing chaos, not surprisingly, is considerable.

If all of this is not ammunition enough against the belief in the balance of nature, there is now considerable evidence that instability is woven into the very fabric of ecological systems. Even if the environ-

Figure 7. The composition of plant communities is shifting continually over time and space; the "hemlock–beech" forests of the north are a quite recent concoction, a result of the very different migration rates of the two species as the glaciers retreated. Note that hemlocks are still spreading westward. Curves indicate the approximate arrival time of each species, in thousands of years ago.

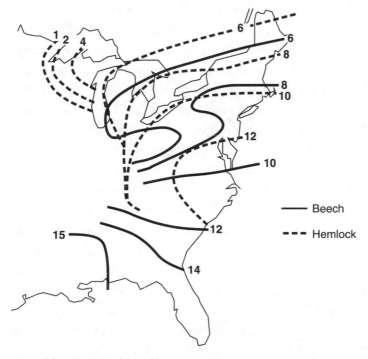

Adapted from Davis, "Stability of Forest Communities," 149; Davis, "Climatic Instability," 277.

ment were absolutely constant, which it is not, the complex, internal dynamics of interacting populations of species are quite capable of initiating mayhem on their own .

Field censuses have long shown dramatic fluctuations in the size of animal populations over very short intervals of time, often for no obvious reason. To take the most extreme example, the lasiocampid moth in German coniferous forests is, at rare peaks in its population, ten thousand times more numerous than in its population troughs. More than a half century ago the British ecologist Charles Elton observed that populations of wild animals are constantly varying in a fundamentally unpredictable way; even when the variations seem to fall into cycles, the cycles are never the same twice. The peaks are higher or lower, and even the interval between peaks is constantly changing. "It is assumed," Elton observed, "that an undisturbed natural animal community lives in a certain harmony, referred to as 'the balance of nature,' and that although rhythmical changes may take place in this balance, yet that these are regular and essentially predictable and, above all, nicely fitted into the environmental stresses without." This nice picture, he went on, "has the advantage of being an intelligible and apparently logical result of natural selection in producing the best possible world for each species. It has the disadvantage of being untrue."[28] Real populations just don't behave themselves.

Recently, a number of mathematically inclined ecologists have found that such unpredictable behavior may be an inherent mathematical property of even the simplest ecological communities. When the factors that control the growth of a population are described in a set of mathematical equations, the solutions to these equations can behave in an extremely bizarre fashion. The populations oscillate, cycle, or, under the right circumstances, exhibit the mathematical phenomenon known as chaos: Instead of settling down to a constant level, or even a cyclically repeating pattern, they burst forth with a multiplicity of possible answers. The population then jumps back and forth unpredictably between two, or four, or eight, or an infinite number of possible values.[29] The term "chaos" was well chosen.

Mathematical models of animal populations are hardly new. But for half a century or more, ecologists pursuing the will-o'-the-wisp of balance tended to look only for stable solutions when they studied such equations. And in pre-computer days, they also tended to make very simple assumptions about how populations grow and interact with other species, in order to keep the equations mathematically tractable. A good example is the logistic growth model—a single, simple equation that purports to describe how a population grows until it reaches the carrying capacity of its environment. This model still appears in virtually every ecology textbook. It has been used in literally hundreds of ecological research papers. It has neat, stable solutions. It makes intuitive sense. Ecologists, not a group renowned for their love of solving nonlinear differential equations, can understand it. According to this model, a small population at first grows exponentially. It continues reproducing at full tilt until it begins to approach the carrying capacity; then, as crowding starts to limit the amount of food or other resources available to each individual, the reproductive rate slowly and smoothly tapers off. The growth rate hits zero precisely at the point that the carrying capacity is reached. From that point hence, the population remains in a state of eternal equilibrium, never rising or falling.

Only in the last few years has there been a general acknowledgment that the neat, stable picture that emerges from this canonical model is terribly misleading. One of the major defects with the logistic equation is that it assumes that a population has the ability to react instantly. In real life, though, there are often time delays. As the amount of food per head decreases, birthrates will drop; but it will be a whole generation before that depression in birthrates can show up as a decrease in the actual adult population.

If the logistic equation is modified to reflect such time delays, that change alone is sufficient to produce wild and unstable solutions. What happens in effect is that the population cannot react quickly enough to diminishing food supplies, and as it grows it overshoots its carrying capacity. Starvation then takes hold and the population begins to crash, but again the time delay does its mischief and the population overcompensates, dropping lower than it needs to before beginning to grow once again. If the time delay is small, this back-and-forth cycle of overshooting and overcompensating eventually damps out and the population in the end settles down at the carrying capacity, as in the simpler model. But if the time delay is substantial, the result is what is known mathematically as a stable limit cycle: The population bounces back and forth over and over in an endlessly repeating pattern. With even longer time lags, chaotic behavior emerges, and the cycles break down into fluctuations that continue without any pattern whatsoever (see Figure 8).

Interestingly, entomologists and fisheries scientists did study these modified logistic equations as early as the 1940s and 1950s; using mechanical calculators, they even discovered cyclical and chaotic solutions. But they were looking for stable solutions and simply ignored or rejected the more bizarre results that they stumbled across as biologically "unrealistic."[30]

A recent computer model of Dungeness crab populations that

Figure 8. In the classical "logistic" growth theory, a population rises smoothly to its carrying capacity K, then levels off. More realistic assumptions generate erratic behavior, even chaos, as the population overshoots its carrying capacity, then overcompensates and crashes.

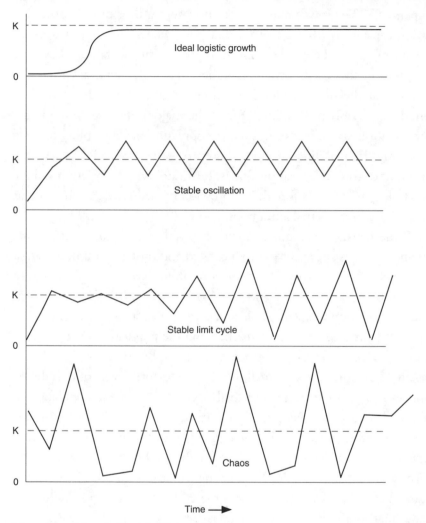

Adapted from May, ed., *Theoretical Ecology*, 16.

added a further small dose of reality—the spatial distribution of the animals—produced even more bizarre behavior. The model assumed that the adult crabs along a coastline reproduced at a rate governed by a logistic-type growth equation. In densely populated spots competition for food depressed the reproduction rate; in sparsely populated areas adults reproduced at their maximum potential. The larvae released at each point then dispersed, spreading themselves out in a bell-shaped distribution from their point of origin. Upon reaching maturity, they then repeated the process. These assumptions are biologically realistic for Dungeness crabs and a number of other marine species with relatively sedentary adults and "pelagic," or seagoing, larvae. In a typical run of the model, the total population showed no apparent pattern for a thousand years, then cycled more or less stably for about ten thousand years, then suddenly burst into chaotic behavior after sixteen thousand years. There was no indication that this erratic behavior would ever settle down, at least not on time scales relevant to ecosystems; detailed examination of the results showed that chaotic behavior, or abrupt shifts from cyclic to chaotic behavior or vice versa, were just as likely to occur after the passage of tens of thousands of years as during the first few thousand years. The results suggested that researchers who have been concentrating on the "asymptotic" behavior of mathematical models of populations—that is, how the population behaves after all of the erratic fluctuations, or "transients," settle down—may be missing the boat. Even if the equations describing animal populations do eventually approach an asymptote, the time it takes to get there is so vast as to make it ecologically irrelevant. It is the transients that more truly characterize how a population behaves in the real world. Indeed, sudden and inexplicable eruptions of Dungeness crab, sea urchin, plankton, and insect populations that have long puzzled biologists may be a manifestation of such transients.[31]

Whether these and other unpredictable fluctuations observed in nature are in truth a manifestation of the chaos found in mathematical models remains controversial; the most recent theoretical work suggests that biological systems that can in theory give rise to chaos have certain mathematical properties that also work to reverse the process, causing chaotic behavior to break down as soon as it starts.[32] These results suggest that erratic fluctuations of populations in the wild may be largely due to random climatic and environmental changes. (Models that incorporate a fluctuating environment certainly exhibit volatile behavior of their own. If, for instance, the factors that represent the environment in a two-predator, two-prey model are made to vary in a random fashion, mimicking the way weather actually changes from year to year, for example, the population cycles undergo such violent fluctuations that the extinction of one or more of the species becomes a near certainty.)[33]

But whatever their cause, there is no doubt that instabilities of one kind or another are the rule, not the exception, in the real world. The simple explanation for this inherent mathematical instability of populations is that nature is extremely nonlinear. "Nonlinear" simply means that a change in one variable can trigger a quite disproportionate change in another. Real animals don't adjust their birthrates or feeding patterns by smoothly turning a knob on a control panel; if the analogy holds at all, the knob is at best a sticky one. It turns and turns and nothing happens at all for a while, then all of sudden the volume shoots up or down. The lag between the time that birthrates decline and the time the adult population drops is one such sticky knob. Another is the abrupt shift in feeding behavior of two predators that compete for some of the same resources. When prey is abundant, each will specialize in catching one type of prey. But instead of smoothly adjusting their food preference to match changes in the prey populations, the predators may show no change in their preference at all as the relative abundance of prey changes. Then, suddenly, a critical point is reached; beyond that point even the smallest additional change in prey abundance triggers a total flip-flop in the predators' behavior. A predator that had been a total specialist, feeding on a single prey species, will abruptly shift to opportunistic behavior, feeding on all prey indiscriminately.

Another nonlinear phenomenon is the "paradox of enrichment." Consider two species that spend their time competing for a limited food supply that they share in common while also trying to avoid a predator that feeds on both of them. Under normal circumstances things remain linear, stable, and well-behaved. Competition for a limited food supply keeps each population in check; so, too, does predation—if one of the species starts to become more abundant, it becomes an easier target for the predator. But if the limiting resource is increased (imagine an unusually mild winter or the Friends of the Deer arriving with their hay truck), nonlinearities can trigger a paradoxical result. Instead of increasing the number of deer, as one might expect, supplying extra food can actually drive the deer to extinction. What happens is this: The extra food removes the competitive check on the two prey species. As their populations start to grow, the increase in the population of one now *benefits* the population of the other; each additional elk means one less hungry wolf, and one additional, now well-fed deer that escapes being eaten. The faster the elk increase, the faster the deer increase, and vice versa. But such fast growth will rapidly outstrip even the augmented food supplies; in the end a drastic crash in population is inevitable. A relatively stable situation is thus sent into unstable and potentially catastrophic fluctuations by the addition of food supplies.

A mirror-image situation may occur when one predator keeps the population of several competing prey species low. If the predator population drops, one might naturally think that all of the prey species would benefit. But instead, a drop in predation can simply give competition, which had been held in check, a free rein. In a classic experiment in which starfish were removed from a shoreline ecosystem, the half dozen species the starfish had preyed on were suddenly thrown into vicious competition as their numbers grew. In the bloody aftermath only one or two species were left in possession of the field; the rest were wiped out.[34]

Nonlinearities produce chaos even in simple systems; it should hardly be surprising that adding more species and more interactions between them results in even more chaos. Again, Charles Elton made the point well in his 1930 critique of the "balance of nature" idea; he observed that not only are populations continually varying, but moreover, "each variation in the numbers of one species causes direct and indirect repercussions on the numbers of the others, and since many of the latter are themselves varying independently in numbers, the resultant confusion is remarkable." Giving the familiar metaphor of nature as a clockwork a mischievous twist, Elton said such an analogy was apt only "if we imagine that a large proportion of the cog-wheels have their own mainsprings, which do not unwind at a constant speed" and if "each wheel retains the right to arise and migrate and settle down in another clock, only to set up further trouble in its new home."[35]

Yet for many years it was accepted as an ecological truism that simple ecosystems—those with a single predator and a single prey, such as the lynx and Arctic hare—are unstable; systems with many interacting species are able to stay on a much more even keel. This argument is still often advanced as a prime "scientific" justification for the preservation of biological diversity; diversity is seen as a sort of insurance policy that guarantees the stability and resilience of such complex ecosystems as tropical rain forests. It also features in ominous warnings against the practices of modern agriculture; planting vast "monocultures" of a single crop is, by this argument, an invitation to ecological disaster. The idea is that in a system with many potential interactions between species, no one species holds the key. If a predator can switch from one food source to another, then a drop in the population of one prey species will be of little consequence to the predator or the ecosystem as a whole. Redundancy equals stability.

The idea appeared to receive confirmation from mathematical models that were originally developed in the 1950s to assess the resilience of telephone-switching networks. These models, a product of the then-new field known as information theory, concluded, not surprisingly, that a network with many redundant links was less liable to suffer a catastrophic crash than one with only a single line connecting point A and point B.[36] The only trouble with all of this commonsense analysis is that common sense often has nothing to do with the complex reality of biological systems. It is now clear that, far from adding to stability, increased complexity only adds additional sources of fluctuation. Consider a population of moose in Canada. An increase in the number of beavers might increase the amount of favorable habitat for moose. An increase in deer might reduce the available food supply through competition. An increase in wolves will reduce the population through predation. An increase in the population of intestinal parasites in wolves might decrease wolf numbers and increase moose numbers. And so on. A better analogy than swinging pendulums (or telephone-switching networks) might be dogs on a water bed. Every time one dog manages to get to its feet, it stirs up a wave that knocks the others down, which in turn starts another wave going that knocks the first dog down. Throwing more dogs on the bed is not a promising way to stabilize the situation.

Even the simplest mathematical models that directly incorporate the effects that one species has an another (predators eating prey or competitors vying for the same resource) confirm this pattern of decreasing stability with increasing complexity. The simplest model of a single predator and a single prey species (known as the Lotka-Volterra equation, after the two mathematical ecologists who independently developed it in the 1920s), for example, exhibits a neat and stable behavior. The equations assume only that the reproduction rate of the predator is proportional to its food supply (the number of prey) and that the death rate of the prey is proportional to the number of predators. Solving the equations, one finds the familiar swinging pendulums. As the prey population increases, the food supply for the predator grows; the predator's growth rate increases, which leads to more predation and a drop in the prey population; fewer prey then triggers a decline in the predator population, at which point the cycle starts all over again. (This model is clearly too simple even for the one predator–one prey case. It assumes that all of the individuals within each population behave exactly the same way, with the same reproductive and feeding patterns; it ignores nonlinear responses of predators, in particular the satiation of predators at high prey densities, which causes such destabilizing effects as the "paradox of enrichment" described above.) But what is interesting is what happens even with this very simple model when the number of interacting species is increased. All it takes is one additional species—three instead of two—for the full array of weird and chaotic behavior to appear, including nonperiodic fluctuations that come and go in no predictable pattern.[37]

The idea that diversity makes for stability is not only wrong but backwards. It is instability that makes for diversity. The instability of populations is just another example of the disturbance processes that are continually creating new biological opportunities. Understanding this role that change and chance play in nature is clearly vital if humans are ever to make intelligent decisions in the management of natural systems. (As we shall see in chapter 8, the failure of managers to face up to the biological reality in all its mathematical complexity— and inherent uncertainty—has led to some spectacular management failures.) One thing is clear: To leave nature to her own devices is no guarantee that what is here today will be here tomorrow. Nature has no eternal plan, no timeless purpose. It is ever changing, a creature of the endless geologic upheavals that are as old as the planet itself, of the instabilities and chaos that are the fate of all complex systems, and of chance. Were it not for the repeated blows of chance, in fact, it would be a very different place. Without disturbance, much of life on the planet could not even exist.

The idea of a risky nature is one that is hard for many people to swallow. Environmentalists recoil at the notion precisely because it seems to give man license to transform nature at will. If what is here could just as well have been something completely different, then what is wrong with turning forests to deserts or prairies to cattle ranches or wetlands to sugarcane fields? The honest and uncomfortable answer is that from a scientific point of view, there is nothing at all wrong with these things. The specter of ecosystems collapsing like a house of cards to the destruction of all life on the planet, ourselves included, if but one piece is tampered with is one of the more successful myths of the modern environmental movement, but it is a distortion of ecological reality. An ecosystem is not a living organism that dies of infection if it gets a scratch or even bleeds to death if it loses a limb. Ecosystems are ever changing, dissolving, transforming, recombining in a kaleidoscope of new forms.

Anti-environmentalists do sometimes take this argument to an absurd extreme and claim, in effect, that nature is so robust and resilient that it can withstand any assault that man can dish out. They are right only in the sense that "nature" can take on an infinity of forms. What they do not acknowledge is that many of those forms are ones we will not very much care for. They will be devoid of the wild animals we love for their wildness or landscapes we love for their beauty or plants that we value for the medicinal or agricultural richness of their genes. But even the weeds growing in a city junkyard are a functioning ecosystem. And certainly a well-managed cattle ranch is no less "sustainable" than a well-managed rain forest. In the end it is purely a value judgment which we will have. There are plenty of good reasons to want some of both, but it is a false argument to claim that nature has a preference herself. The nature we have at any moment is a product of history. For every road taken there were an infinity of others that were no less possible and many that were no less leafy and green.

There is no denying that man's potential to alter the course of nature is greater than ever before. But so too is our ability to learn the laws of nature that govern how species interact and how ecosystems assemble themselves, so that what we value we can keep and what we have lost we can even recreate. And in truth there is nothing terribly new in this. Because, as we shall see, for at least a hundred thousand years it has been largely man who has chosen nature's path for her.

FIVE

Footprints in the Jungle

This is the forest primeval. The murmuring pines and the hemlocks,
Bearded with moss, and in garments green, indistinct in the twilight,
Stand like Druids of eld . . .

So Longfellow wrote in 1847, and nature lovers have been lamenting
its disappearance ever since. Francis Parkman, whom we have already
encountered as the great nineteenth-century popularizer of cowboys,
Indians, mountain men, and sundry other icons of the romanticized
American wild lands, scarcely missed an opportunity to portray the
ancient forests of the New World as vast, dark, and untrodden. In "the
depths of immemorial forests, dim and silent as a cavern," "wrapped
in the shadow of the tomb," not a flicker of sunlight ever touched the
ground; they were "ancient as the world," to whose "verdant antiquity
the pyramids are young." Only where Europeans had intruded was it
otherwise. Between the bits of rough civilization the settlers had
carved out of the virgin land lay "a broad tract of wilderness, shaggy
with primeval woods."[1] A squirrel, it was said, might in the days before the white man arrived have traveled from Maine to Louisiana
never once setting foot on the ground, leaping from tree to giant tree.

A very different metaphor came to the mind of more than one early explorer who actually set foot in America's forests primeval. A stagecoach, said one, might be driven from the east coast to St. Louis without clearing a road. Peter Kalm, a Swedish botanist sent by Linnaeus to collect specimens of New World plants, made a similar observation; he described the forests of New Jersey in 1750 as so free from underbrush that one could drive a horse and carriage through them. "A man may gallop a horse amongst these woods any waie, but where creekes or Rivers shall hinder," agreed Captain John Smith of the Jamestown, Virginia, settlement. If there is one point on which the early European travelers and settlers who set down their observations of the New World agree, it is that the forests of eastern North America reminded them of nothing so much as the carefully tended parks of the great estates of their homelands. An explorer in 1607 observed the trees around present-day Portland, Maine, "growing a great space asunder one from the other as our parks in England and no thicket growing under them." In the early days of the Plymouth colony, the Pilgrims found the woods "thin of Timber in many places, like our Parkes in England." In New Jersey in the mid-seventeenth century, the woods were described as "but thin in most places, and very little Underwood"; another explorer noted an abundance of high grass and trees that "stand far apart, as if they were planted." In such open, parklike wood, deer and turkey could be seen a mile away, cattle three miles.[2]

Others told of vast, open grasslands with hardly a tree even in sight. Passing through western Virginia in 1722, William Byrd noted, "There is scarce a shrub in view to intercept your prospect, but grass as high as a man on horseback." A seventeenth-century settler of Salem, Massachusetts, told of a place nearby where one could stand upon a little hill "and see divers thousands of acres of ground as good as need be, and not a tree in the same." Parkman romantically portrayed the sixteenth-century Italian navigator Verrazano lying off the coast of New England, espying one of his mighty literary forests, full of "shadows and gloom." Yet Verrazano himself told of marching inland fifteen miles from Narragansett Bay, in what would become Rhode Island, and finding "open plains twenty-five or thirty leagues in extent, entirely free from trees or other hindrances." Where the explorer did encounter forests, they grew so open and unencumbered by underbrush that they "might all be traversed by an army ever so numerous," he marveled.³

The Europeans were uniformly impressed, if not surprised, by these open woods and meadows, but they did not have to search far for an explanation. If the land reminded them of carefully tended parks at home, it was for a good reason. The great American wilderness was no less a product of human will. One of the earliest explanations was set down in 1632 by Thomas Morton, an English fur trader and adventurer, who traveled the backwoods of eastern central Massachusetts and settled in what is now Quincy, Massachusetts. (He did not remain long. A freethinker, he was always in trouble with the local authorities. After being repeatedly arrested and being sent back to England more than once, he was finally expelled for good for licentiousness, selling firearms to the Indians, and penning a satiric tract against the New England Puritans). Morton was a keen observer, and his travels off the beaten path gave him a firsthand knowledge of the ways of the Indians. He explained that it was deliberate management by the native inhabitants that kept the woods as they were:

> The Salvages are accustomed to set fire of the country in all places where they come; and to burn it, twize a yeare, vize, at the Spring, and at the fall of the leafe. The reason that moves them to do so, is because it would be otherwise so overgrown with underweedes that it would be all a copice wood, and the people could not be able in any wise to passe through the country out of a beaten path. . . . The burning of the grasse destroyes the underwoods, and so scorcheth the elder trees, that it shrinks them, and hinders their growth very much: So that hee that will look to finde large trees, and good tymber, must not depend upon the help of a woodden prospect to find them on the upland ground; but must seeke for them . . . in the lower grounds where the grounds are wett when the country is fired. . . . For when the fire is once kindled, it dilates and spreads itself against as with the winde; burning continually night and day, until a shower of raine falls to quench it. And this custome of firing the country is the means to make it passable, and by that meanes the trees growe here and there as in our parks: and makes the country very beautifull, and commodious.⁴

The practice appears to have been extremely widespread. Accounts of Indian-set fires exist from Virginia to Maine. Even well in from the coast and rivers, where the Indian settlements were concentrated, explorers reported seeing either the effects of Indian fires or the fires themselves. The Indian population of southern New England was estimated to be some eighty thousand, spread over an area of thirty to forty thousand square miles; but because of seasonal migrations as well as occasional wholesale relocation of villages, the impact of this population on the environment was disproportionately great. Exhaustion of fuel wood supplies was a major force that drove Indians to periodically uproot their villages. The Pilgrims found thousands of acres near Boston stripped bare; the early settlers had to row out to the harbor islands to cut their firewood. Indeed, so large did the constant search for firewood loom in the minds of the Indians that the Narragansetts of Rhode Island believed that the English had come to America because they had run out of firewood at home (a belief which actually contained a grain of truth). In Virginia, through a combination of burning and fuel wood cutting, the Indians had managed to clear some thirty or forty acres of land per capita at the time the first Europeans arrived; three centuries later, although the total area cleared was obviously much greater, it amounted to considerably less per capita—only six or seven acres of treeless land per person.

Even supposedly uninhabited regions were frequented regularly by Indian war or hunting parties that left their mark. In southwestern Virginia William Byrd reported seeing the sky filled with smoke so dense that it blocked out the mountains. "This happened not from haziness of the sky," he said, "but from the firing of the woods by the Indians, for we were now near the route the northern savages take when they go to war with the Catawbas and other southern nations. On their way, the fires they make in their camps are left burning, which catching the dry leaves which lie near, soon put the adjacent woods in a flame."[5] Other travelers reported finding vast, open savannas far inland; the only trees that they found growing there were confined to low swamps or wet areas along streams, which escaped the flames. The Shenandoah Valley, where a thousand square miles of unbroken grassland grew, and likewise the areas that settlers in Maryland, Pennsylvania, and New Jersey called "barrens" for their sparse, stunted oaks and pines, were apparently the direct product of frequent burning, too. Fire scars left in the annual growth rings of old trees in these areas confirm the settlers' observations, testifying to fires every ten to fifteen years.[6]

Careful studies of the fire history of the Rocky Mountains offer convincing evidence for frequent Indian-set fires in that region, as well. Although the ecological role of fire in the Rockies has been understood by specialists for some time, it had been assumed that nearly all of these fires were set by lightning. However, when tree rings of old-growth stands in western Montana were analyzed, it became clear that fires were much more frequent in areas that had been heavily used by Indians than they were in similar but remote areas. The areas frequented by the local Salish and Kootenai Indians had burned on average every nine years, as compared to eighteen years for the more remote sites. The frequency of fires before 1860 (determined by tree-ring scars) was also compared with the known frequency of lightning-set fires for the area since 1930 (meticulously recorded by the Forest Service); again, the results indicate that fires occurred two to three times as often during the period Indians occupied the land than one would expect from lightning strikes alone. The evidence is also clear

Figure 9. The hand of man: Tree ring analysis shows that forest areas in western Montana that were heavily used by Indians were burned twice as often as remote sites. The arrival of European settlers led first to an increase in fire as land was cleared, then, after 1910, to a rigid fire-suppression policy.

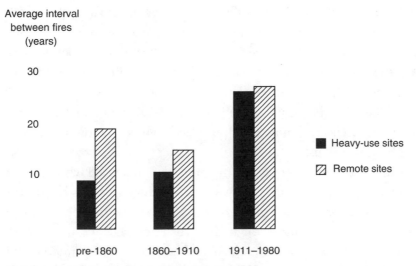

Average interval
between fires
(years)

■ Heavy-use sites

▨ Remote sites

pre-1860   1860–1910   1911–1980

Data from Barrett, "Indian Fires in Western Montana," 39.

that the frequent fires the Indians set had a transforming effect on the landscape. Stands that burn every seven years or so are dominated by tall ponderosa pines and a grassy undergrowth. Older stands, however, become rapidly clogged with woody shrubs, an understory of shade-tolerant Douglas fir, and a buildup of insect and disease pests.[7]

Perhaps the most telling evidence for the dominant role that Indian-set fires played in shaping the American landscape is what happened when the Indians were pushed off the land. One early Massachusetts settler, after duly noting the Indians' practice of setting fire to the wood each year, observed that "in some places where the *Indians* dyed of the Plague some foureteene yeares agoe, is much underwood, as in the mid way betwixt *Wessaguscus* and *Plimouth,* because it hath not been burned."[8] One of the great ironies in the myth of the forest primeval is that the dense, thick woods that later settlers did indeed encounter and arduously cleared were not remnants of the "forest primeval" at all. They were the recent, tangled second growth that sprung up on once-cleared Indian lands only after the Indians had been killed or evicted and the Europeans began to suppress fire. What later settlers took for the forest primeval was nothing more than an abandoned ranch. "The virgin forest was not encountered in the sixteenth and seventeenth centuries," writes one historian; "it was invented in the late eighteenth and early nineteenth centuries."[9]

The reasons that the Indians themselves gave for burning the woods varied. One objective that seems to have been almost universal, however, was to clear underbrush around villages so that an enemy could not sneak up on them. The villages themselves often occupied considerable land; the Iroquois would clear as much as 100 or 150 acres around their dwelling sites. Along well-traveled routes, burning similarly was used to eliminate hiding places where enemy war parties might lie in ambush.

Other accounts frequently mention the improved visibility for hunting afforded by burning. Twentieth-century accounts by Indians in southern Oregon affirm this traditional explanation. "Now I just hear the deer running through the brush at places we used to kill many deer," one Klamath Indian told a scientist who interviewed him. "When the brush got as thick as it is now, we would burn it off."

Fire was also used to drive game; deer in the east, bison on the Plains, alligators in the Everglades, rabbits in the southwest, moose in Alaska—even rats and grasshoppers. Captain John Smith at Jamestown left an eyewitness account of Indian hunting parties of two to three hundred killing deer from canoes after they had been driven by fire onto a peninsula. Throughout North America, fire was also employed to control summer insect pests and drive out snakes.

As William Byrd observed, Indian campfires, especially those set by parties passing through enemy territory, were often left unextinguished, either out of carelessness or simply with the aim of leaving a fire going in case they returned in a few days. Either way, it seems to have been standing operating procedure never to put one out, and not infrequently this led to extensive wildfires. As one authority who has made an extensive search of the literature notes, there is not a single reference to be found of native peoples anywhere in the world ever taking care to extinguish campfires.

Fires were sometimes set as signals, and this was typically on a grand scale. That hoary staple of Western movies, the Indian signaling with puffs of smoke as he waved a blanket over a campfire, is apparently a myth; Indian signal fires, usually intended to gather bands together for hunting or battle, in reality consisted of torching an entire hillside, at a minimum. On at least a few occasions, fires were deliberately set as a weapon of war; the Crees used fire against early Hudson Bay Company posts on the Plains or set fire to the grass to deprive an invading force of fodder for horses. And sometimes fires were set just for the hell of it. Lewis and Clark reported that Indians in the Rocky Mountains set fir trees ablaze as after-dinner entertainment; the huge trees would explode like Roman candles in the night.[10]

As the European settlers also would discover, fire was the quickest way to clear ground for crops, too. Although the eastern Indians practiced a shifting agriculture, it was on a scale much vaster than most people appreciate. In New England, fields were cleared by piling wood around the base of standing trees and setting it ablaze, destroying the bark and thus girding the trees, which would die and eventually fall. Burning provided a short-term injection of nutrients into the soil and transformed the acidic forest litter to alkaline ash that crops such as corn prefer. But within eight to ten years the soil would be exhausted and new land had to be cleared. The story of Squanto notwithstanding, there is no convincing evidence that the Indians knew to fertilize their crops with fish or other artificial amendments; and with no domesticated animals other than the dog, they had no manure to spread over their fields. (Squanto, who had been kidnapped by a ship's captain and taken to Spain as a slave in 1614, later returned to Massachusetts; the trick that he taught the colonists of fertilizing hills of corn with a buried fish was probably something he had picked up in Europe.) Hundreds of acres of cornfields surrounded Mohawk and Seneca villages in New York. John Smith reported thousands of acres of cleared ground near Jamestown. The Massachusetts Pilgrims found they did not need to clear their own cropland, but merely took over cleared fields that had recently been abandoned by the local Indians, who had died in great numbers of disease introduced by the crews of European ships that had visited the area a few years earlier. There were few places in the forest primeval that had not been repeatedly touched by the hand of man for thousands of years.[11]

The net effect of all of this activity was to establish and maintain a mosaic of forest and other vegetation types across the landscape; it also kept the average age of the forests much younger than is at present the rule in many parts of North America. "Old growth" was a rarity. Environmentalists fighting today to preserve the old-growth forests in the Pacific Northwest regularly paint a picture of a "sea of old growth" that once covered the region. Yet early surveys of the forests in southwest Oregon, now the focus of much attention as spotted owl habitat, show that before European settlers arrived in the nineteenth century, stands older than two hundred years occupied as little as five percent of the area. This was almost certainly due to the frequent Indian-set fires and other disturbances to the woods, both natural and man-made.

Frequent burning also prevented the buildup of the large quantities of dead and decaying wood that could fuel a great conflagration; most of the Indian-set fires (and also lightning-set fires in areas that had been frequently burned by the Indians) would have quickly consumed the underbrush without ever reaching a high temperature or setting the crowns of the trees ablaze. These were light ground fires

that burned quickly and moved on quickly. Burning increased the cycling of nutrients, causing a burst of growth of grasses, as well as
blackberries, raspberries, and other edible plants that grow well along
the forest edge. This food in turn attracted an abundance of game:
deer, beaver, hare, grouse, turkey, elk. And also, incidentally, the
predators that fed upon this abundance: bear, wolves, lynx, fox, eagles.

Indians who lived on the Great Plains also appeared to understand
the importance of regular burning in attracting game; Lewis and
Clark's journals are full of references to a pall of smoke covering the
plains as the Indians set fire to the grass in order to encourage new
grass that would attract bison. A history of DuPage County published
in 1857 reported that Indian fires were still encountered regularly in
the Chicago area in 1834; after a farm family spent several days' hard
labor cutting and stacking hay, "they were advised to burn the grass
for several rods around it in order to protect it from the annual fires
set by the Indians." And an English traveler in Indiana in 1823 told of
riding all day through "fire and thick smoke"; near Harmony, "the
everlasting sound of falling trees, which, being undermined by fires,
are falling around almost every hour, night and day, produces a sound
loud and jarring as the discharge of ordnance."[12]

This was game and forest management on a truly sweeping scale.
As one historian has put it, the Indians "were harvesting a foodstuff
which they had consciously been instrumental in creating."[13]

Some of the consequences of such landscapewide alteration of the
environment may still be seen today in southern New England.
Conifers are to this day rare along the coastal areas that were heavily
used by Indians. The present-day range of the oak–hickory forests coincides well with the areas of Indian settlement—which date to at
least nine thousand years ago. Oak and hickory, while not fire-resistant, do have the ability to resprout from stumps. The only conifers
regularly found in these areas today are pitch pines, which have fire-
resistant cones and which are observed today to often colonize burnt
areas. It is thus not improbable that thousands of years of artificial selection through burning by Indians effectively eliminated fire-sensi-
tive species from the landscape.[14]

The extent to which the landscape of America prior to 1492 was
the artificial creation of its native residents is almost impossible for us

Figure 10. The present-day extent of oak–hickory and oak–pitch pine forests in New England coincides closely with areas of Indian settlement. The Indians' practice of frequently burning the woods may have selected for these fire-adapted species.

Oak–Hickory

Oak–Pitch Pine

Adapted from Jorgensen, *Guide to New England's Landscape,* 143.

to grasp, so encumbered are we with the nineteenth-century myth of the forest primeval and the more recent myth of the Indian as an ecological hero who trod softly through the forest on moccasined feet without snapping a twig. But at a minimum the Indian was the dominant source of fire, and "fire is the dominant fact of forest history" in North America.[15] The idea has not been easy for historians, ecologists, or even anthropologists to accept. Despite the overwhelming documentary evidence of Indian fire practices, the suggestion that Indian-set fires had any significant part to play in shaping the North American landscape was almost scornfully rejected by early twentieth-century foresters.[16] Climatic determinists of the Clements school were especially resistant to the notion that fire (and thus man) rather

than climate (and thus nature) was the force that shaped the grasslands. When mesquite, juniper, sagebrush, and scrub oak began over-
running the grasslands of the Midwest and Southwest—by 1960
some seventy-five million acres of grasslands in Texas and surrounding states were a tangle of mesquite jungles, and sagebrush and juniper were invading drier grasslands from the west—many ecologists
and range managers were quick to blame it on overgrazing by domestic livestock that had weakened the native grasses. Yet even in areas
fenced off from stock, the shrubs appeared and took over. It gradually
became clear that a substantial extent of the native North American
grasslands had climate and soils perfectly suitable for deciduous
forests to grow. Groves of trees and shelterbelts planted by settlers not
only survived droughts on the prairies but reproduced viable
seedlings during moist years. Trees were also found to be growing
naturally within the grassland zones along escarpments and other
topographic breaks where they would have been sheltered from
sweeping prairie fires. Only on the high plains, which are too dry for
anything but the native short-grass prairie to grow, are trees not viable. Everywhere else, it was *only* regular burning that kept the ever-
spreading forests at bay.

The manufactured grasslands of North America extended from the
plains, southwest into the desert prairies, and even into fingers of
grassland in the East: the "barrens" of Kentucky, the Shenandoah Valley of Virginia, western Pennsylvania, and upper New York. Bison appeared east of the Mississippi around 1000 A.D. and had even spread
as far as Massachusetts and Pennsylvania by the seventeenth century.
The extensive manufacture of grasslands by the Indians seems the
only convincing explanation for this otherwise inexplicably recent
phenomenon.[17]

The same pattern was repeated not just across America but
throughout the world. "Wherever primitive man has had the opportunity to turn fire loose on a land, he seems to have done so, from time
immemorial; it is only civilized societies that have undertaken to stop
fires," observed the geographer Carl Sauer. Fire has been introduced
by man onto every continent on the earth. Hunting peoples in Argentina, South Africa, New Zealand, Ceylon, the South Pacific, and
Southeast Asia all set fire to the brush to improve grassland for game.

(As one researcher observed of the Australian aborigines, "Perhaps never in the history of mankind was there a people who could answer with such unanimity the question, 'Have you got a light, mate?'")[18]

Even the tropics, long seen as the last true untouched wilderness, appear to have been heavily shaped by man. Charcoal has been found buried in the soil virtually everywhere in the tropics. Radiocarbon dating of charcoal samples from a seemingly unspoiled tropical wilderness in Costa Rica and Panama shows that slash-and-burn agriculture began as much as six thousand years ago.[19] In many tropical grasslands man may indeed have long been the *only* significant source of fire. The tropical savannas and grasslands are not so much a wilderness as a garden. A grasslands animal himself by evolution, man "literally burned down the forests" to expand his habitat.[20] Hunter-gatherers in sub-Saharan Africa have known how to use fire for at least the last sixty thousand years, and as in other places where fire has exerted a sustained selective force on the landscape, the plant species that survive there are fire-adapted. Most savanna trees in Africa are resistant to fire; some species of acacia have evolved a remarkable symbiosis with biting ants that not only defend the trees from grazing animals but also strip bare all nearby vegetation and so form a defensive perimeter against fire. Controlled experiments in Malawi and Zimbabwe have established the importance of regular burning for the well-being of grazing animals such as zebra and antelope.

Again, in places where artificial burning has been halted, significant changes have taken place. In Panama, the destruction of the native Indians by the Spanish resulted in an invasion of the savannas by dense jungle; areas that in the early sixteenth century could be ridden through with ease on horseback are now accessible only by river. In Kruger National Park in South Africa, the eviction of the natives (in line with the standard imperialist model of the nature preserve that the British introduced to Africa in the 1930s) likewise led to a progressive encroachment of grasslands by bush. The carrying capacity of the parkland for grazing animals declined. Controlled burning has now restored the grasslands.[21]

In some cases, however, wildlife flourished as local human populations dwindled. Just as American settlers hacking through tangles of overgrown brush thought they were encountering the forest primeval, so twentieth century white preservationists in Africa mistook the abundance of wildlife in places like the Serengeti for the eternal African wilderness. What each took as the natural state of an unspoiled continent was in fact a very recent development, in both cases brought on by the very intrusion of the Europeans themselves. For thousands of years before the wildlife preservationists evicted all humans from the land in the name of wildlife protection, agriculturists and pastoralists occupied, and heavily managed, the Serengeti plains. The most recent occupants of this niche, the Masai, arrived some four centuries ago. They practiced a shifting system of rotational grazing of cattle (and seasonal burning) that maintained the grasslands. By keeping down the brush, the Masai were also controlling the favored habitat of the tsetse fly, which carries a disease fatal to cattle (but not to wild animals), trypanosomiasis. Wildlife hunting by other tribes also checked the spread of the disease to cattle by controlling the hosts of the fly.

Things began to change, however, when smallpox and other diseases arrived with Europeans. Epidemics in the late nineteenth century decimated the Masai and their cattle; as the ungrazed and unburned brush advanced, the tsetse spread, launching a second wave of destruction. Africa's populations of native cattle and native people probably reached a minimum in the early twentieth century, just as the great push for African wildlife preservation by Europeans was beginning. The Africa that the preservationists found fit perfectly with their mythical image of a land teeming with great wild beasts and devoid of humans or domestic livestock. They did not realize that this wild Africa was one that they themselves had created, albeit unintentionally.[22]

We have a natural reluctance to acknowledge the artificiality of much of the nature that surrounds us. Manufactured landscapes are often very beautiful, for one thing, a trait that seems incompatible with human interference in nature; they often, too, support a diversity of life, including rare and endangered species, an even more confounding fact. We are also uncomfortable with the idea that ancient or primitive man could wreak a degree of havoc that we would prefer to believe is the defining sin of the industrial age. Yet evidence for the antiquity of man's transformation of his environment is overwhelming. Man's hunting alone laid down an environmental template that shaped the course of evolution for at least the past one million years. The pressure of constant culling by skilled and effective hunters selected for species that were able to adapt with evasive and defensive tactics; those that could not were repeatedly hunted to extinction. All of the North American mammals that became extinct shortly after the appearance of humans in North America around twelve thousand years ago—camels, woodland musk oxen, mammoths, mastodons, stagmoose—were descendants of lines that had evolved on the North American continent for a million years in the absence of man. By contrast, the large grazers that survived—bison, moose, elk, caribou, deer, sheep, goat—were all recent arrivals from Asia, where they had evolved in the presence of human hunters for hundreds of thousands of years.[23]

That the Indians and their fellow ecological saints of antiquity were quite capable of hunting species to extinction is no longer seriously questioned by specialists. The arrival of the Polynesians on islands of the South Pacific was invariably accompanied by the disappearance of dozens of bird species. Archaeological work on Hawaii and other Pacific islands has established that 80 to 90 percent of bird species in the region were gone forever by the time Captain Cook explored the islands in the eighteenth century. On Hawaii some fifty now-extinct bird species, including parrots, pigeons, and flightless geese, have been discovered in the fossil record. In some cases, the extinct birds survive on a few isolated islands; in other cases, they live on only in the legends of islanders, who have names for birds they have never seen. Their descriptions of these legendary birds often closely match the fossils that archaeologists have dug up.[24]

Semi-agricultural and pre-agricultural societies had an equally profound effect on the distribution of plant species. Although the Indians of eastern North America had only a handful of domesticated plants, they deliberately influenced the range and abundance of countless other wild plant species through their food-gathering and land-use practices. Early European settlers of Virginia noted the abundance of mulberry trees around Indian villages. There is no evidence that the Indians ever deliberately planted these trees; but they were known to highly prize their fruit, and there is little doubt that by maintaining clearings around campsites and by protecting seedlings that might have sprung up from discarded seeds in village rubbish heaps, the Indians substantially altered the abundance of the species in the forest as a whole. Hickory and black walnut were also reported to exist in a surprising abundance in Virginia's forests; these shade-intolerant species may have been incidentally favored by the regular burning practiced by the Indians, but they may also have specifically been singled out for special protection and attention as a valuable food source. In the tropical rain forests of Costa Rica, repeated harvesting of the Iriartea palm, valued for its edible heart, appears to have profoundly skewed its distribution. Because harvesting the heart of palm means killing the entire plant (the heart is the plant's growing tip), the plant has all but vanished from easily accessible parts of the forest. It is the only one of seven species of palm whose distribution cannot be readily explained by soil or topographic factors.[25]

We have already seen how forest structure was altered and grasslands manufactured on a sweeping scale by primitive man's use of fire. Landscape-level changes accelerated further as agriculture spread during prehistory and antiquity. In Europe and the Mediterranean, whose "natural" landscape remains one of the most artificial on earth, the arrival of the axe and the plow betokened a wholesale transformation of the land. Lest anyone repeat the mistake of underestimating the destructive prowess of the noble savage by underestimating the industry of the Stone Age farmers of Europe, experiments in Denmark have shown just what a few determined axemen can do. Using nothing but stone axes, three men were able to clear a five-thousand-square-foot birch forest in four hours. One hundred trees, in fact, were felled using an original Neolithic stone axe head—which had not been sharpened for four thousand years.[26]

Several millenniums before earnest young men and women in United Nations offices and Washington environmental think tanks began fretting over "deforestation," the primitive agriculturists of Europe and southwest Asia had effectively wiped out the woodlands that once covered much of those regions. The banks of the lower Nile have, for six thousand years, been "a human artifact rather than the swampy African jungle which nature, apart from man, would have made it."[27] Some 4,600 years ago, Phoenicians were doing a lively trade in cedar timber with Egypt and Mesopotamia. The fossil pollen record of Britain shows a precipitous drop in tree pollen beginning

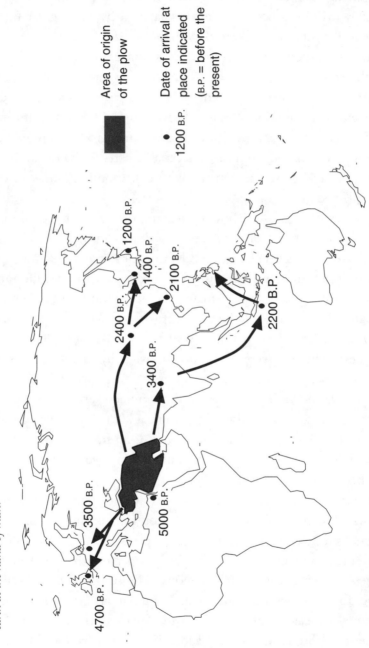

Figure 11. The invention and spread of the plow accelerated the agricultural transformation of the face of the earth at the hand of man.

Area of origin of the plow

Date of arrival at place indicated (B.P. = before the present)

1200 B.P.

4700 B.P.

3500 B.P.

5000 B.P.

2400 B.P.

1200 B.P.

1400 B.P.

2100 B.P.

3400 B.P.

2200 B.P.

Adapted from Goudie, *Human Impact*, 19.

116

nearly 4,000 years ago in northwest Scotland and, sweeping southward, reaching England and Wales by 2,000 years ago. For some time archaeologists spun all sorts of theories about climate change to explain the shifting vegetation patterns they had discovered in the fossil pollen record: The climate, they concluded, had turned colder and moister about 5,000 years ago, which explained the sudden spread in the range of alder across Britain at that time. But then, it was the spread of alder that had led them to conclude in the first place that the climate had turned colder and moister. It is generally agreed now that the extensive changes in the vegetational cover even at this earliest stage of human occupation were the result of human activity.

But man did not merely strip the ground bare. He created, intentionally or not, entirely new ecosystems. The unique "chalk flora" of the British chalk downs—an assemblage of shade-intolerant species that could never have flourished in the presettlement forests—are a product of agricultural clearing, a process greatly accelerated by the arrival of the Roman iron plow, which permitted heavy valley soils to be broken for the first time. The characteristic heather moorlands of England and Scotland are an artifact, too. Although some moors are natural—for example, along exposed coasts or at high altitude, where trees compete poorly—the extensive treeless tracts of heath that cover the Scottish highlands and the low and medium altitudes of Britain and the entire western seaboard of continental Europe only appeared with the arrival of man and sheep grazing. Burning and grazing have kept the heaths from reverting to forest for thousands of years—though over the last century and a half, with the decline in profitability of sheep grazing, heath is now being replanted with more profitable forests along much of its range.[28]

Is this a return to the "natural" state of these lands? Britain and Europe were heavily forested before the arrival of agriculturists. Yet burning and grazing for such a continuous and ecologically significant stretch of time has fundamentally and, in one sense, irreversibly altered the definition of what is natural for these lands. On many heaths, tree seed is so scarce that even when burning is halted and sheep are removed, forests do not immediately return. Many wild species have in the meantime grown dependent upon these artificial ecosystems, including a number of endangered Arctic birds.

Figure 12. Lowland heath is a largely man-made ecosystem, maintained by grazing and burning.

Lowland heath

Adapted from Goudie, *Human Impact,* 59.

Or consider the situation in northern Italy, where the age-old hedges and tree rows that have been used to divide fields since Etruscan times are now also a major habitat for many species of birds. Some preservationists have argued that, with the clearing of the continent's forests, hedgerows are simply the last remaining refuge for woodland species forced out of their native habitat. But that, apparently, is not uniformly correct: Studies found the greatest diversity of bird species in those parts of northern Italy where agriculture dominates, rather than in pure woodlands. The ancient mosaic of olive groves, open fields, hedges, and residual woodlands that characterize the traditional agriculture of the region has come to support many migrating and overwintering birds, including a number of trans-Saharan migrants which feed on the olives and fruits. Where fields are abandoned and woodlands take over—increasingly the case as the economy shifts away from agriculture—the number of bird species actually drops precipitously. Likewise, studies in Britain have found that many artificial "linear features" in the landscape—hedges, roadside verges, even walls, fences, and ditches—often support a significantly greater diversity of plant life than is found in much larger areas of open countryside.[29]

The situation becomes even more tangled when one finds little ringed plovers nesting in sand and gravel pits in England—indeed, the increase in the number of nesting pairs that summer there correlates well with an increase in the number of pits—or American oystercatchers nesting in the Everglades in stands of Australian pine, an exotic tree much despised by concerned environmentalists for its ability to displace mangroves and other native vegetation. And what are we to make of the decline of the large blue butterfly in Britain? This is a species that does well solely on wild thyme, a weed of close-cropped grasslands. Since the decimation of rabbits in the 1950s by the introduction of the viral disease myxomatosis, the grass has grown taller, wild thyme is scarcer, and the butterfly is in trouble. Yet the rabbit was itself an alien introduction of medieval times; it was imported from the continent and kept for food and fur. By 1950 the free-ranging population of rabbits in Britain numbered one hundred million. Which is "natural"? A landscape with alien rabbits and native blue butterflies or one without either?[30]

It may be too much to expect that we will soon see the formation of a group styling itself Save the Gravel Pits. But Save the Prairies is not hard to imagine, nor, in Britain or Italy, Save the Hedgerows. Many artificial landscapes are both ecologically important and aesthetically pleasing. And many, such as grasslands, have clearly been a part of the template that has shaped "natural" ecological relationships for thousands upon thousands of years.

We have a particular difficulty figuring out how to incorporate farming into our feelings about nature, and for good reason. Agriculture has been a part of the natural landscape for as long as there has been civilization and writing and philosophy—and cities to flee from. In

Europe and America in particular, farming is full of wholesome and nostalgic associations. The lure of the pastoral long predates the age of wilderness worship; even now, "back to nature" often has the operative meaning of moving to the country to raise goats and organic vegetables. (Those who head to the hills to take up a more truly Paleolithic lifestyle of pre-agricultural hunting and gathering are generally of a different social class; they usually speak more about resisting the IRS and the Bureau of Alcohol, Tobacco & Firearms than they do about seeking oneness with nature.) With the rise of the nature-preservation movement, however, there has come an increasing tendency to lump agriculture with other forms of "development" that are destroying nature. With no more than the usual amount of hypocrisy, well-fed American preservationists have of late taken to bemoaning the advent of European agriculture on the American continent as an environmental catastrophe; cattle in particular have been singled out for the host of ecological sins that they brought with them. Perhaps because intensive agriculture is a so much older and virtually inextricable part of the European countryside (agriculture affects some 80 percent of the land area of Britain, for example, and 60 to 70 percent of northwestern Europe), and perhaps because Christopher Columbus presents a more suitable target for vilification than the anonymous agriculturalist imperialists who first invaded Europe some thousands of years earlier, European nature lovers have always been more accepting of farming as a part of the "natural" landscape.[31]

In the American environmental battles that agriculture has figured in, preservationists often present the issue as simply one of competing land *use*. Should a piece of Western rangeland be for cattle or bison; should a piece of the Everglades by a sugar plantation or a swamp. The underlying assumption is that human perturbations can always, given enough political will (or enough money), be exorcised from the landscape. Or at the very least, they can be held at bay at the park's boundaries.

Yet agriculture has changed the game in ways that reach far beyond the farm fence. The changes agriculture has brought are not merely on the land; they are woven into the land, into the very fabric of ecological relationships. Farms may go, but the ecological shadows they cast remain.

Much of New England, for example, has returned from agriculture to forest in the last century. In 1850 woods covered 30 to 40 percent of the land area of southern New England; today the forested area is close to twice that. Yet the very act of clearing and then abandoning fields proved to be a novel selective force that has created a new and quite different distribution of many woodland flowers and shrubs from what had existed before the colonists arrived. The woods today are not the woods that were here before. On cleared fields, groves of white pine and red-cedar spring up where they never did in the past. Poison ivy, abetted by the colonists' forest clearing but then long kept in close check by the colonists' grazing cattle, today is spreading out of control. The black-eyed Susan, which seized the opportunity presented by open farm fields to invade the East from its native grasslands of the West, has now firmly established itself even as the fields vanish (it is no less than the state flower of Maryland). Two wildflowers, the arethusa (a small orchid) and the fringed gentian, are now quite rare in New England, their decline a cause of concern and comment among nature lovers; yet their abundance a half century ago was due only to the thousands of acres of abandoned fields that provided the full sun that these plants require. As wood now replaces the fields, they have been displaced by more shade-tolerant competitors.[32]

An even greater ecological legacy of agriculture is the thousands of new species that are now loose upon the land. Longfellow may have relied too much on his imagination when it came to the forest primeval, but he did manage to get another tale of the ancient North American woodlands right. In Hiawatha's dream of the coming of the English, the Indian foresees the appearance of a mysterious new plant in the woods he has known so well: "Wheresoe'er they tread, beneath them / Springs a flower unknown among us, / Springs the White-man's Foot in blossom."

We know it as plantain; the Indians of New England and Virginia did indeed call it Englishman's Foot. They believed it literally grew only where the white men had walked over the ground. Plantain was one of at least forty weeds that, in the first few years of English settlement, arrived in the New World mixed with crop seeds, strewn among shipboard cattle fodder or hay or straw used to pack cargo, clinging in bits of mud to farm tools, or—perhaps the Indians were right—even lurking on the soles of the boots of the invading English-men. Dandelions, shepherd's purse, chickweed, knot grass, stinging nettles, sow thistle, wormwood, and mullein were all noted on a list "Of Such Plants as have sprung up since the English Planted and kept Cattle in New-England," made by John Josselyn on his visits to New England in 1638 and 1663. Ragweed, daisies, most buttercups, Queen Anne's lace, clover—indeed, the overwhelming majority of the American continent's most familiar weeds—are European imports, too.[33]

All told, according to the best recent census of exotic species, the United States is host to more than 2,000 species of imported plants and a like number of insects and spiders; more than 140 land animals; 70 species of fish and 90 terrestrial snails and slugs; and more than 200 microscopic plant pathogens (fungi, viruses, bacteria, and nematodes). As many as one quarter of the total number of wild plant species now found in New England are aliens, almost all of them

Figure 13. An influx of foreign plants has transformed local ecosystems throughout the world. Yet the distinction between native and exotic species is ultimately an artificial one; after a thousand years it is impossible to distinguish the two. The charts show the present-day makeup of local flora.

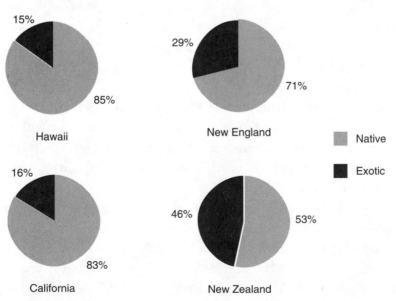

Data from Heywood, "Invasions by Terrestrial Plants," 40; U.S. Congress, *Harmful Non-Indigenous Species,* 95.

from Europe. Australian botanists count about two thousand introduced plant species there, too; in New Zealand, nearly *half* of the flora, some fifteen hundred species, are alien.[34]

Many invasive exotics were incidental stowaways, but many others began their careers as cultivated plants or domesticated animals that, once introduced to the land, continued to multiply and spread without further human assistance. Escaping over the garden fence, fennel, parsnip, and celery readily colonize wasteland in California; potatoes grow wild in southern Africa, peaches in New Zealand, coffee in Haiti, oranges in Paraguay, guava in the Philippines. Repeating a pattern well established in Chile, Argentina, South Africa, and Australia, European grasses brought to America quickly displaced almost entire ecosystems of native grasslands. Bluegrass and white clover may have been deliberately sown at first to improve pastures or may have been inadvertently brought over in cattle fodder, but in either case it was not long after these plants first made their appearance on the east coast of America in the seventeenth century that they swiftly began to spread west by natural dissemination, filling clearings and displacing native grasses. Today many American grasslands, from abandoned New England cow pastures to the western rangelands, are almost entirely composed of non-native species.[35] European honeybees almost literally formed an advance guard of the American settlers; the Indians soon learned that wherever the stinging "English flies" appeared, real trouble, in the form of the white man himself, was not far behind. "As they discover the bees," one contemporary observed, "news of this event, passing from mouth to mouth, spreads sadness and consternation in all minds."[36] Cattle formed another advance guard, often raiding Indian corn and vegetable patches, in a sense speeding the ecological transformation that the colonists themselves were to complete.

In South America and Mexico, cattle in fact spread with astonishing rapidity without the agency of humans at all. Columbus carried cattle to Hispaniola in the West Indies in 1493; by the end of the sixteenth century, their descendants in northern Mexico were running wild on the land in vast herds that doubled their numbers every fifteen years as they continued to move northward. On the pampas of South America, where five thousand cattle were abandoned by a Jesuit mission that pulled up stakes in 1638, free-ranging herds of even more astonishing proportions were soon seen. By the mid-nineteenth century one traveler recorded seeing plantations and orchards in Argentina whose walls were built entirely of the skulls of cattle, stacked "seven, eight, or nine deep, placed evenly like stones, with the horns projecting."[37]

In the American West horses and burros have shown a like proclivity to expand and spread without assistance. Although horses originally evolved in North America, they passed into extinction in the New World at the end of the Ice Age. The Spanish reintroduced the horse to America, and a free-ranging population soon was established. Western ranchers periodically rounded them up or shot them; during the 1849 California gold rush, they drove thousands of wild horses off the cliffs of Santa Barbara to make room for their more profitable cattle. But since 1972, when, in response to the outcry of horse lovers, federal legislation turned ownership of the herds over to the U.S. government and the shooting was halted, the population grew from an estimated 17,000 to more than 50,000 in 1980. The Bureau of Land Management has since removed 100,000 wild horses and burros and placed them with individual owners under its Adopt-a-Horse program, but that has barely made a dent in the population, such is its natural increase. And it is likely that the official figures for the size of the wild horse and burro herds are gross underestimates. Death Valley National Monument, which had been particularly hard hit by overgrazing by burros, originally estimated that it had a population of 1,500 burros; by the time its control program was finished, 6,000 had been trapped and removed.[38]

These invaders form a body of facts on the ground that pose an especially difficult philosophical dilemma for preservationist ideals. If we accept these species as a legitimate part of local ecosystems—and many exotics are so firmly established or so essential for the well-being of other species within an ecosystem that it is ludicrous to pretend otherwise—then their very existence is an admission that what we take for wild and pristine nature has been shaped by man, sometimes in quite dramatic fashion. If conversely we choose to fight them off as artificial intrusions, we have got a management problem of stupendous proportions on our hands.

Preservationists, clinging to the idea that what they want to preserve is nature untouched by man and that the best way to do that is to keep man's hands off, have not surprisingly proved inconsistent on the subject of exotics. A survey of national parks in the United States not long ago found that managers ranked exotic species as the greatest threat to their parks' natural resources, even greater than poaching and over-crowding. Eighty-eight parks reported problems with exotic plants, and forty-four with exotic animals. Japanese kudzu has inundated many parks in the Southeast; Australian melaleuca trees advance through the Everglades; salt cedar forms dense thickets along the banks of the Col-orado River, drying up springs that desert bighorn sheep drink from; tangles of honeysuckle on Theodore Roosevelt Island in Washington, D.C., strangle the dominant forest trees while blankets of English ivy suffocate low-lying native herbs; feral pigs root through the underbrush of Great Smoky Mountains National Park, uprooting and trampling at least fifty species of native plants, disturbing the habitat of voles and shrews, and gobbling up threatened salamanders and snails.[39]

But doing something about these problems is never free from con-troversy. The case of the feral horses and burros in the American West is a prime example of the confusion that reigns when the preserva-tionist philosophy meets invasive exotics. The destructiveness of the burros in particular is undeniable. Originally brought to the West as pack animals, they became widely dispersed when the mining boom ended in the second half of the nineteenth century and many prospectors simply turned their animals loose. A native of North Africa, the burro is well adapted to the desert mountains along the Colorado River where they now flourish. They have no natural predators there; most females breed in their second year; they live ten to fifteen years; their young have very high survival rates. A careful study of burros and bighorn sheep in western Arizona mountains found that the range of the two species overlapped considerably, as did their diets. The burros, which numbered sixty to ninety within the study area, reproduced at a rate of 20 percent a year, with extremely low natural mortality; the bighorn sheep, which numbered seventeen, produced a total of three lambs, of which only one survived its first year. The news obviously does not look good for the native sheep. Nor does it look good for many of the plants that the burros feed on voraciously and indiscriminately. The researchers could find no re-ports of burro numbers declining or even leveling off anywhere in the West; human predation, until outlawed by the 1971 Wild Free-Roaming Horse and Burro Act, appeared to have been the only effective check on its numbers. "We would predict from fundamental ecological theory that uncontrolled burro populations would reach equilibrium only after severely depleting and perhaps eventually bringing to extinction several species of native flora and fauna," the researchers concluded. At Lake Mead National Recreation Area in Nevada and Arizona, burros have already nearly destroyed the northernmost stand of palo verde trees in North America.[40]

On Atlantic barrier islands where horses have been turned loose, the devastation is, if anything, worse. Salt marshes have been grazed down to stubble; the bare sand quickly erodes. What is left, in the words of one biologist, is "a sandbox with horses" and little else. "If a developer damaged these islands the way the horses do," concluded another scientist studying the islands, "he would be put in jail."[41]

Nonetheless, the 1971 federal act recognizes wild horses and burros as "an integral part of the natural system of the public lands" and declares that they "contribute to the diversity of life forms within the Nation." This was language that the horse and burro lovers worked hard to have included in the bill; in the battle for preservation, the label "natural" still serves as an unimpeachable seal of approval.[42]

If herds of non-native horses and burros that are driving bighorn sheep to extinction and destroying the vegetation of barrier islands are natural, it is hard to imagine what is not natural. On the other hand, if half the wild flora of New Zealand is artificial or if the only remaining nesting places for endangered birds are hedgerows planted by farmers, what is there left that *is* natural? The truth is that thousands of years of human history have effectively blotted out the very meaning of "artificial" and "natural." We cling to these terms at the cost of endless confusion and muddled thinking. Man's influence is inextricably woven into the most "natural" ecological relationships, even into evolution itself. The eight thousand species of weeds that have spread throughout the world in the company of agricultural man owe their very evolution to man. The act of clearing land and sowing and reaping a crop made these plants what they are and then guaranteed their existence. Many weeds have the remarkable habit of ripening simultaneously with the crops whose fields they invade and producing seeds indistinguishable from those that man painstakingly collects, saves, and replants, thus guaranteeing themselves a free ride. Other weeds closely resemble crop plants as seedlings, thereby escaping the hoe until they can mature and cast their thousands of seeds on the ground. Weeds have evolved in the presence of man and his habits and have adapted accordingly. They are free-living—that is, they are "natural"—but they are simultaneously the direct product, albeit the unconscious product, of man's artifice.[43]

Piggybacking on human patterns of disturbance and movement, most weeds, not surprisingly, are especially well adapted to a habitat that field guides generally refer to as "waste places." The verges of Roman roads provided a prime avenue for the spread of many weeds across ancient Britain, just as the canals of North America later provided the means for the propagation of purple loosestrife, now a major problem weed that ousts native vegetation from wetlands, destroying the native cover and food for waterfowl.[44]

The long, natural coevolution of the native flora of Europe and Asia with agricultural man probably explains why so many North American (and African and Australian) weeds are of Eurasian origin, while so few weeds have made the return journey. Some 80 percent of the alien plant species found on other continents are Eurasian in origin; annuals most, followed by biennials and perennials, shrubs, and trees. These were species that long ago went through the rigors of adapting to the new environment of agriculture; when the colonists of North America and Australia and southern Africa began to clear woods and plow fields, they were merely expanding an ecological niche that these plants were already adapted to exploit. On the other hand, the native weeds of North America, though they might have been as readily transported to the Old World in ships' cargoes as European weeds arrived in the New World, found there an alien ecosystem with few opportunities.[45]

The many "weedy" animals that have come to exploit the niche created by man's domestic habits have a similarly hybrid, natural-artificial history. Rats and mice have spread throughout the world, sheltering in man's houses and feeding off his refuse; even the success of dogs in and around human society is explained as much by their natural excellence as scavengers as by any conscious efforts we made to breed and keep them. Our mere existence has irreversibly altered the course of evolution of "wild" things.[46]

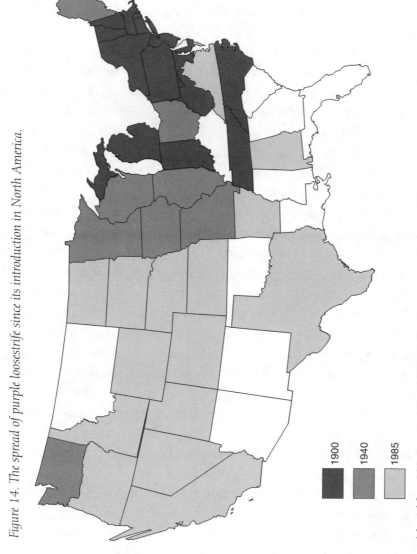

Figure 14. The spread of purple loosestrife since its introduction in North America.

Adapted from U.S. Congress, *Harmful Non-Indigenous Species*, 86.

Although the notorious examples of kudzu and brown tree snakes and burros suggest that invaders are always destabilizing, in fact most invasions are followed by adjustments that cause no net loss of species. Europe was certainly invaded by weeds that arrived from the Near East with the first agriculturists thousands of years ago; yet botanists note that after a thousand years it is virtually impossible to distinguish in any ecologically significant way between natives and in- vaders. Islands have clearly suffered extinctions (or local extinctions) at the hands of exotics, but no mainland species has ever been extir- pated solely as a result of the introduction of an alien species. A theo- retical model of biological invasions in fact suggests that ecological communities structured by long (and supposedly stabilizing) coevo- lution are more susceptible to extinction through competition than are invasion-structured communities, where new species appear sud- denly on the scene but fill relatively unoccupied niches.[47]

In other words, at some point weeds and other invaders become in- distinguishable from any other species: They are just folks. In some cases it may be possible, even desirable, to eliminate exotic species from certain landscapes; in many other cases it will be futile or even unthink- able, given the adaptations that nature has already made—"naturally"— to their presence. "Attempts to exclude all exotic species inevitably conflict with the existence of continual dispersal and adaptation of new arrivals to communities," argues one environmental scientist.[48] The ex- tremely high failure rate of human efforts to remove exotics is certainly suggestive; sometimes it seems a matter of outwitting not just a species but evolution itself. There is apparently no nature reserve on earth, save for Antarctica, that can claim to be free from one or more invasive species. A survey of three hundred African nature reserves found an av- erage of eight invasive species per park; an average of two per park were the object of control efforts; fewer than one, on average, had been suc- cessfully eradicated. The National Park Service recently spent $250,000 in an unsuccessful five-year campaign to eradicate fountain grass in Hawaii Volcanoes National Park by hand weeding.

The few successes on record have been herculean (and sometimes quite bloody) affairs. Rabbits were wiped out on Santa Barbara Island through an intensive program of shooting from 1979 to 1981. One Scottish nature reserve managed to eliminate the giant hogweed through a ruthless campaign of cutting and herbicide sprayings. At Kaloko-Honokohau National Historic Park in Hawaii, the Park Service spent fifty thousand dollars *per acre* to remove exotic mangroves.

Many invasions indeed appear to be simply irreversible facts. An alien rhododendron that has moved into oak and holly woodlands on the British Isles not only thrives in this climate, but it shades out the natives, preventing their regeneration while ensuring its own further spread. Feral mallards from domestic stock have spread into the northeastern United States, interbreeding with the American black duck and so creating an entirely new, and wholly irreversible, genetic fact on the ground. Domestic cats have likewise interbred with African wildcats; introduced marsh grasses have even hybridized with native British varieties. Every farm, every cow, every corn plant could disappear from the world tomorrow and the earth would still never return to what it was ten thousand years ago.[49]

"There is a kind of irrational xenophobia about invading animals and plants that resembles the inherent fear and intolerance of foreign races, cultures, and religions," one biologist, James H. Brown, told a recent scientific conference devoted to exotics. He went on to note that no matter how scrupulous humans may try to be, some species will continue to invade under their own power, moving into favorable niches created by human activity—as indeed they have for thousands of years. Moreover, in some cases, exotics may be the only species capable of thriving in drastically altered landscapes: "The choice may be between exotics or virtually no wildlife at all," Brown said. But he went to the heart of the matter in recognizing that "pristine" and "artificial" are terms of the past. "It has become imperative . . . that we use our expertise as scientists not for a futile effort to hold back the clock and preserve some romantic idealized version of a pristine natural world, but for a rational attempt to understand the disturbed ecosystems we have created and to manage them to support both humans and wildlife."[50]

That is a lesson that many entrusted with the care of the land have yet to take to heart.

SIX

The Science,
but Mostly the Politics,
of "Natural Management"

"We tried a lot of different things here in the past eighty years." John Varley, chief biologist for Yellowstone National Park, was speaking about elk. It is hard not to at Yellowstone. Elk are everywhere. A few dozen yards from Varley's office at Mammoth Hot Springs, the old headquarters town of America's oldest national park, elk were grazing, snoozing, hanging around. On a September afternoon, they outnumbered the waning stream of late summer tourists on their way to see the sputtering and steaming cascades of Yellowstone's famous hot springs at the end of the town. Scattered amid the neat green lawns and tidy headquarters buildings and Park Service residences of Mammoth, the loitering elk put one in mind more of lawn ornaments than of wild animals.

A few urbanized elk grubbing for handouts may always have hung around Mammoth, to be sure. But throughout the rest of the park something is clearly happening. Elk, bison, and moose are so abundant these days that it would take an exceptionally unlucky or obtuse visitor to go home disappointed, having failed to get his fill of wildlife-viewing experiences and several rolls full of exposed film to prove it. From the 1970s to the 1990s, the number of elk increased from five thousand to more than twenty thousand. They—and the picture-snapping tourists—are the clearest beneficiaries of the latest "thing" that the Park Service has tried in its ever-controversial management of America's flagship park. "From the turn of the century until as late as 1941, we tried to feed the animals," Varley explained. "We tried to farm them. Then we tried to kill 'em—kill 'em to save them—that was done in the forties, fifties, and sixties. And the public didn't like that. When Congress started hearing from forty thousand schoolchildren about that, the Park Service decided there must be another way."

That other way, a policy variously termed "natural management" or "natural regulation," is the closest thing to complete hands-off management that has ever been tried for a natural area the size of Yellowstone. It has also become a showcase of the wilderness ethic on a spectacular scale. Leave the animals be, zealously eradicate all visible traces of man's heavy hand, and let nature reign. Environmentalists have responded enthusiastically, seeing in natural regulation a practical vindication of their basic philosophical beliefs. The very prominence of Yellowstone—2.5 million visitors pass through every year, and the park has hardly been shy about explaining its program to them—has given heft and a seeming scientific imprimatur to the idea that nature will take care of itself if only it is left undisturbed.

To implement the policy, elk are no longer shot by rangers to control their numbers; instead, their population is governed only by the amount of food available on their winter range. Grizzly bears are no longer allowed to feed from garbage dumps; the dumps have been shut, and the bears forage for themselves across the park—and beyond. Fires started by natural causes are allowed to burn. Insect infestations of lodgepole pine forests are left to run their course.[1]

When pressed to justify this hands-off policy, which began in 1969, park officials have their scientific defenses ready. (Even if, recently, they have somewhat more cautiously taken to calling the policy an "experiment" or even a "great experiment.") But the discussions invariably drift back to history and politics and letter-writing schoolchildren. "This has never been a biological question," Varley said. "It has always been a political question."[2]

Whatever its merits in the eyes of forty thousand schoolchildren or their parents' elected representatives, natural regulation is a policy that cannot, biologically, succeed. As elk have multiplied, they have literally destroyed the park's vegetation on a massive scale. Aspen and willow stands have failed to reproduce. Beaver and other small mammals have dwindled as the elk strip their food supplies. Meanwhile, the abrupt shift to a let-burn policy after decades of fire suppression set off the massive 1988 Yellowstone forest fires, fueled by a huge buildup of a century's worth of dead wood on the forest floor and a wholesale shift in the structure of Yellowstone's forests to old, mature stands that go up like tinder.

The objections to a policy of hands-off management are so fundamental that it is disconcerting to read the blithe confidence with which park officials explain that "the pristine ecosystem relations" of most national parks are "comparatively intact" and that they can be maintained indefinitely in that state simply by permitting "ecological processes . . . to proceed as they did under pristine conditions."[3]

The realities of nature that we have encountered in the preceding chapters of this section point to at least five basic reasons why a policy that is determined to fly in the face of those realities must fail in practice. First, change is natural and unavoidable. The idea of a "pristine" wilderness loses some of its saintly glow once we realize that there has been a succession of quite different pristine wildernesses occupying the same space over time. Setting aside dinosaurs, saber-toothed tigers, and glaciers and concentrating only on the extremely recent postglacial past, which southern New England forest, say, do we deem to be pristine? The one of twelve thousand years ago, dominated by spruce? The one two thousand years later, when a suddenly accelerating warming brought a wave of pine, birch, and oak? The one three thousand years later when hickories appeared, completing their slower migration? The one a thousand years later when hemlock practically disappeared, wiped out most likely by an insect or disease outbreak? Or perhaps the one that existed during the "little ice age," the five-hundred-year cold snap that began around 1350 A.D., causing still more shifts in the ranges of tree species? A policy of taking whatever nature has to dish out can defeat the very purpose for which a natural area was set aside—as a habitat for particular rare or endangered species or as a vignette of a unique landscape prized for reasons of aesthetics, history, or biodiversity in general.

The internally unstable dynamics of animal populations, even in a constant environment, are another source of trouble. A park the size of a continent might fare reasonably well without meddling, save for the odd extinction every few years. But even the largest parks are biological islands. Park boundaries cut across migration routes. They cut off animal populations within from other subpopulations that might have served as a source for recolonization after a population crash. They close off safety valves that might have allowed for dispersal after a population boom. They genetically isolate populations of park animals under all conditions, hastening inbreeding and increasing their genetic vulnerability.

Third, the limited size of protected natural areas makes it impossible to capture the full scope of natural disturbance processes. Fire, windstorms, landslides, floods, disease outbreaks—all are necessary to maintain the mosaic of habitats that life depends on. Yet disturbance becomes catastrophe when it occurs on a scale that approaches the size of an entire protected area. A reserve that is to have any chance of maintaining its existing complement of species without human management must be large enough to give free rein to disturbance processes without ever losing its own internal recolonization sources in the bargain.

Moreover, many natural disturbance processes have been artificially suppressed across the landscape. Simply giving them free rein within a park or reserve may not be sufficient. Fires that once swept through now-protected lands arose at least at times from beyond park boundaries. It would be a remarkable and unprecedented act of selflessness on the part of homeowners, ranchers, and businesses who now abut park borders to allow such fires to rage unchecked for the good of landscape diversity. Thus, even allowing lightning-set fires to run their course within a park, as Yellowstone set out to do under its natural management policy, may fail to reproduce the pattern and frequency of fires that once occurred.[4] Other biological components that formed the putative "pristine ecological relationships" of these lands have been more thoroughly expunged from the landscape. Key species are extinct; a New England forest may be zealously guarded from all "consumptive" use, but it will never again harbor thousands of passenger pigeons. At the same time, artificial disturbances cross park borders with impunity. Exotic plants and animals, air and water pollution, even stray dogs and cats have altered "pristine ecological relationships," rarely to the benefit of the species and landscapes parks were created to preserve.

Finally, for many key landscapes and habitats, most notably grasslands, man's hunting, burning, and farming, as we have seen, have been a part of the ecological template for thousands of years. Species have adapted to the niche man has thus created; entire landscapes valued for their beauty and biodiversity are the "artificial" creations of human behavior.[5]

All of these arguments lead to but a single conclusion. Hands-off management shows, in the words of the pioneering conservationist Aldo Leopold, "good taste but poor insight." (This is, incidentally, one of many such statements by Leopold that are never quoted by environmentalists these days; they have sought to canonize Leopold's "land ethic" while either failing or refusing to grasp that his entire vision was premised upon the need for active and vigorous human intervention in the management of natural systems.) Leopold continued: "Every head of wild life still alive in this country is already artificialized, in that its existence is conditioned by economic forces. Sane management merely proposes that their impact shall not remain wholly fortuitous. The hope of the future lies not in curbing the influence of human occupancy—it is already too late for that—but in creating a better understanding of the extent of that influence and a new ethic for its governance."[6]

Leopold wrote those words in 1933. It is thus not exactly a new idea that man may from time to time need to intervene in the management of natural areas—intervene to counteract perturbations he himself has irrevocably let loose on the landscape; intervene to supply disturbances he has suppressed or circumscribed by the artificiality of park boundaries; intervene to regulate populations during eruptions or crashes; intervene to maintain landscapes that he himself was instrumental in creating.

The point has been reiterated many times since, often in the form of very pointed criticism of the National Park Service. In 1941 Victor Cahalane, a biologist with the U.S. Fish and Wildlife Service, delivered a searing critique of management policies at Yellowstone at the North American Wildlife Conference, the major annual meeting of experts in the field. Cahalane duly noted that Park Service regulations and policies that aimed "to protect the parks and to maintain them as nearly as possible in their natural condition" reflected both the original legislation that established the parks and broad public sentiment. "The effects of natural forces are a desired part of the picture," he added. But Cahalane quickly proceeded to put his finger on the source of Yellowstone's ills. "We are all accustomed to consider our national parks as vast wildernesses, in which conditions are ideal for animals. Unfortunately that is not always true because the boundaries of a number of our best-known parks were determined solely on the basis of scenery. They are mountain-top or high plateau areas, which although they may have plenty of midsummer range for herbivores, contain little or no winter habitat." The twelve thousand elk in Yellowstone were roughly twice as many as the small and severely overgrazed winter range within the park could support, he calculated. The historic winter range of the park's northern elk herd had stretched north some seventy miles along the valley of the Yellowstone River, reaching as far as the present-day town of Livingston, Montana. But by 1900 ranchers up and down the valley had cleared away the willows, sage, rabbit brush, and aspen the elk had once fed upon. Fences, ranch buildings, and villages cut across the elk's migration routes. When thousands of starving elk descended on the ranches trying to get at hay that had been cut and stored for winter feeding of livestock, they were shot. The remaining elk were effectively sealed within the northern border of the park. Cahalane suggested that continued pressure from hunters and ranchers outside the park might even have begun to effect an evolutionary change in the remaining population, selecting against animals with a strong instinct to migrate to lower elevations in search of winter forage. The survivors, he speculated, were all descendants of elk that had always stayed on the colder, snow-covered high lands, eking out a marginal existence.

Thus, human action had artificially driven back and concentrated elk on what had then, inevitably, become a severely overgrazed winter range. "Over-solicitude for the ungulates—deer, elk, and bighorns—was the reaction from a period of wholesale slaughter throughout the country," Cahalane concluded. "Unfortunately, anxiety to maintain as much game as possible blinded early park administrators to the now obvious realities of range-capacity limitations."[7] Cahalane urged that additional winter range be secured where possible, with protected corridors to provide migration routes. But where that was not possible, ungulate populations should be deliberately reduced through live-trapping and removal or through shooting. Cahalane circumspectly hinted that the "strictly protective legislation" that established the parks and the larger public feeling that the parks and their resources should be "sacredly reserved from commercial or other interference" might need to be modified to allow more vigorous action to correct the elk and deer surpluses that were damaging vegetation in many parks. He stopped short of arguing for public hunting within national parks but suggested that broader legal authority needed to be given rangers to remove or kill excess animal populations. Legislation specifically allowed removals of elk, bison, and bear in Yellowstone, but most other parks were granted no exception to the law forbidding "killing, wounding, or capturing at any time of any bird or wild animal."

Much the same points were uttered, though in a much more authoritative voice, two decades later by two separate bodies of experts. An international conference on the management of national parks issued a report in 1962 that recognized all of the key flaws in the laissez-faire philosophy:

Few of the world's parks are large enough to be in fact self-regulatory ecological units; rather, most are ecological islands subject to direct or indirect modification by activities and conditions in the surrounding areas. These influences may involve such factors as immigration and/or emigration of animal and plant life, changes in the fire regime, and alterations in the surface or subsurface water. . . .

Most biotic communities are in a constant state of change due to natural or man-caused processes of ecological succession. In these "successional" communities it is necessary to manage habitat to achieve or stabilize it at a desired stage. For example, fire is an essential management tool to maintain East African open savanna or American prairie. . . .

Where animal populations get out of balance with their habitat and threaten the continued existence of a desired environment, population control becomes essential. This principle applies, for example, in situations where ungulate populations have exceeded the carrying capacity of their habitat through loss of predators, immigration from surrounding areas, or compression of normal migratory patterns. Specific examples include excess populations of elephants in some African parks and of ungulates in some mountain parks. . . .[8]

A committee appointed by Secretary of the Interior Stewart Udall that same year to examine management of the national parks—generally known as the Leopold committee after its chairman, A. Starker Leopold (a zoologist and the son of Aldo Leopold)—is most often cited today by environmentalists, and indeed by the Park Service itself, for its recommendation that the parks should strive to represent "a vignette of primitive America." The flora and fauna of the parks, the report urged, should be maintained or recreated "as nearly as possible in the condition that prevailed when the area was first visited by the white man." The committee strenuously rejected any deviation from this "single-minded" purpose, frowned on proposals to share management responsibilities over animals in the parks with state fish and game departments, who, it said, had very different interests at heart, and argued that any thought of introducing public hunting or other "multiple uses" on park land was unjustifiable, illegal, and a betrayal of the purpose for which the parks were established.

But that said, the Leopold report was also a ringing, unambiguous endorsement of aggressive, intrusive, assertive, hands-on management. It urged burning and even bulldozing to create and maintain important vegetation habitats. It urged the artificial reintroduction of native plants and animals that had been lost to overgrazing or hunting. It unstintingly urged the draconian removal or killing of excess elk and deer, as well as feral goats, pigs, and burros, where their unnatural concentration was destroying vegetation. The committee recommended specifically that one thousand to eighteen hundred elk from Yellowstone's northern herd be trapped or shot every year to keep the population at about five thousand, the estimated carrying capacity of the northern winter range. "Protection alone, which has been the core of Park Service wildlife policy, is not adequate" to achieve the parks' primary goal of reproducing the primitive landscape, the committee concluded.

Again, the well-established reasons for this fact were enumerated:

Many of our national parks—in fact most of them—went through periods of indiscriminate logging, burning, livestock grazing, hunting, and predator control. Then they entered the park system and shifted abruptly to a regime of equally unnatural protection from lightning fires, from insect outbreaks, absence of natural controls of ungulates, and in some areas elimination of normal fluctuations in water levels. Exotic vertebrates, insects, plants, and plant diseases have inadvertently been introduced. . . . The resultant biotic associations in many of our parks are artifacts, pure and simple. . . .

The report's authors concluded that "reluctance to undertake biotic management can never lead to a realistic representation of primitive America"—the officially adopted goal of the Park Service for the lands it is charged with managing. And the authors noted, with a certain zest even, that "management may at times call for the use of the tractor, chain-saw, rifle, or flame-thrower."[9]

So how, in the face of overwhelming scientific arguments to the contrary—arguments voiced with such singular unanimity by the world's leading wildlife experts—how did a prejudice, a sentiment, a public relations gesture even, become the guiding policy of America's premier national park? How did "the traditional, simple formula" of protection—the words are those of the Leopold committee—become elevated in 1969 to the status of a fundamental scientific principle? A partial answer is to be found in another one of the Leopold committee's recommendations. The committee did not doubt the Park Service was the proper agency to conduct the scientific research that would be needed to inform and guide its own management decisions. There was only one hitch. The Leopold committee was polite enough about it, but one didn't have to read very closely between the lines to get the message: The Park Service's research staff was not exactly full of Einsteins. Or anyone else, for that matter. What little research was being done was aimed largely at "interpretive functions"—signs, pamphlets, and ranger talks for the tourists. Real scientific research was the definite exception.

Thus had it always been. When the National Park Service was established in 1916, ecology was in its infancy. Park superintendents rarely had any formal training in biology. They were outdoorsmen at best, and they conceived of their role in custodial or even military terms. (Prior to the founding of the Park Service, the superintendents of Yellowstone were in fact military officers; the U.S. Army had been deemed the only institution capable of controlling the poaching hunters and trappers that were seen as the primary threat to the park.) These were not men who, by their training, background, or conception of the world, were likely to place great stock in scientific research, at least not when it came to setting budget priorities. A scientific research program briefly got off the ground in 1932, when George M. Wright, a former park naturalist who three years earlier had used his own money to conduct a survey of wildlife management problems, was named to head a new Wildlife Division within the Park Service. But Wright died in 1936, and the new organization quickly lost what influence it had managed to acquire; by 1939 the staff had dwindled to three as a result of Depression-era budget cuts, and the program was disbanded. The surviving staff was packed off to the Interior Department's Fish and Wildlife Service.[10]

The situation had changed little by the time of the Leopold committee report. Nor did it change dramatically afterward. Despite repeated reorganizations and declarations of good intent, science has never achieved much prominence within the Park Service, in terms of either funding or political influence. Since the Leopold report, literally a dozen additional major reviews by outside experts have urged the Park Service to strengthen its research program. The same recommendations appear time and time again. A note of frustration is all too apparent in the latest such effort, a 1992 report by the prestigious National Research Council: "The recommendations of many serious reviews over nearly three decades reveal both a unanimity of opinion about the need for research to support resource management in the national parks and an abysmal lack of response by the NPS. . . . Many of the suggested improvements were recommended repeatedly, yet few have been effectively or consistently implemented. . . . Despite repeated admonitions, the importance of a strong science program— although recognized by some regions, parks, and personnel—simply has not garnered servicewide support."[11]

Many of the reports went further, sharply criticizing the service for its continued failure even to recognize the importance of scientific knowledge in making management decisions. A number took aim directly at the Park Service's "natural management" philosophy. A 1977 review co-authored by A. Starker Leopold at the request of the Park Service's director included the usual criticisms of the failure to implement the Leopold committee's recommendations (of fourteen years earlier) for a strong research program; it then added this warning: "Seat-of-the-pants guesses in resource preservation and management are open to challenge and do not stand up well in court or in the forum of public opinion." The report found that even when scientific data was available, it was not necessarily considered by officials charged with setting management policy. And a 1989 investigation conducted by a blue-ribbon panel funded by the Andrew W. Mellon Foundation concluded with a more pointed barb: "The concept of 'naturalness' is not a simple and comprehensive guide for management and will not anywhere substitute for identification of well-defined, park-specific, and research-based objectives."[12]

The criticism intensified in the wake of the 1988 Yellowstone fires. The old policy of total fire suppression had been abandoned in 1972; in keeping with the spirit of the new philosophy of natural management, fires would henceforth be allowed to burn if they were started naturally and if they did not threaten life, property, or unique park features. Although the policy allowed the use of prescribed burns, Yellowstone managers decided not to deliberately set any fires. The decision appeared to have been at least in part a further obeisance to the gods of "naturalness."

The fires that raged through the park in the summer of 1988 burned 45 percent of the park's area. Subsequent studies showed that a century of fire suppression had caused an unprecedented shift toward old, decaying forests with huge loads of dead wood on the forest floor. A fire that starts in this type of forest under dry conditions, even without wind, will readily propagate to the crowns and turn into an intense, fast-moving firestorm. By contrast, the younger stands that dominated Yellowstone in the century before the fire suppression policy began in 1872 are the product of frequent low-level fires and will rarely or only under extremely windy conditions propagate crown fires. "It is not enough to withdraw aggressive fire suppression from wild areas," concluded yet another blue-ribbon panel of experts that reviewed the fires. "Rather, fire management must blend various forms of suppression with various forms of prescribed fire." The panel added: "Avoiding the influence of people may no longer be a realistic or desirable wilderness management goal. . . . [W]e have learned enough to know that wilderness landscapes are not predestined to achieve some particular structure or configuration if we simply remove human influences. . . . [J]ust as human presence in and around wilderness landscapes is inescapable, human intervention and manipulation will be necessary to preserve [natural] processes." The report ended with the all-too-familiar call for support of scientific research programs that can inform management decisions.[13]

Yet science is just not part of the culture of the Park Service. The spirit of "protection" is, though. The 1916 "Organic Act," still the basic law which guides the Park Service today, faithfully reflects the reformist, conservation ethic of that earlier day. The overriding philosophy was one of saving resources from the rapaciousness of private commercial interests; the legislative charge to the Park Service was, and is, to "conserve the scenery and the natural and historical objects and the wildlife therein and to provide for the enjoyment of the same in such manner and by such means as will leave them unimpaired for the enjoyment of future generations." Park officials have a way of quoting those words as if they were the Holy Writ, and indeed they are not bad words. But they carry the clear message that simple protection, or in the censorious words of the National Research Council report, "passive management," will suffice.

The history of appalling overhunting in the American West was also clearly a formative influence on the Park Service's conception of its mission. Journals of early travelers through the Yellowstone area at time seem to be nothing so much as scorecards of the numbers of animals they slaughtered—deer, elk, antelope, moose, grizzly bear, black bear, mountain lion, wolverine. Even after the park was founded, sport hunting of this sort was considered just part of the visitor's experience. But even sport hunters were appalled by the depredations of the professional hunters who descended on the region in 1871. Thousands of sheep, deer, and elk were slaughtered for their hides, their carcasses left to rot where they fell. General W. E. Strong, who visited

Figure 15. Yellowstone's policy from 1872 to 1972 called for complete fire suppression. As a result, the proportion of the forest occupied by mature stands—characterized by pine, fir, and spruce of all ages—increased dramatically. In these stands, a high density of young spruce and fir and dead trees can ignite sweeping crown fires even under dry conditions and no wind.

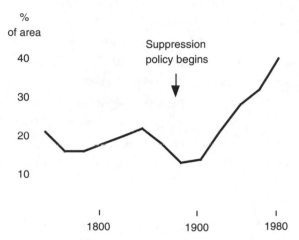

Adapted from Romme and Despain, "Yellowstone Fires of 1988," 696.

the park in 1875 in proper military style with a party of thirty-two, recorded his outrage at the carnage: "But few years will elapse before every elk, mountain sheep, and deer will have been killed, or driven from the mountains and valley of the National Park. . . . It is an outrage and a crying shame that this indiscriminate slaughter of the large game of our country should be permitted. The act of Congress setting aside the National Park expressly instructs the Secretary of the Interior to provide against the wanton destruction of the game and fish found within the limits of the Park . . . unless some active measures are soon taken looking to the protection of the game there will be none left to protect."[14] To be sure, Strong was lobbying to get the job turned over to the army, as subsequently happened. But his comments were by no means atypical of the time. Such scenes of carnage were indeed instrumental in the later decision to ban all hunting within national parks.

The zeal with which the army and later the Park Service pursued their policy of protection of game animals led to its own excesses; these form another part of the political and historical backdrop to the

1969 decision to adopt natural management. Having won the war against poachers, the army turned its sights on the next enemy: predators. A series of military superintendents left no doubt that they viewed predators—wolves, mountain lions, coyotes—as a threat to game animals and urged their control or extermination. Official reports chronicled with satisfaction the destruction of these and other carnivores; in one particularly lurid account, an early park superintendent described how a grizzly bear was blown up with dynamite planted in a pile of garbage set out as bait. Traps and poison were routinely used in Yellowstone and other parks; a pack of hounds was even acquired by Yellowstone in 1893 for hunting cougars. The Park Service continued the army's effort with enthusiasm, adding lynx, bobcat, foxes, otter, marten, mink, weasel, and fishers to the list of undesirable species. Bounty hunters were hired, and in a number of parks, including Glacier, Grand Canyon, Mount Rainier, and Zion, the services of the Interior Department's Biological Survey, which had initiated a zealous campaign of predator eradication of its own on public lands, were employed. It was not until 1931 that the Park Service, finding itself under increasing criticism from outside scientists who had begun to understand more clearly the role of predators in ecological relationships, finally dropped its extermination efforts and issued a policy directive declaring that "predatory animals are to be considered an integral part of the wild life protected within national parks."[15]

Since the Park Service had just stopped shooting wolves, it would be too much to expect that the service would turn around and immediately start shooting elk, however much of a problem they were becoming. From the 1930s the park began an intensive program of live-trapping elk in Yellowstone and removing them to restock game ranges throughout the West. All told, 11,000 elk were trapped. When the population of the northern herd was found to still exceed the estimated carrying capacity of 5,000 animals, the Park Service finally faced up to the inevitable and in 1949 began shooting elk within the park. By 1961 nearly 9,000 elk had been shot, but the herd was still at roughly twice the carrying capacity. Rangers that winter shot 4,300 more elk (under arduous conditions that included deep snow and temperatures of forty degrees below zero) in what was termed a "definitive" reduction down to the carrying capacity.

But the policy was to be the victim of the Park Service's own earlier public relations successes. Having instilled in park visitors the message of protection as an almost sacred trust, the Park Service found that the public had a hard time fitting rifle-toting rangers into that picture. Perhaps more important, sport hunters in Montana, who from 1934 to 1968 had shot some 44,000 elk of the northern herd that migrated out of the park, began to complain that the rangers were spoiling the fun. Montana hunters bagged only 760 animals from 1960 to 1964, roughly a tenth the number they had shot in every previous five-year period back to the 1930s. The area's congressional delegation began leaning on Park Service officials, and at a March 1967 hearing Senator Gale McGee of Wyoming opened the proceedings by announcing that the Secretary of the Interior had agreed to an immediate halt to the "direct kill" of elk by rangers within Yellowstone.[16]

It was an unabashedly political decision. But perhaps taking to heart the admonitions of the Leopold committee, in spirit if not in substance, the Park Service was very soon offering up a scientific rationale for it all. Or at least a scientific-sounding one. Invoking broad and, in the context, meaningless concepts such as "dynamic equilibrium" and "ecological homeostasis," park scientists were suddenly putting forth the opinion that the elk would seek their own balance with available vegetation: "Accumulated knowledge on natural ecosystems tells us that the Northern Yellowstone elk and other native wildlife would have had to be in some dynamic balance with each other, their food sources, and the environment several thousand years before modern man first visited the region."[17]

Where the Leopold committee had stated explicitly that its goal for the parks—the maintenance of "primitive" conditions—required active management, the Park Service was now arguing that, by its very definition, "primitive" conditions meant the exclusion of all human influence.[18] This was the exact opposite of what Leopold had said; indeed, Leopold reiterated the point at the very same Senate hearing where the Park Service announced it would no longer shoot elk. Leopold told the senators that the control of elk was the "keystone to maintenance of the habitat" and that direct reduction by shooting within the park was "absolutely essential." He concluded: "I have no reason whatsoever to alter my views that this is the manner in which that herd has to be regulated."[19]

To the extent a scientific case was made for the new policy at all, the argument was that elk automatically reduce their reproductive rate as populations increase, thus insuring that they never destroy their own food supply. But references to actual scientific data are virtually nonexistent in the Park Service's publications explaining these new scientific revelations; the few papers published in scientific journals by park scientists at this time cite unpublished or mimeographed reports by Yellowstone scientists as their primary references.[20] Most often, however, the argument took the form that one philosopher has aptly termed "self-sealing." Because elk free from human interference must naturally regulate themselves, then *however* a "natural" elk population behaves must, by definition, be natural. It is hard to disprove such a hypothesis. (Even park scientists were not always able to steer clear of tautologies in explaining the concept. For example: "Over a series of years, naturally regulated ungulate populations were self-regulating units.")[21]

Since by definition naturally regulated elk were incapable of becoming out of balance with their environment, then elk could not overgraze the range or suffer from overpopulation. Thus, the ensuing population explosion was merely evidence that the elk were in the process of seeking a dynamic equilibrium with their environment. As elk numbers climbed upwards toward twenty thousand, the park reversed its previous long-standing contention that the carrying capacity of the northern range was five thousand and began to argue that elk populations had historically been much greater, perhaps as large as fifteen thousand.[22]

Explaining away the problem of overgrazing required some slightly more elaborate intellectual gymnastics, especially as the park had been arguing for years that the winter range *had* severely deteriorated, with aspen stands having declined by 50 percent on the northern range since the park was established a century ago. It was impossible to deny the deterioration, but park scientists claimed to have found a new culprit—not elk, but climate.

The only trouble was, as Charles Kay of Utah State University persuasively demonstrated in research he carried out for his 1990 Ph.D. thesis, that aspen stands outside the park were doing just fine. So were stands within the park protected by exclosure fences—fences that had been constructed many years earlier expressly for the purpose of providing controls for evaluating the effects of ungulate browsing. Outside the park or inside the protective fences, trees of all different sizes were found growing, indicating that the aspen stands were successfully reproducing on a continuing basis. On the park's northern range, by contrast, the trees came in only two sizes: small suckers that never get above six feet and very large trees that appear to be at least eighty to one hundred years old. Even more convoluted arguments were forthcoming from the park to explain away these uncomfortable facts. Some park scientists suggested, for example, that the exclosure fences themselves altered the microclimate within the exclosures by causing "unusual drifting of snow . . . thereby concentrating moisture near the fences." Since some of the exclosures are as large as three hundred acres, this seemed to be reaching a bit.

The only factor that is actually different from one side of the fence to the other is, of course, elk. Kay found similar inside-outside differences in willow stands protected by exclosure fences. Reviewing nearly fifty thousand historic photographs of the park, Kay also was able to document that the healthy growth of tall willows within exclosures today closely resembles the conditions that existed across the entire northern range from the 1870s to the 1890s, when "innumerable dense thickets" were noted along river banks; successive photos taken over the intervening years show the steady disappearance and deterioration of these stands—a 98 percent decline. The photos similarly suggest that aspen have declined by far more than the 50 percent reduction the Park Service acknowledges; the area covered by aspen in the photos has dropped by as much as 96 percent since the period 1880 to 1910. In some photos Kay was able to count individual aspen trees, and tallied an 85 percent drop in actual numbers of trees in specific stands within the park just from 1947 to 1988. The photos also confirmed what the size-distribution data strongly suggested: Aspen stands within the park have not successfully regenerated for at least eighty years. (Aspens rarely, if ever, grow from seed in the wild; stands that were established shortly after the glaciers retreated ten thousand years ago have continued to reproduce ever since vegetatively, sending up new suckers from old roots. Thus, once a stand is wiped out by overgrazing, it is permanently lost.) Finally, the photos show progressively more severe "high-lining" of conifers—the stripping away of

Figure 16. As the elk population exploded, aspen in Yellowstone National Park failed to regenerate and mature to larger-size classes. The histograms show the age distribution of aspen protected by exclosure fences ("inside") and exposed to browsing by elk ("outside") at two sites in the park.

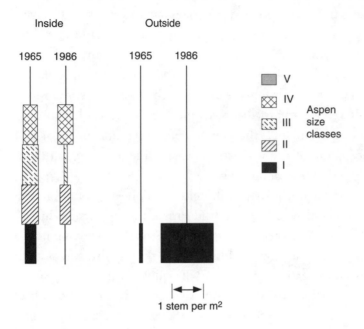

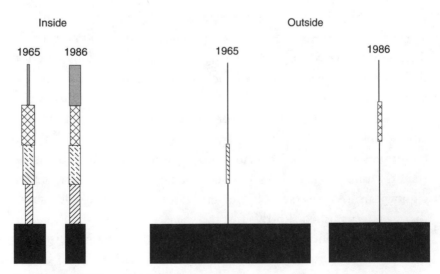

Data from Kay, "Yellowstone's Northern Elk Herd," 86, 92.

lower branches—over the last century, another strong piece of evidence that the deteriorating state of Yellowstone's vegetation is anything but "natural."[23]

The lingering consequences of predator-control programs, which had exterminated wolves, and the artificial confinement of the elk's winter range by the park's boundaries partly explain the increase in elk numbers and the resulting vegetation damage over the last century. But Kay's research suggests an even greater factor. The reason elk historically were scarce in the Yellowstone area, he argues, is that they had been heavily hunted by Indians for thousands of years. The much-cherished idea these days that Native American religious beliefs and taboos served to harmonize their impact on the environment is apparently without basis. Rather, at every opportunity they exploited resources to maximize the immediate benefits, regardless of the long-term environmental consequences. It would indeed be astonishing if they did not: It is not just a human characteristic but a universal biological characteristic that organisms tend to follow a strategy that maximizes individual fitness.

Specifically, the claim made by some authors that Indian hunters selectively spared female elk or deer in order to protect the future supply of game is contradicted by archaeological data, historical accounts, and anthropological studies. All indicate that the Indians, like aboriginal hunters throughout the world, if anything selectively killed prime-age females, which were highly desired for their higher fat content and their superior hides. (The hides of males are often scarred from fights during the mating season; female hides are also easier to tan.) Such a harvesting strategy is, of course, precisely the opposite of what is required to maximize future game numbers. In fact, calculations show that even relatively modest amounts of predation that selectively takes females of reproductive age can lead to an abrupt collapse in the population. There is no evidence at all that Indian religions even made a connection between their harvest practices and the future abundance of game. "If a Native American could not find any game, it was not because he had overharvested the resource, but because he had done something to displease his gods," writes Kay. "Their system of religious beliefs actually fostered the over-exploitation of ungulate populations. Religious respect for animals does not equal conservation."[24]

The overwhelming effect that Indian hunters had in limiting the populations of game animals in North America is well documented in historical sources. Lewis and Clark found an abundance of wild animals only in buffer zones that separated warring Indian tribes, where hunting was severely curtailed. In one instance that has been recorded, warring Chippewa and Sioux tribes reached a truce; the buffer zone between the tribes, which had served as a refuge for deer, was then hunted by both; the deer population crashed and starvation gripped both tribes. But most of the time the consequences were not so drastic. Indians in the intermountain West had many other, if less desirable, sources of food to turn to, including fish, small mammals, and vegetables. Overhunting that led to a drastic drop in elk and deer populations would not have resulted in any compensating loss in human population; it would just have meant a less tasty diet.[25]

Kay has gathered considerable evidence to show that this is precisely what happened. Historical accounts and archaeological remains suggest that elk were indeed quite rare in the Yellowstone area in the decades and centuries before the park's establishment. Elk currently account for 80 to 90 percent of the ungulate population of the park; at archaeological sites in and around the park, elk bones are rare, while bighorn sheep and mule deer appear in vastly greater proportion than they do today.[26]

So committed are Yellowstone officials to their belief that huge elk herds are natural that, in proposing to reintroduce wolves to the park, they have scrupulously avoided any suggestion that wolves might be needed to bring down the elk population. In so doing, they have deprived themselves of a potentially persuasive argument in support of a controversial proposal. But having insisted for the past twenty-five years that, in the absence of wolves, elk were capable of regulating themselves, it would be rather awkward now to start ascribing a major role to predators. Thus, officials generally insist that bringing back the wolf will have *no* effect whatsoever. (Except, that is, on perceptions. Since the public incorrectly believes the range is overgrazed and often attributes this fact to the loss of predators, bringing back predators may change all that, according to a recent scientific paper published by the park.)[27]

Yet according to population models that the park itself has published, the zero-effect scenario depends on some rather restrictive as-

1. The dark and dense "forest primeval" was largely the invention of nineteenth-century artists, poets, and nature lovers; the real forests of presettlement America were open and parklike. (Asher B. Durand, *In the Woods*, 1885)

2. Romantic nature: In Britain, wealthy landowners fashioned their own soul-stirring land-scapes and filled them with unkempt copses, faked-up Gothic ruins, and the occasional hermitage—complete with live hermit hired to play the part. (Samuel Hieronymus Grimm, *The Hermitage at Selbourne, Hampshire, with Henry White as the Hermit, 1777*)

3. Patriotic nature: Thomas Jefferson, who sang the praises of—and purchased—Virginia's "Natural Bridge," was a leading voice among American nature-nationalists, who saw in the New World's natural grandeur proof of its superiority to decadent Europe. (Caleb Boyle, *Thomas Jefferson at the Natural Bridge*, c. 1800)

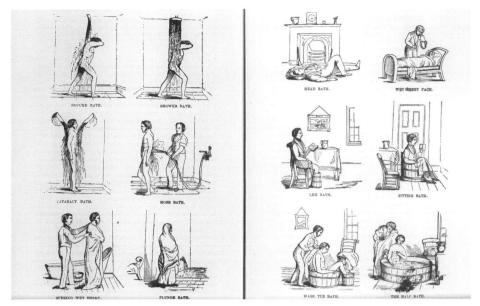

4. Nature as cure-all: The surge of interest in nature owed much to nineteenth-century cults and fads that promised physical or spiritual salvation through a return to "natural" ways. Cold–water enthusiasts claimed that liberal applications of water would cure gout, consumption, alcoholism, and unhappiness. (Front papers from Joel Shew, *The Hydropathic Family Physician*, New York: Fowler & Wells, 1854)

5. John Muir's nature religion was incomplete without nature evangelism. On an outing in 1909, members of the Sierra Club received a natural history lesson from Muir.

6. The scouting movement promoted outdoor activities as both nostalgia and hygiene, a way to cling to the romance of the frontier while combating the widely feared physical and moral degeneration of urban life: Building a bridge at Camp Recreation, Ohio.

7. Indians regularly set fire to the woods and plains for a variety of reasons: to encourage fresh growth to attract game, to increase the sight distance for hunting, to keep down insect pests and snakes, and, as depicted in this turn-of-the-century painting by Charles Russell, *Blackfeet Burning Crow Buffalo Range*, as a weapon of war.

8–9. The brilliant—and all too successful—propaganda campaign waged against forest fires by the U.S. Forest Service created a huge psychological barrier to the later acceptance of controlled burns as a necessary management tool. Posters appealed variously to sentiment, guilt, and patriotism.

10–12. The elk that ate Yellowstone: To monitor the effect of elk, Park Service researchers in 1936 took down an abandoned corral near Yancy's Hole where aspen trees had begun to grow; half of the trees were then enclosed within a fence that protected them from browsing. Within a year (top) elk had already "highlined" the exposed trees; in five years (above) nearly all of the browsed trees were dead. A half century later, the protected trees stand sixty feet high (left).

13–14. The elk that ate Yellowstone II: Tall willows at Round Prairie in Yellowstone's Pebble Creek Valley were already heavily browsed by 1949 (above); by 1988 they had virtually disappeared (below).

15. The Scottish moors are man-made creations, maintained by constant burning and sheep grazing. Strips about thirty yards wide are burned on a rotating schedule; the light-colored patches that cover the hills indicate the most recently burned areas.

16. Oak savannas once covered thirty million acres of North America; regular fires kept them clear of underbrush. Today, remnants survive largely by fluke. Tank and infantry maneuvers at Fort McCoy Army Base, Wisconsin, disrupted the vegetation to maintain this stand, which contains the largest population of the rare Karner blue butterfly known in the United States.

sumptions. *If* elk hunting outside the park is reduced by 27 percent, *if* the wolf population in the park peaks at seventy-eight, and *if* wolves kill an average of only nine ungulates a year each, then, yes, elk populations will remain virtually unaffected. But equally plausible scenarios—no reduction in hunting outside the park, a hundred wolves, and fifteen ungulates per wolf per year—lead to a predicted drop of more than 50 percent in elk numbers on the northern range.[28] It is an exquisite dilemma for the park. In fealty to its belief in natural management, it wants to bring back wolves—a natural component of the "pristine" ecosystem that has been missing for a half century. Yet if thus restoring the ecosystem to its natural state causes elk numbers to drop by half, the only possible conclusion is that the high elk populations the park has so staunchly defended for the last quarter century were unnaturally high. Ergo, wolves *must* have no effect.

A few park scientists whose research ran afoul of the party line found quickly that their views were not welcome. When one researcher was about to produce a paper reporting that grizzly bear populations suffered a much higher mortality rate than park officials acknowledged, his research data were confiscated from his office by his superior. While denying that he had conducted a "raid," the superior explained in a memo that he was "responsible for" the data and had retrieved it "before it was used to further criticize the government." In a subsequent newspaper interview the official explained that the researcher had become too critical of the government's policy. "It's called biting the hand that feeds you," he told the *Los Angeles Times*. Another Yellowstone scientist who strayed from the fold with a study on elk damage of cottonwood trees in the park was also criticized by a higher-up, who was quoted in the same article; he denounced the researcher's work as "dabbling," and said that to challenge the natural regulation theory was "improper, unscientific, and immoral."[29]

In other places where natural regulation has been tried, the consequences for both ecosystems and intellectual honesty have been equally disastrous. One of the worst cases was Tsavo National Park in Kenya, where antipoaching efforts, the digging of wells to provide an artificial water source for wildlife, and other artificial perturbations led to a huge eruption in elephant populations in the early 1960s.

Outside scientists recommended shooting three thousand elephants if the park was to be saved from severe overgrazing. An adult male elephant eats three hundred pounds of plant material daily, uprooting trees, stripping shrubs, and leaving behind what more than one observer of overgrazed African parks has described as a "lunar landscape." Tsavo's warden, David Sheldrick, disagreed, however, insisting that nature should be left to take care of itself; all that managers should do is eliminate what he viewed as human interference—poaching and fires, mainly—to allow attainment of the "natural ecological climax." The inevitable ensued, and six thousand elephants starved to death in 1969 and 1970. The story has been repeated in other East African parks where hunting is strictly banned, and even a die-hard protectionist like Richard Leakey, until recently head of the Kenya Wildlife Service, now concedes that culling may be necessary to keep elephant populations under control lest they destroy the habitat for impala, giraffes, monkeys, and other species in the parks. In southern Africa, where a strict program of culling and slaughtering surplus elephants has been practiced in the parks for some time, there are no such problems of habitat destruction.[30]

The wilderness lobby remains unfazed by the history of Yellowstone or Tsavo; it sees no problem with natural regulation that could not be solved by bigger parks. Larger reserves could certainly address one of the five flaws in natural management outlined at the beginning of this chapter—the inability of most parks to capture within their artificially circumscribed boundaries the full scope of natural disturbance processes. The debate over how much land society ought to set aside for parks quickly enters realms of politics and economics that are well beyond the scope of this book. Yet the theoretical studies that have been done on the minimum size of such a reserve or network of reserves ought to suggest to all but the most visionary that there is not much chance of it ever happening. The "minimum dynamic area" for a self-sustaining park would have to be considerably larger than the largest natural disturbances that occur, even those that occur quite infrequently; and such a minimum dynamic area would be required for every separate habitat type found within the park. In some habitat types, such as boreal forests, fires as large as two million acres—about the entire size of Yellowstone, the largest park in the lower forty-eight states—have been known to occur under presumably "natural" conditions.[31] Its name notwithstanding, the Greater Yellowstone Ecosystem, the thirteen million acres of public lands that surround the park proper, supports a mix of timber, mining, grazing, and other commercial uses that unavoidably conflict with any preservationist purposes that it might be devoted to. The economic and political realities that those who dream of a self-sustaining wilderness face are even more formidably apparent in the blueprint issued by the North American Wilderness Project. The project, a serious effort by conservation biologists to define the scope of the problem, concluded modestly that an area equal to half the land area of the lower forty-eight states would have to be set aside as "core reserves" and corridors to link them. The core reserves would be completely stripped of all human presence— roads, power lines, dams, farms, ranches. These inner areas would be surrounded by further buffer zones where human activities would be allowed but only on a limited scale. "Our goal is to create a new political reality based on the needs of other species," explained one of the project organizers. What the effort is much more likely to accomplish, however, is to establish conclusively that self-sustaining nature reserves are a political, indeed a physical, impossibility.[32]

Biologists who have led the fight to save in toto the tropical rain forests and other species-rich habitats of the world have a strange habit of not grasping the political implications of their calls to arms in the name of wilderness. In an article in *Science* magazine, overpopulation guru Paul Ehrlich and Harvard biologist Edward O. Wilson, the man who made *biodiversity* a household word, issued a manifesto calling upon mankind to "reduce the scale of human activities" in order to save the planet's biodiversity. The "first step," they said, "would be to cease 'developing' any more relatively undisturbed land."[33] Some readers were probably inspired by their bold vision, but most were probably struck more by the naïveté of the suggestion that development can simply be made to cease. The world's population is continuing to expand, and the best efforts in the world will not prevent it from growing from 5.5 billion in 1995 to more than 8.5 billion before finally leveling off. (If every woman in the world immediately decided to have no more than two children and if all the technical and cultural obstacles to that end were removed in a flash, world population would still continue to surge upwards until sometime in the middle of the twenty-first century. This is the result of demographic "momentum" in the population that arises from the current young, skewed age distribution.) Nor is there any detectable sentiment anywhere in the world in favor of limiting economic growth.[34]

To be sure, the more-developed nations continue, through technology, to delink economic growth from the exploitation of natural resources. And because tropical areas that support the greatest biodiversity have generally poor agricultural soils, it may be possible to preserve these areas from development at relatively low economic cost even as populations grow. Free trade, industrialization, and the shift to market economies in developing nations should tend to shift economic incentives away from further agricultural exploitation of tropical forests and other biodiversity-rich areas; on a global scale the economic incentives will be to concentrate agriculture in those areas where it is already most productive, namely, the temperate regions where farming has gone on for hundreds or thousands of years and where all the recent gains in production have come through technological improvements rather than clearing more land. Similarly, some 75 percent of the total world production of commercial timber and other forest products comes from temperate forests, almost entirely from lands that have been intensively managed for sustained timber production for more than half a century. These sorts of high-yielding, sustainable timber plantations could meet the entire world's timber needs on a mere 5 percent of the area of all the world's existing forests. Much of the recent loss of tropical forests, indeed, has been driven not by rational economic development but by government subsidies that encouraged farming or logging on lands where it would never pay to do so in a free market.

All of that said, it would be hard to find any knowledgeable economist who believes that twice as many people a century from now will occupy less of the globe's land area or have less of an impact on its resources than they do at present. Displaying a realism that many devout preservationists lack, the World Conservation Strategy of 1980 recognized that the world's impoverished billions are not going to place the goal of self-sustaining wilderness preserves above their own survival: "Hundreds of millions of rural people in developing countries, including 500 million malnourished and 800 million destitute, are compelled to destroy the resources necessary to free them from starvation and poverty." That is a simple way of saying that it is too late in the day to leave nature to its own devices. The world will not stand for it—and nature won't either. Only by active management will the world be fed; only by active management will such goals as preserving biodiversity come even close to being realized.[35]

PART III

Nature Management

SEVEN

Waiting for Newton

It says much about the state of ecology as a predictive science that one of the few clear-cut applications of ecological theory to the real world in the scientific literature is a disproof of the existence of large mythical monsters. Working only from fundamental mathematical considerations, the ecologist Peter Brussard was able to demonstrate that a population of twenty Loch Ness monsters (the maximum number of one-ton animals that the loch's food supply could be expected to support) would rapidly dwindle to extinction due to the process known as demographic stochasticity. That is another way of saying that a small population runs a great risk of falling victim to bad luck. One generation might be born with all males or all females, for example. Or every individual of breeding age might suffer an accident and die young. The odds of these demographic accidents are readily calculable from basic statistical formulas. Brussard concluded that a population of twenty individuals would be extremely unlikely to have persisted from prehistoric times; if it somehow had, it would be "precipitously close to extinction" right now.[1]

Theoretical ecologists need to take their victories where they can find them, and being able to predict the nonexistence of nonexistent creatures is something, anyway. The successful management of natural systems by man, however, poses an inordinately greater challenge. Arguing that humans need to intervene in nature is one thing; making the case that humans have, or will have, the wisdom to do it right is quite another. A physician prescribing a drug can call upon a vast storehouse of knowledge, both specific to the drug and general to the biology and chemistry of the body, that links biochemical cause with symptomatic effect. He can know with a very high degree of confidence whether the prescribed treatment will cure the condition and what side effects it may cause in the process. An engineer designing a bridge can apply the even more straightforward laws of mechanics to calculate what a high wind or a heavy load will do to his structure. The would-be manager of ecosystems is somewhere back in the Middle Ages on this scale of things; if he doesn't quite believe that ailments are brought on by an imbalance in the humors or that buildings collapse because of demons, still he must rely to an uncomfortable degree on experience and hunches. He proposes to lead a party across a trackless moor based on the experience of once having seen *Wuthering Heights;* it is an act of folly forgivable only because the rest of the party knows even less. And then the moor, it turns out, is not trackless but, worse, is crisscrossed with thousands of false turns, hidden valleys, and, of course, treacherous bogs. Understanding the workings of ecological systems may be a more difficult problem, theoretically speaking, than those a chemist or physicist encounters. "It is as if chemistry found itself faced with a periodic chart of *millions* of elements, thousands of which may be present in any reaction, all of which are bizarrely different from one another, all of which are badly behaved from a statistical standpoint, and all of whose properties may change with history," writes one despairing ecologist.[2]

What the ecosystem manager longs for is the ecological equivalent of Newton's laws of motion. He needs general principles that can answer specific questions: What determines the abundance of a species? How do changes in the population of one species affect others? What makes a species vulnerable or resistant to extinction? Are there a few key species that play a critical role in larger ecosystem processes? Under what circumstances are exotic species innocuous and tolerable, and when are they disruptive? When are extraordinary measures, such as culling or control of predators or captive breeding and reintroduction, required? And above all, how can we be sure that an intervention will not trigger unforeseen side effects or even worsen the original condition it was intended to correct?

The inherently chaotic properties of biological systems, compounded by an ever-changing environment, thoroughly dashed hopes that natural systems would achieve a self-sustaining equilibrium on their own; the same properties might appear to render equally remote the hope that ecosystems will respond in predictable ways to human perturbation. History is littered with the failures of ecological theory to provide the correct answers. The confident generalizations of earlier eras have proved spectacularly wrong; management strategies based on these generalizations have, more often than not, been disastrous or at the very least ineffectual. There was no grander generalization than the theory of succession and climax, and none that more consistently led to the wrong results in practice as Norway maples invaded protected forests, as Kirtland's warblers vanished, as prairies were consumed by brush and trees, and as Yellowstone was consumed by elk.

Environmentalists, who are still rather fond of climax and succession, prefer to point to the failures of game and forest management to make the case that man lacks the wisdom to intervene in nature. Here the story is less clear-cut, however. Policies such as the enthusiastic persecution of predators early in this century in America were certainly disastrous, but they had as much to do with unexamined tradition as with misbegotten ecological theory. It is not entirely fair to blame science for the actions of those who were at best ignorant and at worst contemptuous of science. Aldo Leopold noted that the "pre-biological stages" of game management follow an invariable pattern. First come restrictions; in America these go back to 1639, when Rhode Island established a closed season on deer from May to November. By the time of the Revolution, twelve of the thirteen colonies had closed seasons on certain species. A century later all of the states had hunting laws, and many had introduced bag limits as another rough attempt to regulate the harvest. (Actually, as Leopold pointed out, the first recorded hunting restriction appears in Deuteronomy 22:6–7: "If, along the road, you chance upon a bird's nest, in any tree or on the ground, with fledglings or eggs and the mother sitting over the fledglings or on the eggs, do not take the mother together with her young. Let the mother go, and take only the young." Leopold added that "the phraseology is as circumstantial and repetitive as the act of any modern legislature.")

Sometimes these restrictions worked, and sometimes they did not. It was a matter of luck, really. None were based on an accurate census of populations, an understanding of habitat requirements, or consideration of the species' reproductive potential, though the choice of closed seasons at least demonstrated a basic grasp of the animals' breeding cycles.

The next step, predator control, was equally commonsensical and equally unscientific in its application. Henry VIII placed bounties on crows and rooks; Elizabeth added wildcats, stoats, weasels; the list kept growing. Wolves were exterminated in Britain by the eighteenth century. In America the misleadingly named Bureau of Biological Survey was established in 1905 with the mission of achieving a similar success on the North American continent and not just for wolves, either. In 1907, for example, the bureau oversaw the destruction of twenty-three thousand coyotes, eighteen hundred wolves, and hundreds of bobcats, mountain lions, bears, and lynxes. Bureaucracies and politics being what they are, the bureau survives today (as the Animal Damage Control program of the U.S. Department of Agriculture) and enjoys the strong support of western sheep ranchers, despite near-unanimous disapproval by wildlife experts.

It was not always thus, to be sure. In the early years of this century, wildlife biologists ranked among the staunchest advocates of predator control. It seemed obvious that reducing predators would increase the animals they preyed upon, many of which were undergoing a precipitous decline. But that is literally as deep as the "scientific" analysis of the issue went. William Hornaday, the director of the New York Zoological Park in the early years of the century, was one of the most prominent cheerleaders for the search-and-destroy operations, and his 1913 book, *Our Vanishing Wildlife*, effectively publicized the campaign. A picture of a Cooper's hawk in the book is captioned "A Species to be Destroyed," and Hornaday meant it.[3]

When even rudimentary science arrived on the scene, it quickly became apparent that predator control suffered from two sorts of unintended consequences. First, it sometimes didn't even work. It is now clear that in some cases prey numbers are kept down by food supplies or disease or competition or predation by another species—kept down to a level below any limit set by the predator in question. In other cases the very high reproductive potential of the predator (this appears to be the case with coyotes) can thwart control efforts. And in still other cases, as we saw in chapter 4, removal of a predator can paradoxically lead to the extinction of the species that the well-meaning manager is hoping to save, when a second prey species that had been kept in check by the same predator surges upward in an uncontrolled growth spurt and outcompetes the target species. Overall, the picture is profoundly mixed. A review of fifty-eight studies of North American predators found thirty-one cases in which they seemed to have a limiting effect on prey populations and twenty-seven in which they did not. Common sense is a poor substitute for detailed scientific research.[4]

The other unintended consequence was that predator control sometimes worked too well. The explosion of deer, elk, bison, and other grazing animals has become a tired refrain in the history of American—indeed, global—wildlife management. Moose were on the verge of extinction in Sweden in the eighteenth century; today they stand at three hundred thousand and rising, even though a hundred thousand are shot every year. American white-tailed deer surged from half a million at the turn of the century to more than twenty million today. At mid-century Aldo Leopold was able to document more than a hundred cases in which deer populations had exploded. In half the cases the deer were harvested to avert disaster, in the other half severe overbrowsing and mass starvation was the consequence as the deer ate all the new shoots off woody plants, effectively wiping out their principal food source for both the present and future.[5]

All of these miscalculations were a mixture of bad policy and bad or inadequate science. In effect, they were a series of not very well controlled experiments in which politicians, bureaucrats, ranchers, hunters, foresters, the humane society, and the occasional blue-ribbon panel were all permitted to traipse through the lab, twiddling the dials and shaking the test tubes. Hardly a referendum on science, science rarely even entered the picture.

One might think that modern ecologists would resent being tarred with the past sins of others. Yet a perusal of the present-day scientific literature in ecology reveals an almost neurotic degree of guilt and self-doubt. "The serious societal issue," writes one theoretical ecologist, "is whether ecological expertise, as it is currently employed, leads to better or worse decisions."[6] It is hard to imagine a theoretical physicist ever uttering such words.

Some of this is honest self-examination and honest frustration with the state of knowledge. But like all neuroses, the real cause lies deeper. Reading the scientific literature, one sometimes gets the feeling that ecologists have perhaps taken too much to heart the image of ecology as a subversive science. Many (though by no means all) ecologists were attracted to the field in the first place out of sympathy with the environmentalist political agenda of saving the planet from the evils of technological society and its "mechanistic" worldview. And just as science students who can't stand the sight of blood gravitate towards physics or chemistry, the ones who can't stand the sight of a mathematical equation head for ecology. In an odd sense, the very failure of ecology as a predictive science was part of the attraction. It is what set ecology apart from the rest of modern, mathematical science; it freed the field ecologist to study nature more as an artist than as an engineer; it reinforced the environmentalist taboo that man dare not meddle with nature for fear of bringing down upon the world unknown and unknowable disaster.

So like an anarchist who wins an election and keeps on issuing manifestos against the authorities, himself now included, ecologists seem to have a hard time always accepting the idea that their science is starting to become a science—however far it still has to go.

Indeed, the most well-publicized effort of late to apply basic ecological theory to conservation and ecosystem management is, upon closer inspection, little more than a bomb thrower's polemic masquerading as science. The effort in question is principally that of one man, Harvard biologist Edward O. Wilson, a relentless popularizer of the theory that "we are in the midst of one of the great extinction spasms of geological history."[7] Most people may be forgiven for being unaware that it is only a theory; such are Wilson's credentials and so effective has been his publicity campaign that the belief that fifty thousand or more species a year are being driven to extinction has attained the stature of received wisdom. Such statistics are cited repeatedly as verified fact not only in environmental groups' fund-raising literature but in newspaper op-ed pieces and in the utterances of government officials. Vice President Al Gore regularly invokes the specter of mass extinction in his environmental speeches, warning, for example, that "more than half of all the creatures God put on this planet may disappear within the lifetimes of people now living."[8]

The fact that the actual, observed rate of extinction is not fifty thousand species per year but *one* species a year thus comes as a surprise to many. And the fact that Wilson uses different figures in different contexts—low numbers in scientific journals, high numbers in his popular books and magazine articles, and the highest numbers in newspaper interviews and other carefully orchestrated media events—and, finally, the fact that his conclusions are usually accompanied by calls for an immediate halt to economic development are uncomfortably suggestive that something closer to politics than to science may be at work here.[9]

For those who get beyond the impressively alarming numbers, Wilson does offer a theoretical justification for his predicted extinction rates. The predictions are based on what is rather grandly termed the theory of island biogeography. This "theory," however, consists of but a single equation that attempts to relate the number of species found on an island with the size of the island. The version of the equation that Wilson uses (there is more than one) is $S = CA^z$, where S stands for the number of species, A stands for the area, and both C and z are constants chosen arbitrarily to try to make the formula come out right. So to calculate the number of species found in an area A, one raises the area to the zth power and multiplies the result by C. Ecologists who have studied the distribution of species on ocean islands have found that they can usually get a pretty good fit to the observed data by setting z in the range of 0.2 to 0.4. What that translates to in practice is that an island ten times as big typically has twice as many species.

Claims by a few researchers that the factors C and z have some literal biological significance have not been widely accepted; most agree that they are, to put it simply, fudge factors. Unlike Newton's second law, for example, which expresses a precise, immutable law of nature—force equals mass times acceleration—this so-called species-area relation is what scientists call an empirical formula. It is not derived from any fundamental principles. It is just a mathematical attempt to fit a curve to a vast body of scattered experimental data points.

Wilson's global-extinction calculations, however, are a huge leap from this already shaky ground. He assumes that the species-area formula is not merely a rough generalization of scattered data, but a fundamental law—a rigid connection between area and the number of species that can be found therein. What is true for an island is true for the world. Cut the area of, say, the world's tropical rain forests, and species will vanish unwaveringly according to this mechanical relationship. This is how Wilson derives his global extinction-rate figures. This is also how Wilson derives so many *different* figures. In an article in the sober scientific journal *Science,* using what he calls a "conservative estimate" of the number of species currently found in the rain forests and the lowest value of z, he calculates 4,000 species a year are lost. In his popular book *The Diversity of Life,* again using "the lowest z value permissible" but assuming five times as many species exist in the forests, he obtains the "maximally optimistic conclusion" that 27,000 species are lost each year. In interviews with journalists the number magically grows to 50,000, or even 100,000.[10] Actually, there is no magic about it—the "theory" is so loose and sloppy that one can derive almost any answer one wants, according to the assumptions one chooses to start with.

This is but a caricature of mathematical ecology, one that does little justice to the rigorous and sophisticated work that has been done in recent years on population dynamics, ecosystem stability, extinction probability, and predator-prey interactions. Although Wilson insists that the species-area relationship has been verified by "hundreds of independent studies," the literature is replete with criticisms of the entire concept. One major review of, in fact, a hundred published data sets of species-area relations found that only half of the variation in the number of species encountered from one island to another could be accounted for by differences in area according to the formula Wilson uses. The same review concluded that the tendency of z values to fall in the range of 0.2 to 0.4 was probably nothing more than a mathematical coincidence. The entire "theory," the authors concluded, may be nothing more than a "sampling phenomenon," totally lacking in predictive power.[11] The wider you search, the more species you will find. This is about as profound an insight as noting that one is likely to encounter more different colors of automobiles the farther one travels from home. A recent paper by two distinguished conservation biologists concluded: "The species-area curve (in a mainland situation) is nothing more than a self-evident fact: that as one enlarges an area, it comes eventually to encompass the geographical ranges of more species. The danger comes when this is extrapolated backwards, and it is assumed that by reducing the size of a forest, it will lose species according to the same gradient."[12] A formula that roughly holds for isolated islands may have nothing whatever to say when it comes to predicting what will happen on millions of square miles of mainland.

An apparently unintended, but nonetheless telling, parody of the entire concept appeared two decades earlier in *McKay's Bees,* a novel by Thomas McMahon, a Harvard University engineering professor who studies biomechanics:

> He made a game of elaborating the species of beetles to be found in a limited space. In Edward and Jiffy's garden alone, he found thirty-seven species. Within the range of a hundred feet of the hotel in any direction, he found more than fifty. If he extended his circle to a half-mile radius, his number of beetle species exceeded two hundred. . . . If fifty species could be found in an acre, and two hundred could be found in a square mile, Sewall estimated that half a million different species of beetle were lurking in the bushes within a day's ride of the hotel.[13]

One reason the species-area curve tends to exaggerate so wildly is that it ignores the texture of habitats. Species are not distributed randomly but in patches. Reducing all of a forest's multiplicity of habitats to a single mathematical variable representing "area" is a biological absurdity. For one thing, a little bit of conservation in the right place may be much more important than the loss of thousands of square miles of forest elsewhere. The species-area curve also ignores conservation measures already taken, which have, for example, preserved habitat crucial to 95 percent of the tropical birds of Africa. And it ignores the possibility that at least some species can survive in secondary forests that regrow on deforested land.

(It also is contradicted by actual experience. Almost ninety percent of the Atlantic coastal forests of Brazil have been cleared in the last five hundred years; the species-area equation would predict a loss of half of all species. Instead, a survey by Brazilian zoologists found that not a single known species could be declared extinct. Several birds and six butterflies believed twenty years ago to be extinct have been rediscovered. The reason for their persistence, Edward O. Wilson notwithstanding, appears to be simple and unsurprising: Many of the rarest species are rare because they are restricted to tiny microhabitats that occur in widely dispersed, isolated patches across the landscape. Even with the loss of 90 percent of total forest area, representative samples of all of these microhabitats survive in the remaining twenty thousand square miles of parks, reserves, and remote areas. "An insect fauna already accustomed to appreciable isolation and disturbance in nature, on both long and short time scales, has met with *savoir faire* the challenge of human occupation . . . essentially all the original species seem to be persisting," concludes one recent study by a biologist who has the advantage of actually living and working in Brazil.)[14]

But perhaps the greatest failing of island biogeography as a basis for ecological guidance is that it is virtually insight-free. One square mile is indistinguishable from any other square mile as far as the species-area formula is concerned. The theory offers no practical or realistic guidance for a conservation planner or ecosystem manager at all. It is nothing more than a restatement of the most extreme preservationist sloganeering in scientific-sounding language. The *only* lesson that one can draw from the species-area relation is "save everything." And indeed that is precisely how Wilson and other scientist-advocates have tried to use the results—to elevate a quixotic crusade against economic development to the status of a scientific imperative.

Meanwhile, back in the real world, more practical conservation organizations and governments would like to know which areas to focus their conservation efforts on—because, in the real world, most of us know that we cannot save everything. Park managers need to know how to effectively maintain disturbance processes and how to compensate for the disruption of migration routes, for the loss of key species, and for the invasion of exotics so that the species in areas already "saved" will actually have a chance to survive.

"It is sad," one prominent conservation biologist, Daniel Simberloff, has concluded, "that the unwarranted focus on island biogeography theory has detracted from the main task of refuge planners, determining what habitats are important and how to maintain them."[15]

Despairing of generalizations, many, indeed probably most, ecologists have sought refuge in the study of individual species. It is an approach that temperamentally, scientifically, and even, thanks to the Endangered Species Act, legally, is in favor these days.

The complexities of biological interactions between species are enormous. Breaking down the problem to its most basic level is a logical reaction. There are countless examples that ecologists can cite of crucial insights that were only attained by the exhaustive study of the habits of an individual species. What an organism feeds on, what species it tries to avoid, which species it competes with, where it makes its nests, where it migrates in the winter—the answers to such questions are usually full of surprises. At bottom, it seems, every species is unique.

There are sound evolutionary reasons for this to be so: In the competition for survival, the name of the game is to do something that no other species does. The whole idea is to develop a way to make a living that defies the rules. Every strategy in nature has its counterstrategy; predators have a keen sense of sight and smell, prey are fleet. The trick, then, is to develop a nongeneralizable tactic, the more outlandish the better—think of the skunk's spray or the opossum's death-feint—that minimizes the chances of an effective counter. It is the very fact that every species has one place or one season or one sort of "business" where it is more effective than any potential rivals that permits the enormous diversity of life to exist—in other words, that keeps competition and predation from turning into wholesale slaughter and extermination.

The species-by-species approach offers many practical advantages over the broad generalizations of island biogeography. A careful study of a single species' behavior is likely to reveal specific characteristics of the landscape that need to be maintained or created for its benefit, such as the low-lying branches of young jack pines that the Kirtland's warbler nests in or the decaying trunks of old hardwoods that the red-cockaded woodpecker nests in. These revelations in turn translate very clearly into management practices—prescribed burns to maintain a turnover of pines for the warblers; leaving old and dead trees standing or perhaps even setting out nest boxes to aid woodpeckers and other cavity-nesting birds.

But how many acres to burn? How many dead trees to leave standing? How many nest boxes to set out? Intensive field studies sometimes offer clues; radio-collar tracking studies can establish the territorial range of a nesting pair, or quantitative assessments of food supplies can be used to calculate carrying capacity of a given area. But that only shifts the question: how many individuals do we need? A single breeding pair is clearly a bad bet; even ten pairs, as the Loch Ness monster analysis showed, is unlikely to weather the vicissitudes of nature and the dice rolls of genetic recombination. Are there fundamental rules that transcend the outlandish peculiarities of individual species? In other words, are there consistent patterns that emerge through the fog of biological chaos?

The benefits of discovering such patterns—assuming they do exist, that is—are enormous. Trying to tackle the problems of wildlife conservation one species at a time is cumbersome, time consuming, and if experience is any guide, futile. It is a bit like setting out to build a watch each time we want to know what time it is. By the time we've fashioned all of the separate gears and figured out how they go together, the original question may be rather moot.

In fact, the Endangered Species Act, which conceives of wildlife conservation as the sum of protecting individual species, has become an unintended monument to the practical failure of this species-by-species approach. Under the act, the U.S. Fish and Wildlife Service is charged with identifying endangered species and developing recovery plans to ensure their survival. The act states, and Supreme Court decisions have affirmed this interpretation, that every species in effect is of incalculable value. The economic and political implications of this are breathtaking, and indeed much of the criticism of the act has focused on its failure to rationally consider costs and benefits and on the enormous political weapon the law has become in the hands of those who don't particularly give a damn about snail darters or spotted owls but who have strong aversions to dams and logging.[16]

But even the most well-meaning efforts to implement the act have demonstrated the shortcomings, on purely biological grounds, of trying to manage nature one species at a time. The main problem is it simply doesn't work, even for the species on which so much individual attention is lavished. Despite claims of success trumpeted by the Fish and Wildlife Service and environmental groups, it is difficult to make a case that the act has made any difference at all. Of the more than fourteen hundred species listed as endangered or threatened since the original act was passed in 1966, only twenty-two have ever been "delisted." Of those, eight were removed from the list because it was found that the original data used to justify their listing was in error, usually when additional populations were discovered; seven were removed from the list because of their extinction. That leaves seven supposedly bona fide success stories: the Pacific grey whale, the American alligator, the Arctic peregrine falcon, the Rydberg milk vetch (a plant found in Utah), and three birds found on a single South Pacific island. But even here the evidence is not clear-cut. The milk vetch and the alligator are thought by some to have been listed in error and never to have been truly endangered; grey whale populations have been increasing steadily since the nineteenth century, as demand for whale products evaporated; and the birds of Palau Island may have recovered largely due to the (unassisted) regrowth of vegetation wiped out in bombing during World War II.[17]

There is much sleight of hand in the arguments for the success of the Endangered Species Act; a Wilderness Society publication, for example, points to the comeback of the American alligator, brown pelican, peregrine falcon, bald eagle, and grey whale as examples of the act's "remarkable successes." Elsewhere the same publication acknowledges in passing that the birds on this list owe their recovery to the banning of DDT, while the alligator and grey whale started to come back when overhunting ceased. What the publication does not mention is that none of these actions had anything whatever to do with the Endangered Species Act.[18]

Biodiversity boosters who concede that the act has failed blame it on insufficient funding. Yet even when millions of dollars have been lavished on recovery plans, often for extremely labor-intensive captive-breeding and release programs, failure has been the rule. In one of the most expensive efforts, more than four million dollars was spent to airlift eggs of the Kemp's Ridley sea turtle to Texas, where they were hatched, raised in captivity for nine months, and then released back to the sea. Even some of the original founders and proponents of the program now concede it has been an unmitigated disaster, with no evidence that a single one of the eighteen thousand "headstarted" turtles survived to return to the shore and reproduce.[19] As in many other such cases, the real problem seems to be that by the time a species makes it to the endangered species list, much of its critical habitat is already destroyed. The consistent failure of such heroic recovery efforts suggests that some fundamental ecological principles that determine survival or extinction are still eluding us.

The species-by-species approach suffers from another major flaw. Championing an endless list of individual species is, in the end, no different from championing "biodiversity" in toto. It offers no help in setting priorities. The Fish and Wildlife Service has tried a series of more or less absurd methods of ranking endangered species, based on the degree of threat, the potential for and cost of recovery, and even the amount of political "support" a particular species enjoys. Numerical scores are awarded on each of the scales, then added together, a methodology that one agency official has termed the "apples plus oranges minus grapes equals fruit salad" approach.[20] The want of biological insight is painfully obvious.

But perhaps the greatest shortcoming of this way of thinking about wildlife conservation is that it is terribly narrow and, as a consequence, haphazard. Nature consists of considerably more than the handful of ecological basket cases that make it onto the endangered species list. The number of species that inhabit the earth is unknown, but few creditable estimates place the number below three million; there are plausible arguments, based on extrapolations from the number of insects that have been found to associate with particular tree species, that insects alone may account for as many as six million species. (Wilson, in his relentless pursuit of ever more alarming statistics, has speculated that the total may approach a hundred million— remember, the larger the starting figure, the larger the rate of loss according to the species-area formula—though he offers no evidence or argument to substantiate this conjecture and the number is not widely accepted by experts.) In any case, the total is large enough to give pause to anyone who hopes to complete a species-by-species conservation plan before the next comet crashes into the planet, much less before the next ice age arrives.[21]

Focusing on the requirements of a single species tells us nothing about the bigger picture. The ubiquity of disturbance processes and the evolution of life to exploit them in all of their dimensions mean that different species will always have conflicting, if not completely contradictory, habitat requirements, even within the same general landscape. What's good for moose, which browse on the new shrubs that spring up following a fire, is bad for caribou, which feed mainly on lichens that grow only in older forests. An abundance of forest edge benefits species that shelter in woods and feed in clearings (or vice versa), such as deer, rabbits, grouse, and songbirds; at the same time, it is detrimental to some nesting birds that are vulnerable to edge-dwelling predators.

So peculiar are the needs of some rare species that to meet their particular requirements would turn the entire landscape upside down. The rare California fan palm, for example, is an extremely ancient species; the fossil record shows that it was once widely distributed

Figure 17. Take your pick: Young forests favor moose, which feed on shrubs; old forests favor caribou, which eat lichens. The numbers on the vertical scale refer to an indirect but faithful measure of population: the number of pellet groups found per hectare.

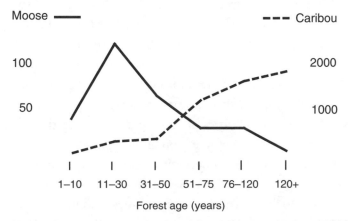

Moose ——   – – – Caribou

Data are from northern Canada. Adapted from Robinson and Bolen, *Wildlife Ecology and Management,* 218.

from the West Coast to the Mojave Desert. But its habitat has largely vanished with the climatic changes that have taken place over the last ten million years, and it is now restricted to a few small groups found in oases along the San Andreas fault. The current population is so small that it is probably not viable. To expand its habitat would mean a massive transformation of the landscape, which is neither practical nor, more to the point, desirable. Meeting the needs of single species, even rare, endangered, valuable, and politically popular species, is hardly the same thing as developing a sound, landscape-wide conservation *strategy*. It is literally a case of not seeing the forest for the trees.[22]

And so we seem no closer to a Newton's first law of ecosystems. Generalizations based on the species-area curve are useless because every species is different; focusing on individual species is futile because there are too many of them and they are too contradictory in their requirements; and neither approach tells us a thing about where to concentrate our efforts or how to effectively manage an area once it is protected.

This dismal situation began to improve in the 1980s, however, with the publication of a flurry of papers in what has become an entire new subdiscipline of conservation biology called population viability analysis. Although still focusing on the individual species as the unit of study, viability analysis marked the beginnings of a systematic theory that explains how populations survive or go extinct. Virtually unprecedented in the checkered history of theoretical ecology, it has the hallmarks of a genuine theory: general enough to be broadly applicable, powerful enough to make specific predictions. The theory has already been used to suggest the optimal design of nature reserves, to identify populations that require extraordinary management interventions, and to predict what sorts of interventions are most likely to succeed. The fact that the theory also appears to correctly explain the historical persistence of species through geologic time (and the absence of the Loch Ness monster) is an encouraging sign, too.

Viability analysis starts by asking a deceptively simple question: *Why do species become extinct?* The deceptively simple answer—bad luck—turns out to be the key to transforming the randomness and uncertainty of nature into a useful set of predictions. For there are different kinds of bad luck, and each one can be reduced to a useful statistical form.

The first kind of bad luck is the kind we saw in the Loch Ness monster analysis: demographic stochasticity. There is always a chance in a small population that every individual will be doing the wrong thing at the wrong time and the entire population will simply fail to reproduce itself. It is a matter of straightforward statistics to calculate the odds of this happening. Consider, for example, the probability that a small population of N individuals will in one generation be made up entirely of members of one sex. This is exactly the same statistical problem as calculating the odds that N coin tosses will produce all heads or all tails. The odds of coming up with two heads in two tosses is $1/2 \times 1/2$; for three heads in three tosses it's $1/2 \times 1/2 \times 1/2$; and so on. The odds of coming up with all tails is the same, so the overall odds of winding up with all heads or all tails is twice the chance of either one, or 2 multiplied by $1/2$ a total of N times, which can be written in the mathematical shorthand $2(1/2)^N$.

When N is very small, the chances of hitting this particular demographic dead end are quite serious—one in eight for a population of four, one in four for a population of three, and fifty-fifty when the population is down to two. But such an exponential relationship decays very rapidly as N increases; by the time N hits ten, the odds are down to less than one in a thousand; by the time N grows to twenty, it's one in a million.

This is an oversimplification of the sort of calculations that are typically made to arrive at the risk of demographic accidents in small populations, but it captures the flavor of it. These analyses suggest that demographic bad luck is a factor only in the very smallest populations, though for such populations it is an overriding factor. As one practitioner put it, "Noah . . . must have been very lucky indeed." Biblical authority notwithstanding, it takes considerably more than one breeding pair to have any confidence of maintaining a rare species.[23]

In larger populations, the danger of demographic bad luck is quickly overwhelmed by that of environmental bad luck. Whereas demographic fluctuations operate on each member of a population individually, environmental downturns can fell entire populations in one swoop. It would be extremely unusual for everyone living in a single trailer park to drop dead from a heart attack in the same year or to give birth only to boys; it is much less unusual for everyone in the park to be wiped out by a tornado. The odds of extinction through environmental bad luck are hard to calculate directly, but some clever analyses of how birthrates vary with year-to-year environmental fluctuations—droughts, floods, temperature, and so on—can be used to obtain plausible values to plug into the equations. As with demographic stochasticity, the odds of extinction drop as population increases. A large population, spread out over a larger area, is less likely to suffer a single devastating blow (this would be like *every* trailer park in the country being hit by a tornado at once). But the margin of safety grows more slowly with increasing population than is the case with demographic factors. In extreme cases, which some researchers break out as a special case, usually labeled catastrophic processes, increased numbers offer *no* extra margin of safety. A catastrophic process is one of those very rare but devastating events that strike across the entire geographic range of a species. In effect, this is an-

Figure 18. Basic processes of survival and extinction. Demographic threats—mainly the risk that one generation will, through chance, produce offspring of all one sex—disappear quickly as population size increases. Environmental threats—the risk of a hurricane wiping out a patch of habitat, for example—fade more gradually but can be mitigated by spreading the risk among a large, spread-out population. Catastrophes that strike over a wide area pose a risk of extinction that is largely independent of population size.

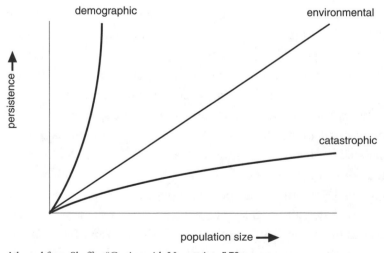

Adapted from Shaffer, "Coping with Uncertainty," 72.

other way of stating the inescapable geologic fact that all species eventually must suffer extinction.

For the processes that matter over the time scales that conservation planners worry about, viability analysis calculations show that the key factor that controls whether a population will make it is environmental fluctuation. The more closely a species' birthrate tracks the swings of its environment—the more susceptible it is to a cold winter, a drought, a sudden food shortage—the larger that population must be to resist extinction. This leads to a number of curious results. Small animals, which typically have higher birthrates than large animals, are in one sense more resilient to perturbation. If they are hit hard one year, their high birthrate allows them to rapidly make good the deficit. A population made up of birds that lay large clutches of eggs in the spring can recover rapidly from a harsh winter that wipes out large numbers of breeding adults. But high resilience also leads to great variability in the population from year to year, since a species that can respond quickly to environmental fluctuations will undergo much more violent oscillations than one that responds only sluggishly. On balance it is this high variability that kills them. Large animals are more resistant to environmental fluctuations on two counts: They tend to have fewer young each year to start with, and so the degree to which their birthrate can vary from year to year is much more confined. And because they tend to be longer-lived, large-bodied individuals can ride out a harsh season to breed again when conditions are more favorable. Overall, calculations suggest that smaller, rapidly reproducing species require much larger populations to buy a given amount of anti-extinction insurance.[24]

When actual numbers are plugged in, the results are, to say the least, sobering. Minimum viable populations required to ensure a 95 percent probability of persistence for as little as a century are typically quite large, from hundreds in the case of large mammals in the stablest environments to millions in the case of the smallest in highly variable climates. Translating these population requirements into area requirements is even more revealing. The area requirements of the largest carnivores tend to drive this calculation; even though the minimum viable population of a large carnivore is much smaller than that of, say, a beetle, each grizzly bear or panther needs an immensely vaster area to meet its food

Figure 19. Back-of-the-envelope calculations using population viability analysis suggest that the area needed to insure a 95 percent probability of survival of the largest carnivores for a thousand years exceeds the size of most reserves and parks. A given population of carnivores needs more space than the same number of herbivores because animal food is generally less abundant than plant food.

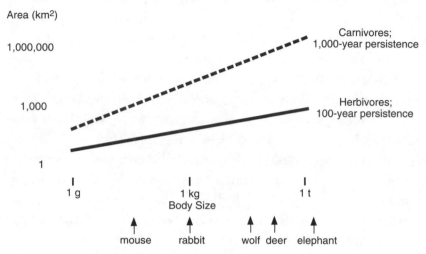

Adapted from Belovsky, "Extinction Models and Mammalian Persistence," 46–47.

needs. (Plant food is more abundant than animal food.) Multiplying the minimum viable population size of the largest carnivores by the area each of these large carnivores needs to live in implies that a reserve must be a minimum of a half million square miles—again, just to ensure a 95 percent probability that the species will persist for a hundred years without being driven to extinction by environmental fluctuations. The vast majority of existing parks are less than a tenth this size. To ensure a 95 percent probability of a thousand-year persistence time for a large carnivorous species would require a reserve larger than any that currently exist. Because the persistence time predicted for any given species by this calculation grows only gradually with population size, extending the boundaries of existing reserves by modest amounts makes little difference; doubling the size of a reserve buys something less than a doubling of persistence time.[25]

This is yet another confirmation of the inescapability of human management of wildlife populations. By way of consolation, the theory offers some clear, practical management implications, however.

One way to reduce the environmentally driven variance in a population's growth rate—which, remember, is the key determining factor in its viability—is to spread out that population among a chain of smaller reserves. A series of populations spaced out far enough from one another so that each experiences environmental fluctuations independently of the others will in effect spread the risk, a concept verified by the economic viability of insurance companies. The ultimate version of such risk spreading is captive breeding in zoos. In any case, the theory strongly suggests that humans will have to play a pivotal and ongoing role in reintroducing species to parks and reserves from other sources (either zoos or other reserves) when the inevitable local extinctions occur.

A puzzle in all of this is how *any* species could have survived for tens of thousands or even tens of millions of years without an astronomically large population. The answer is that nature, in effect, has employed this same strategy of multiple independent "reserves." It is all but certain that at some point in the not too distant past the entire wolf population residing in what is now Yellowstone National Park was wiped out by environmental or demographic bad luck. But other populations of wolves hundreds of miles away survived whatever ill-fated roll of the dice doomed the Yellowstone wolves, just as the Yellowstone wolves at other times survived the local extinction of their neighbors. Population viability calculations imply that small, local populations have almost certainly suffered repeated extinctions throughout their history. Yet the species as a whole—which consists not of any one local population, but rather a "metapopulation" of dispersed local population groups—survives because whenever disaster strikes, there are always other local populations that can serve as a recolonization source.

The significance of metapopulations is one of the most important results of population viability theory. The concept of the metapopulation is in effect a restatement of the overwhelming importance that disturbance processes play in maintaining the continuity of ecosystems and of the folly, if not the impossibility, of attempting to rigidly preserve any single, ephemeral product of those disturbance processes. And it suggests that any sound conservation strategy will have to focus more on processes rather than things. "It is the processes that have generated or that maintain the species, community, ecosystem, or landscape," observe the authors of a recent article in the ecological literature that advocates conservation "above and beyond the species level."[26] In some cases the processes will be disturbance regimes, such as fire or fluctuating water flows on a river; in some cases they will be crucial linkages, such as nutrient cycling or soil stabilization or recolonization. Trying to preserve the rare furbish lousewort (a plant that achieved distinction as the "botanical snail darter" when it held up construction of the Dickey-Lincoln Dam on the St. John's River in Maine) by protecting currently existing colonies would, for example, be surely futile. Colonies are regularly wiped out when ten-to-hundred-yard stretches of river bank collapse. But without such catastrophes, the metapopulation could not survive. Local populations are outcompeted after a few years by invading woody species; only regular upheavals clear the decks for colonization by the low shrubs that the lousewort associates with. Maintaining the seasonal changes in river flows that scour and undermine the banks is clearly a better strategy than putting a fence around a few lousewort colonies. In places where disturbance regimes have been interrupted, it will be up to managers to recreate them.

It will also be up to managers to supply the means of recolonization where local populations are now isolated from one another. A conservation strategy based upon multiple small reserves will have to face up to the fact that local populations of key species will inevitably vanish from time to time and will have to be replenished by importations. (Even absent local catastrophes, some routine interchange between isolated populations may be vital to maintain their genetic diversity and to prevent inbreeding. The problem of inbreeding, however, is usually far less important than the more immediate environmental or demographic problems, and recent studies have shown that in some well-publicized cases, such as that of the cheetah, the role that inbreeding has played in the decline of a rare species has been greatly overestimated.)[27]

At very low population levels, population viability theory suggests that much more direct and continuous intervention may be required. This includes captive breeding and release, supplemental feeding, predator control and disease control, in order to dampen fluctuations in growth rates. "Reintroductions are often portrayed as singular efforts, which need not be repeated," observes Daniel Goodman, a leading ecological theoretician who helped to pioneer population viability analysis. But, he argues, "in a longer perspective, we might think of these introductions as part of a program which augments the species population whenever its local density becomes too sparse."[28]

A pessimist might conclude that that brings us back where we started from: a laborious, species-by-species rescue effort. Although population viability theory has the advantage of offering an objective standard for assessing which species require intervention and a scientific basis for predicting what sorts of interventions are likely to succeed, it is still an approach that addresses the problems of one species at a time.

On the bright side, the concept of metapopulations and disturbance processes contains the seeds of a more general theory of conservation; disturbance processes are in most cases not unique to a single species, and the ecological processes that create one sort of habitat create others, too. Disturbance is the key to the diversity of habitats that supports a diversity of life.

Still, there are many unanswered questions, and many hard choices in want of guidance. The more aggressive interventions that population viability theory suggests may be required for the benefit of a rare species of special concern—control of predators, artificial breeding and release, control of environmental fluctuations—will surely have implications for other species. And all but the largest reserves will demand that some choices be made among which habitat types to maintain. They will simply not be large enough to support the full range of disturbance processes and patch dynamics, even under intensive management.

For a while ecologists presumed—or maybe hoped is a more accurate term—that taking care of the rarest species would automatically take care of everything else. Viability analysis at least hints that that might be so; a preserve big enough to sustain a viable population of the biggest carnivores ought to be more than adequate to hold sustainable populations of smaller species, and even if the big rarities need help, most other species would seem to be able to manage in reserves of reasonable size. The trouble with this reasoning is that it fails to take into account the patchiness of habitats and the inevitably conflicting needs of various species. The idea received a firm kick in the teeth from a study in Britain that exhaustively catalogued the distribution of species. After first noting that selecting sites for nature reserves "would be easier and more effective" if habitats that supported a diversity of, say, birds also tended to be rich in butterflies and also if rare species tended to occur wherever overall biodiversity was greatest, the study concluded that neither of these conditions was true. Dividing all of Britain into ten-kilometer squares, the researchers found that there was no one square where biodiversity "hotspots" (defined as the top 5 percent most-species-rich squares) for birds, butterflies, dragonflies, liverworts, and aquatic plants coincided. In only 26 of the 2,761 squares did hotspots for any three of the groups overlap. Moreover, the most species-rich areas for birds contained only about half of the rarest bird species; the most species-impoverished areas actually contained almost 20 percent of the rare species themselves. A management strategy that emphasizes endangered species will fail to preserve overall biodiversity; a strategy that emphasizes biodiversity will sacrifice many endangered species. There is no easy way out.[29]

That said, what a manager really wants to know is what matters the most, from a community-wide, or landscape-wide, perspective. If he cannot save everything, where should he focus his efforts? Are there certain species or certain processes or certain characteristics of "natural" or managed ecosystems that are more important for the long-term well-being of an ecological community than others?

To doctrinaire environmentalists this question is, of course, heresy. It is a given that all species are equally vital strands in the web of life; to remove one is to risk the collapse of all. Paul Ehrlich often invokes the metaphor (it comes from a grade B science fiction story) of the madman pulling rivets out of an airplane in mid-flight; finding that nothing happens each time he pulls one out, he keeps at it until, loosening the thirteenth rivet, the plane splits apart and crashes.[30] The ecological literature is full of examples of what are termed recondite relationships between species, which often become apparent only after one is wiped out. No one can deny that cascading extinctions have occurred.[31] Many plants cannot live without fungi or bacteria that help them pick up nutrients from the soil; many plants cannot reproduce without ants that collect and store their seeds underground.

Take away the microbes or the ants, and the plants go, too.

But there are also many cases in which extinctions of one species have had no further consequences whatsoever, just as there are cases in which invasions by exotics have been disastrous and cases in which they have been benign (or even beneficial, when they provide cover or food for endangered species, as is the case of eucalyptus in California). In a world where choices are inescapable, it would be useful to have some way of distinguishing the bad choices from the worse choices. There is a whiff of duplicity in the environmentalists' objection to this line of inquiry. They insist the question is irrelevant because all species are vital; but they also suggest it is immoral because it might be used to justify abandoning some species. The argument is reminiscent of the classic tale of the lawyer who, representing a client accused by a neighbor of having damaged a borrowed vase, produced a three-part defense: My client never borrowed the vase; it was in perfect condition when he returned it; and it was broken before he borrowed it. Asking which species are more important than others can be either irrelevant or immoral; it cannot be both.

The search for basic principles which can identify those "keystone" species upon which other species depend has been an arduous and not always convincing process. The connections between species are often complex and obscure, and the effects of one population on another are as a rule counterintuitive and paradoxical. But some general principles are beginning to emerge, and they may prove to be of great importance both in helping managers decide where to focus their conservation efforts and in predicting the consequences of management interventions on the broader ecological community.

The effort began back in the 1960s with a series of competing, and flatly contradictory, theories which attempted to draw general conclusions about the resilience of an ecosystem from its basic structural features. It had been recognized for some time that the basic structure of an ecosystem is constrained by fundamental laws of energy. The amount of solar energy striking an acre of ground limits how many plants that acre can support. Because no animal is 100 percent efficient in converting food to usable energy, the amount of energy available to support life at the next level of the food chain—grazing animals—is correspondingly diminished. Ninety percent or more of the energy taken in by an animal is expended in maintaining its body temperature, in keeping its heart pumping, and in moving about, so the amount of energy stored in protein and fat, and thus available to feed a predator on the next level of the food chain, is once again diminished. After three or four steps, the amount of energy left per acre is simply too small to support a further link in the chain. Although there are some carnivores that feed on carnivores, there are essentially no terrestrial ecosystems with carnivores that feed on carnivores that feed on carnivores.[32]

Given this basic structure—plants at the bottom, herbivores in the middle, carnivores at the top—and the basic functional connections between them, what happens if one link or another is removed? One of the first theories that took a stab at generalizing the effect of species removals was dubbed the "world is green" hypothesis. It postulated that carnivores, which have no predators above them to keep them in check, should tend to keep the populations of the herbivores they eat low; the herbivores, thus limited, should in turn fail to exercise much of a check on the plants they feed upon. The theory thus predicts that removing herbivores should have little effect on plants, while removing carnivores should have a major effect on herbivores.

A second theory, dubbed "the world is prickly and tastes bad," leads to very different predictions. The idea here is that most plants exhibit defense mechanisms, such as toxins or sharp spines, that limit herbivore numbers; a scarcity of herbivores in turn limits the number of carnivores. Removing either carnivores or herbivores would thus have little further consequences for the community as a whole, as the species they feed upon are already acting as a brake on their numbers.

The theories also predict at which levels competition will play a major role. In systems where herbivores strongly compete, removal of one species may have a profound effect on other herbivores; where competition is held in check either by short food supplies or numerous predators, removals will have a minimal effect on other species at the same level of the food chain. Figure 20 summarizes the predictions of these theories and a third, more elaborate one, which distinguishes between the separate cases of low, medium, and high productivity climates—"the world is white, yellow, and green."

Debates have raged for decades over which of these models is best supported by the actual data. One limitation with all of these models

Figure 20. Competing theories of population control. Arrows indicate how trophic layers influence one another, either through predation or resource limitations. Double arrows indicate competition; dashed lines, weak interactions. See text.

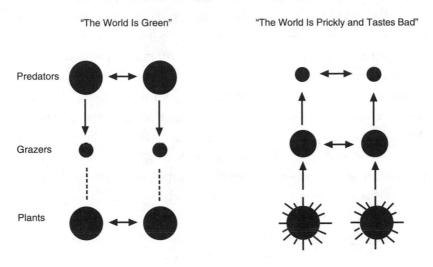

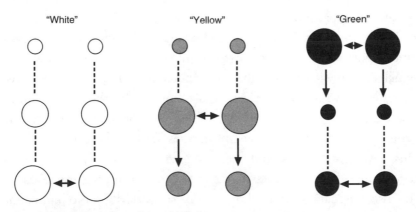

Adapted from Pimm, *Balance of Nature?* 282–84.

is that they really are not capable of predicting what happens when a single species is removed or introduced; rather, they are models of what happens to an entire level of the food chain when another entire level is reduced or augmented. That said, the field evidence does tend to lean toward the "world is white, yellow, and green" hypothesis. It predicts that in regions that support scant vegetation, such as the Arctic, plants will not produce enough food to support many herbivores; removing herbivores or carnivores will have few, if any, further consequences for the ecosystem as a whole. In regions of medium productivity, there will be enough food produced to support a modest level of herbivores, enough to keep down plant numbers but not enough to support many carnivores. In this case, predator removals will have little effect, but herbivore removals will have a significant effect on plants. In the most productive systems, carnivores will begin to control herbivores. Removing carnivores in these systems will have a significant impact on herbivore numbers and thus on vegetation.[33]

This theory begins to explain why predators sometimes seem to matter a lot and why they sometimes seem to matter not at all to an overall ecological community—and why predator control sometimes works to increase numbers of a targeted prey species and why it sometimes does not. Arctic ecosystems do indeed appear to be relatively resistant to major perturbations, as the "white" scenario predicts. And in a "green" system like Yellowstone, as the theory predicts, removal of predators leads to a significant increase in herbivores and a significant impact on vegetation.

A more fine-grained look at food chains can yield some more specific predictions. The near-extinction of the American chestnut, which once made up more than forty percent of large, canopy trees of many eastern North American forests, ought, by the rivet-pulling-madman view of the nature, to have led to a cascading loss of many other species. Seven species of butterflies are known to have fed exclusively on chestnuts, and these indeed are probably extinct. But forty-nine other butterflies that also fed on chestnuts survive, as do the insect predators that feed on all fifty-six butterflies. No higher animals in eastern North America have passed into extinction during the period of the chestnut's decline or since, either. The buck stopped very early on in the food chain.

Why? Apparently because of its detailed structure. A chain with multiple branches has considerable redundancy as one goes to higher levels.[34] Most of the butterflies that fed on the chestnut had alternative food sources they could switch to. And the insect predators that preyed

Figure 21. What goes down does not come up: In a complex food web, removing a single plant (black circle, top diagram) has little effect on a top predator, which draws on many different food sources. But removing the top predator (bottom diagram) creates a major shock that is propagated down the food web to all levels.

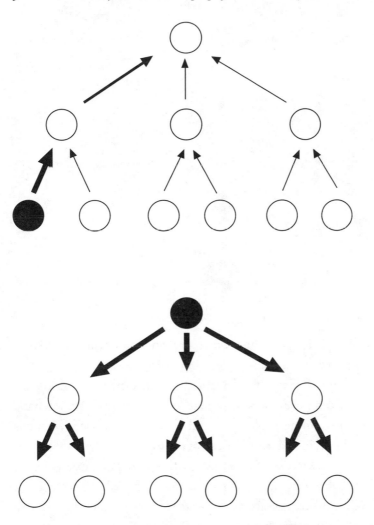

upon the seven butterflies that could not switch had other choices, too. A complex food chain—or, really, a food web—tends to be resistant to changes at lower levels. On the other hand, it is more vulnerable when the loss of species takes place at the top because the very complexity that dilutes a shock on the way up tends to amplify and propagate a shock far and wide on the way down. Loss of a single top predator that

Figure 22. In a simple food chain, removing a species at the bottom will have a profound effect on all levels.

feeds on many species will cause a greater upheaval to the system as a whole than the loss of one of its multiple-prey species.

For systems with simple food webs, the situation is reversed. Extremely specialized herbivores or predators are clearly extremely vulnerable to the loss of their sole food source. That is precisely what has happened in Hawaii, where the destruction of just a few species of plants by the introduction of pigs and goats by the Polynesians led to the extinction of a number of birds that were specialized to feed on the nectar of just those plants. Generalist feeders—which have more complex food-web patterns and which feed on a variety of plants or insects—have by contrast survived.

This analysis has another interesting result, namely, that the introduction of generalists should have more of an impact than specialists: likewise, that introductions of species into systems that contain generalist predators—which can limit numbers of the intruders—should have less of an impact than introductions into systems with specialist predators.[35]

This is all clearly no more than a start. But it offers a glimpse of a coherent conservation strategy. Food-web considerations can help to identify which species are the most crucial in larger ecosystem functions; the keystone species thus identified would then become the logical candidates for the more species-specific business of population viability analysis; that analysis in turn would suggest how a nature reserve should be designed and show when extraordinary intervention is required. If managers are going to get in the business of captive breeding and release and transporting animals between reserves and simulating disturbance processes—as viability analysis suggests they will have to at times—and if they are going to face decisions about where to spend scarce dollars in acquiring more habitat, it certainly would make sense to expend such efforts on behalf of species that affect the existence of many other species rather than on behalf of those populations that have no influence beyond their own kind.

But in the end, all such tools of ecosystem analysis are really just that—tools. They can help to guide decisions in that they can show what is possible and what is not; they can help to ensure that the goals we set are the goals we actually reach; they can help to minimize the element of nasty surprises that has so long plagued wildlife conservation; but they cannot substitute for human judgment. Science is a tool. It is not a moral imperative.

EIGHT

Bioeconomy

There are apparently few things quite so robustly satisfying these days as proclaiming the imminent collapse of an ecosystem or, better yet, the planet. A role that used to be filled by deranged street-corner prophets has now been eagerly taken over by presidents of environmental think tanks, members of the National Academy of Sciences, and the occasional vice president of the United States. Thus does an "urgent warning to humanity" signed by 1,575 leading scientists declare that man's activities may soon render Earth "unable to sustain life in the manner that we know"; thus does Vice President Al Gore warn of "irreparable damage to the global environment" and call mankind's current course a "road to extermination"; thus does Worldwatch Institute President Lester Brown testify before a Senate committee that the human population will simply never reach ten billion, the consensus of demographers notwithstanding. "Well before we get there, systems will start breaking down," Brown said. "First, the ecosystems, and then the economic systems that depend on them."[1]

There is a whiff of almost misanthropic satisfaction in some of these pronouncements, as when Paul Ehrlich asks if there would "be any purpose served" in turning Earth "into a gigantic human feedlot" any-

191

way and calls humanity a "cancerlike disease" growing on the planet.[2] Yet even many nonmisanthropes share the fundamental assumption of the doomsayers, that man's current use of the land is "unsustainable." Stories of overhunting, overfishing, and overgrazing have long been staples of the popular environmental literature; they have been augmented more recently by slightly more complex tales of the ecological instability of farm or forest monocultures. It's not just that fishing or farming or grazing or logging is destroying wilderness habitat or upsetting the delicate ecological balance for other species; these attempts at husbanding nature are not even successful on their own terms. It goes without saying that foresters are killing the spotted owl; but now it turns out they can't even grow trees without messing it up, setting off infestations of spruce budworms that kill their stands or upsetting the balance of soil fungi and bacteria that the trees need to grow properly or attracting invasions of competing weeds or parasites or eroding the soil and destroying the long-term productivity of the land.

To the doomsayers, the conclusion is of course a foregone one: The only possible course is to convert as many acres as possible from cultivation to nature reserves, abandon the "selfish pursuit of materialism," and "tread more lightly" on what is left. (The quoted words happen to be those of Lester Brown but might just as easily have been taken from any of literally scores of manifestos urging us to save the planet by riding our bicycles to work, turning off the air conditioning, becoming vegetarians, and shopping for clothes at the Hadassah Thrift Shop.)[3] In the United States the entire discussion of how successfully man has managed his fields and forests, which ought to be a scientific discussion, has become a proxy for the political debate over whether federally owned timber and grazing lands should continue to be devoted to multiple uses or designated exclusively as "wilderness."

Politics aside, the lands and wild animal populations that have been harnessed to supply the needs of mankind are of unusual significance, and environmentalists are right in starting to single them out for special attention—albeit for the wrong reasons. Roughly one-tenth of the land area of the earth is cultivated; one-sixth is grasslands; another one-sixth is temperate forest, a significant proportion of which is managed for timber production. By contrast, only 3 percent of the world's land area is in parks and nature reserves.[4] The proportion of the earth's surface devoted to meeting human needs is hardly likely to diminish appreciably in the near future. By their sheer extent, lands that are farmed, logged, and grazed have come to dominate the landscape over much of the earth. How these lands are managed will be as important, if not more important, for conservation as the management of parks and reserves.

There are really two separate questions. First is the one that environmentalists think they already know the answer to: Can humans successfully manage these often highly perturbed ecosystems in a fashion that gives predictable, consistent, and—however one defines it—sustainable results? And second, are there management strategies that can reconcile intensive management for production on these lands with other values, especially conservation values?

Intensively managed lands and animal populations pose an especially rigorous test of how well we truly understand what makes an ecosystem tick. We are often attempting to maintain high rates of harvest, in the case of fish or trees, for example; or unusually high densities of animals, in the case of game birds; or accelerated rates of nutrient cycling and the maintenance of exotic species, in the case of row crops and many pastures. The circumstances are more extreme, the room for error less; that will only become more so in the future. Even lands that have been cultivated more or less successfully for hundreds or thousands of years by farmers guided only by the seats of their pants will increasingly require the benefit of ecological insight and scientifically based management as the demands we place upon them increase—both for more intensive production of commodities and for wildlife conservation.

On the other hand, from a purely scientific point of view, such "seminatural" systems have a few things going for them as objects of study that more purely "natural" ecosystems do not, which may make them especially important scientific models—real-world laboratories that can be used to formulate and prove ideas about what controls the numbers, distributions, and interactions of species over time and space. The key to scientific understanding of cause and effect always lies in perturbation: the way to figure out how a clock works is not to stare at it but to fiddle with it. "In ecology, however," one practitioner ruefully notes, "most of the perturbations that would yield far-reaching insights are either immoral, illegal, or impractical. . . . Think, for example, how much faster community ecology would progress if your graduate students weren't restricted to the minuscule field experiments now in favor, but if each of you were permitted to select and burn some part" of an area the size of a city; "or if you could reintroduce wolves into an area of your choice, exterminate the local population of a select species, or dredge and flood a Wisconsin farm and convert it into a marsh."[5]

Agriculture has been precisely such a grand perturbation experiment. High densities place great demands on such ecosystems but also provide great insights into intraspecific competition, nutrient cycling, even multispecies ecology. There is a vast amount of both traditional experience and deliberate experiment that has gone into determining optimal stocking and planting rates on farms, which not coincidentally has proven of great importance to basic ecological theory. Some of the best experiments on how competition for resources within a population varies with population density have been carried out in poultry. How different species of grasses and legumes compete and interact and how the balance between them is affected by fertilization and grazing have also been studied in exquisite detail. Efforts going back a century to control insect and weed pests by introducing natural enemies have been remarkable applied experiments in both population biology and community ecology.[6]

There has, however, been a curious conspiracy of ignorance at work that has tried to deny the knowability—or even the significance—of the ecology of these systems. Ecologists have tended to dismiss agricultural ecosystems as nothing but zoos or gardens. Environmentalists have tended to emphasize the disasters and surprises, the pest outbreaks, the crop failures, the eroded rangelands, as proof that even under seemingly tightly controlled conditions man is playing with fire and cannot control it at all. The combination of biological uncertainty and human greed, they suggest, inevitably leads to disaster.

Even producers sometimes join in, preferring to blame a shortage of grouse or fish on God or fate or the weather rather than admit that humans might actually be able to fix the problem through scientific management—and thus, by implication, admit that humans (such as themselves) are responsible when things go wrong.

The disasters have been real enough. Whether they prove that ecosystems are fundamentally unknowable, beyond human ken and human control, is another matter. Environmentalists, joined by some ecologists of the throw-up-one's-hands school, often point to the collapse of the Peruvian anchoveta fishery as exhibit A. From 1960 to 1972, it was the world's largest single fishery, bringing in as many as twelve million tons of fish a year. But in 1972 the catch plummeted to four million tons; the next year it was down to less than two million; and by 1978 it was virtually zero. Although quotas were set on the total catch during the boom years to a level that fishery experts believed was the so-called maximum sustainable yield—about ten million tons a year—the Peruvian authorities never made any attempts to limit the number of fishing vessels, which led to an interesting result. Attracted by the booming business, more and more fishermen and processors entered the field, resulting eventually in a huge overcapacity. The annual quota, which in the early days of the fishery took almost a full year of fishing to catch, was by 1971 being caught in three months. The rest of the year the boats and the processing factories sat idle. When the crash hit, there were some twenty thousand people whose livelihood

Figure 23. The collapse of the Peruvian anchoveta fishery is a case study of economic and biological inefficiency. Authorities tried to enforce catch limits through shorter and shorter fishing seasons, which resulted in a huge overcapitalization of the fishing fleet and ultimately a biological catastrophe.

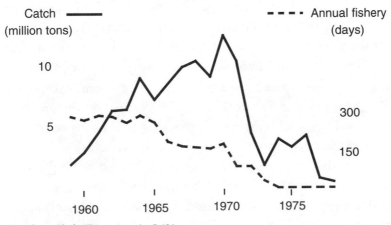

Data from Clark, "Bioeconomics," 401.

depended directly on the anchoveta fishery, an enormous constituency ready to oppose any suggestion of closing the fishery for a year or two to allow stocks to recover and a political and economic nightmare for the government. The fishery stayed open, stocks continued to fall, and the crash became virtual extinction.[7]

This "ratchet effect" is unfortunately typical of marine fisheries. Good years attract new investors, resulting in gross overcapitalization in bad years; the market forces that ought to shake out that excess capacity are then sabotaged by demands for government subsidies to help out the beleaguered producers. The incentives to expand in good years are much greater than the incentives to contract in bad years; each time stocks fall and rise, the overcapitalization is ratcheted up another notch. Much the same fate befell the Pacific sardine fishery in the 1940s and 1950s; indeed, it was the collapse of the sardines that set off the anchoveta boom, as processors looked for a new source of fish meal for cattle feed. The Alaska halibut fishery is well on its way to repeating the pattern, too. Although for now, at least, the halibut stocks appear to be in good biological shape, the halibut fishing fleet is one of the most grossly overcapitalized in the world. The entire annual quota, which once took six months to catch, is now pulled in in two days—a madcap "halibut Olympics" in which boats scramble to make their year's take in two twenty-four-hour "seasons."[8]

"Even well-meaning attempts to exploit responsibly may lead to disastrous consequences," concluded one group of ecologists of the fatalistic persuasion. "The complexity of the underlying biological and physical systems precludes a reductionist approach to management. . . . [S]cientific consensus is seldom achieved, even after collapse of the resource . . . by and large the scientific community has helped to perpetuate the illusion of sustainable development through scientific and technological progress." Even were scientific certainty and consensus possible, the ecologists said, destruction of resources would inevitably occur; human greed being what it is, scientific facts are no match for the prospect of wealth. Their conclusion (no surprises here) is that rather than continue to mislead the public with the false promise that basic ecological research will make sustainable management possible, we should instead focus on "the problems of [human] population growth and excessive use of resources."[9] There's not much point in trying to understand, much less manage, natural resources; the only hope is to put a fence around them.

Is such fatalism justified? Despair over human greed is understandable enough. But greed is not some faceless, unknowable force. There is in fact an entire science devoted to analyzing and even quantifying and predicting the effects of greed: it's called economics. Economic forces affect, in generally predictable and explainable ways, how people exploit resources, and economic analysis frequently can suggest sensible policies or regulations for preventing overexploitation—policies that take human motivation into account, rather than bemoaning or ignoring it.

It is here that environmentalists and fatalistic ecologists notably part company with economists and practical ecologists. The fatalists are forever citing the now all-too-familiar story of the "tragedy of the commons" as proof that man is somehow destined to screw up his environment so long as he continues to think of the world in selfish economic terms. The phenomenon of overuse of common lands is certainly true enough; no one denies that it has happened. Even though the cumulative result is a tragedy for all concerned, individuals behaving in a perfectly rational economic fashion will find it in their individual economic interests to maximize their individual exploitation of commonly held lands. Indeed, one joint owner's overuse can actually act as a goad to others to keep pace, a sort of bidding war familiar to lunch parties that have agreed ahead of time to split the bill—if one person orders a drink or a high-priced entrée, all the others feel they had better, too, so they don't wind up subsidizing the one extravagant member of the group.

But in citing this argument, it is as if environmentalists have observed that their clock is not working right and, rather than simply deciding to get it fixed have concluded instead that there is nothing to be done but to renounce the concept of time. Environmental writers are forever bemoaning the evil effects of capitalism and materialism and adjuring us to adopt a "new ethic" as the only hope for saving nature; the tragedy of the commons is just another illustration of the ecological bankruptcy of the economic system. We must renounce the pursuit of worldly goods and conduct our business affairs on the basis of a new set of values. "Most Americans would be physically, if not spiritually, better off if they consumed less food and beverage, certainly less tobacco, demonstrably fewer paper products, arguably less energy, and clearly less televised entertainment, particularly in the form of professional football and other juvenile programming," is the all-too-typical conclusion of one environmentalist writer who complains that "corporate producers" must learn to serve society first and place profits second.[10] The enemy is not bad policy but "systems of behavior" that must be replaced in a sweeping transformation of human values.

Experience alone might suggest that whenever someone tells us that they don't care about money and are conducting business on a higher spiritual plain, we should check our wallets. But more to the point, there is a very odd blend of cynicism and naïveté in the expectation that mankind will be swept up in a new ethic that renounces materialism and the profit motive. In one sense the fatalists are too cynical; they see profit as such a source of evil that they refuse to believe it can be channeled to achieve a desired end. They argue that someone will always try to get around the rules so long as the profit motive exists. Yet why a new ethic that renounces profit altogether should be exempt from such chicanery is a mystery. The entire economy is a tragedy of the commons, which drives out voluntary self-sacrifice and the renunciation of the profit motive; even if, somehow, the mass of humanity should see the light and renounce profit for the greater good of the planet, the one bastard who doesn't will make a killing. And bastards are not known to be in short supply.

Fixing the clock is certainly a more prosaic solution; it is much more satisfying and ever so much easier to spin out portentous essays (bearing titles like "The End of Time," no doubt) indicting our society for its dearth of spiritual values and predicting the millennium. Making the clock run better also has the disadvantage that it requires taking the clock apart, figuring out why it is malfunctioning, and devising a mechanism to fix it. This may involve hard work and even mathematics. The advantage of this approach is that it actually works.

Adding basic economic analysis to models of biological resources in fact can often explain why a catastrophe such as the collapse of the anchoveta fishery happens in the first place and can suggest sometimes quite simple measures to avoid such catastrophes in the future.

The work that has been done to support the management of fisheries is a good example of how combining biological and economic analysis can lead to practical policies. Whether those policies are implemented or not is, of course, another matter, and politics is always a factor. But even problems that seem quite intractable at first can often be deftly picked apart through rigorous mathematical analysis. The sweeping claim that solutions do not exist—indeed that solutions cannot exist—is simply not borne out by a mounting body of experience.

Typically, it turns out that there are one or two critical factors that determine how greed interacts with population biology. These factors may be far from the obvious ones. In the case of fisheries, mathematical models have revealed that setting a fixed catch quota has a much more destabilizing effect on a fish population than limiting the size of the fishing fleet. The basic argument, which is instructive as an example of how this kind of mathematical analysis can lead to surprising and powerful conclusions, is depicted graphically in figure 24. The first graph, figure 24a, represents the regulatory scheme that has been applied to many fisheries. The vertical axis represents the growth rate, the horizontal axis the population size. The shape of the growth curve embodies the admittedly simple assumptions of the logistic growth model: A very small population grows at a low rate because there simply aren't very many individuals around to reproduce; a very large population has a slow growth rate because it is straining the limits of available food resources; somewhere in the middle the growth rate hits its maximum. The objective of many simple fisheries management schemes has been to set the harvest rate exactly equal to this maximum growth rate, thus achieving what is canonically defined as the maximum sustained yield. Fisheries experts estimated, for example, that the maximum sustained yield of the anchoveta fishery was ten million tons, and the catch quota was set accordingly.

All is well and good as long as the population actually remains at the size that corresponds to this maximum growth rate (the point marked N_{eq}). Harvest and growth will precisely balance, and the population will remain constant, forever and ever. If the population should nonetheless creep up for some reason (which it almost certainly will from time to time, since, as we saw in chapter 4, the logistic model is an idealization of a much more chaotic and chancy reality),

Figure 24. Good policy, bad policy: (a) A fixed catch quota set at the theoretical "maximum sustainable yield" (MSY) leads to collapse if the population being harvested drops below the supposed equilibrium point, N$_{eq}$; (b) by contrast, a policy that sets a fixed level of harvest effort (a set number of boats, e.g.) is automatically self-correcting: if the population drops, so does the harvest rate; (c) even this management strategy can run into biological complications, however, which argues for giving regulators the authority to close a fishery as soon as populations begin to drop. See text for further explanation.

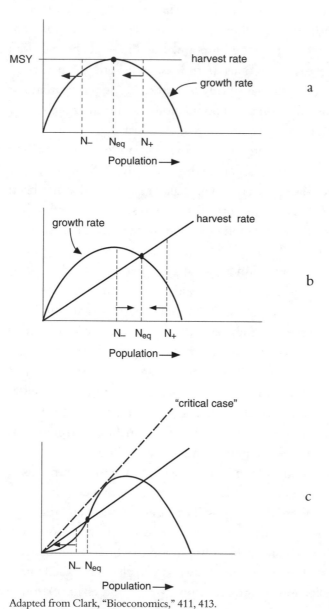

Adapted from Clark, "Bioeconomics," 411, 413.

things are still all right. Consider what happens if the population N shifts upward to the point N_+: The harvest rate is now greater than the growth rate, which will cause a net loss in numbers, forcing N to move to the left; this state of affairs will continue until the population once again reaches N_{eq}, at which point the harvest and growth rates will once again balance and the population will stabilize. This is the property that mathematicians refer to as stable equilibrium—any change is automatically corrected; the inherent properties of the system operate to return the population to its starting point.

The snag comes if fluctuations should cause the population to fall *below* N_{eq}. At N_-, the harvest rate is again greater than the growth rate, but now we are already to the left of N_{eq}. The net loss in population will then shift N farther to the left, which only further widens the gap between harvest and growth rates, causing an even faster loss in population, which in turn causes N to move even farther to the left, and so on until N crashes to zero. The effect is like rolling a marble off a hill. Even the smallest deflection will start it going. This is termed unstable equilibrium: As long as N stays precisely at N_{eq}, it will remain there. But even the smallest deflection will send it cascading inexorably downhill.

This was what happened to the Peruvian anchoveta fishery. The crash was exacerbated, however, by a policy which may have made simple biological sense but made no economic sense. To prevent overuse of a shared resource, a fixed quota was set on total exploitation. But the severe overcapitalization of the fishing fleet and processing industry created enormous pressure to maintain the harvest quota at a fixed level even as N began to drop. All it took was a succession of a few bad years and the result was near-extinction. "It has in practice sometimes proved difficult for the fishing industry to understand that a scientific estimate of 'maximum sustainable yield' does not refer to a catch that can be taken each and every year regardless of natural fluctuations," notes one practitioner.[11]

The ideal solution from a purely biological point of view would be to adjust the harvest rate so that the harvest-rate curve exactly duplicates the growth-rate curve. That way, whatever the population, the catch never exceeds the rate of natural increase. This is clearly impossible, since it would require a degree of precision and detailed knowledge about a wild population that is simply unattainable. Yet there are other still quite practical regulatory strategies that avoid the instabilities that the simple "maximum sustainable yield" approach falls prey to. One step that can help to control both biological depletion and economic inefficiencies is to allocate a quota to each individual boat (or at least to individual countries) rather than simply set a total quota for the entire fishery. The International Whaling Commission set total annual catch quotas from its inception in 1949 until 1960, creating the paradigmatic helter-skelter economic competition and its attendant "whaling Olympics"; it thereafter adopted a policy of allocating national quotas, which increased the profitability of the industry while reducing the intense competition for a fixed resource.[12] Another idea increasingly in favor is to allocate private property rights in resources, which at least in principle avoids the tragedy of the commons pitfall by creating an incentive for the owner to protect his resource, secure in the knowledge that he will be the one to benefit in the future from his own prudence today. (Unfortunately this is not always the case, as we shall see below.)

A fairly simple and promising concept, however, is to regulate a fishery by controlling total fishing effort. This approach is represented graphically in figure 24b. The growth-rate curve is the same as before, rising and falling in the familiar logistic pattern, but the harvest rate has become a sloped line instead of a horizontal line. This is because, for a fixed number of fishing boats and fishing days, the harvest rate will tend to increase in proportion to the total fish population. A very dense population can be harvested more rapidly than a sparse one. The slope of the line is in turn a function of the effort. Adding more boats will make the line rise faster as fish populations grow. In principle, by adjusting the effort, the harvest-rate line can be made to intersect the growth-rate line wherever we choose. (Recall that the point where they cross is the equilibrium point, where harvest and growth rates just cancel each other out and, absent natural fluctuations, result in a population that neither grows nor shrinks.)

But what is especially interesting about this regime is its stability. If natural fluctuation sends the population up, the harvest rate automatically increases (a fixed number of boats fishing a fixed number of days will catch more fish the more fish there are); the harvest rate then exceeds the growth rate, and the population falls until it again reaches N_{eq}. But unlike the case in figure 24a, stability is preserved here even when population falls below the equilibrium point. In that circumstance, the harvest rate dips below the growth rate, resulting in a net gain in the population, which continues until N returns to N_{eq}. This model exhibits a stable equilibrium with respect to fluctuations in either direction from the equilibrium point.

As a final example, this model can be modified to incorporate some real-world complications, both biological and economic. One of these complications is particularly interesting, because it can further help explain the "inexplicable" collapse of the sardine and anchoveta fisheries—and suggest additional strategies for preventing such catastrophes in the future. Many fish form large schools; among other things, this an efficient way to protect against predators. The larger the school, the smaller risk of predation for any one member of the school. (This is the same principle that spawned the idea of sending ships across the Atlantic in convoys during both world wars. The odds that a U-boat will spot a convoy is not much greater than the odds that it will spot a single ship. So long as a predator is unable to kill every member of the school in one encounter, it pays to travel together to cut down on the number of opportunities for discovery.) Conversely, as the size of the school shrinks, the rate of predation per individual goes up. Thus, as total populations drop to low levels, forcing not only the number of schools to shrink but the size of each school as well, there comes a point at which growth rates are depressed below what the simple logistic curve would predict. This is the situation depicted in figure 24c. There are two curious results of this situation. One is that there appears a second point where the harvest and growth curves cross (the one marked N_{eq} here), which exhibits unstable equilibrium properties, just as in the first example we considered where the harvest rate was fixed at a constant value. Second, as the harvest level increases and the steepness of the harvest-rate line grows, there comes a point where a so-called critical case is reached. At this level, the two curves do not cross at all—the harvest rate is always greater than the growth rate, no matter what the population. (Actually, there *is* one equilibrium point where the growth and harvest rates are equal under these conditions: when the population is zero.)

The fatalists will of course say "I told you so," but in fact this analysis also shows how one can detect an impending crash and take corrective action. The harvest rate is proportional to both the fishing effort and the number of fish. One way to tell if populations are heading downward is thus to monitor the ratio of harvest rate to effort, which are both directly measurable quantities. If that ratio begins to fall, that is strong evidence that N is falling, too. This warning mechanism is already being used in the management of some fisheries. The international commission that regulates yellowfin tuna in the eastern Pacific can close the fishery as soon as the catch per unit effort falls below a set value.[13] Fancier models, which incorporate the effects of random fluctuations, have also been developed; these can actually show which of several alternative management strategies is most likely to reduce the risk of a collapse in the fishery over time. Models can also take into account such factors as the competition between two harvested species for food, the effect of harvest rate on price and investment in additional fishing effort, and the effect of selectively harvesting fish of a certain age out of a population.[14]

At the other political extreme from those who insist that man's greed will always ruin nature are those who insist that nature can be saved only through the magic of the marketplace's invisible hand. As we have seen, catastrophes such as the collapse of the anchoveta fishery can ultimately be traced to the lack of a single owner for the resource. The "tragedy of the commons" that is bound to ensue in these circumstances may be averted either by imposing a government regulatory scheme that restricts harvest effort (the solution developed for the yellowfin tuna fishery) or by allocating private property rights to the resource (the solution developed for whaling). The growing number of advocates of free-market solutions to environmental problems have argued that property rights are a less cumbersome and onerous method of achieving this end. The basic argument is that by having a clear and single owner, not only will the tragedy of the commons be prevented but the owner will have a powerful financial stake in carefully husbanding the resource for the future; after all, his continued livelihood depends on it. There is a convincing case, for example, that overharvesting of the African elephant has actually been exacerbated by idealistic attempts to ban the international ivory trade. In Zimbabwe, however, where villagers were given a share in license fees paid by well-heeled trophy hunters, a species that had been seen as nothing but a crop-trampling menace suddenly became a valuable asset to be protected, and elephant numbers in the country actually rose; while in Kenya they continued to plummet, despite a massive, military-style antipoaching program launched by park rangers.[15] This is all certainly consistent with the idea enunciated earlier of harnessing greed for good rather than trying to banish it as an evil.

On the other hand, free-market environmentalists are often quite doctrinaire about their claims in behalf of the market, insisting that private ownership alone will solve the problem of overexploitation of biological resources. Recent bioeconomic analyses have been instrumental in pointing up the fallacy of such sweeping claims on behalf of market solutions. (The fact that some of these free marketeers go so far as to say that if laissez-faire will not cure the problem, it is not even a problem is also a bit of a giveaway as to the real political agenda at work here.)[16]

The analysis is quite complex and mathematically far beyond the scope of this book, but the basic idea is not hard to grasp. A slow-growing population may simply not be worth careful husbanding for the future, even to a single owner: If its reproduction rate is less than the interest rate the bank pays, a perfectly rational economic solution would be to slaughter the entire population at once, put the money in the bank, and live off the interest. Even modest discount rates can have a dramatic effect on how many fish or whales or trees it pays the owner to leave for the future. A model of Antarctic blue whales, for example, found that at a discount rate of zero, the economically optimal population is 85,000; if the interest rate is just 5 percent per year, the optimal population drops to 44,000; at 15 percent, it is 27,000. The blue whale has a very slow growth rate, of about 5 percent per year. Exactly the same phenomenon bedevils other slow-growing resources, notably timber. Private ownership in these cases is no guarantee that overexploitation will not occur. The only thing that prevents the whales from being completely wiped out when interest rates outstrip the animals' intrinsic reproduction rate is the rapidly escalating cost of hunting the few remaining whales as populations dwindle. The marginal cost of finding the last members of a scarce population just isn't worth it.

Again, allocated quotas (which are a "proxy" of private ownership and could in fact be auctioned off and freely traded on an open market) are a way to confer the chief advantages of private ownership (eliminating the incentive for cutthroat competition that effectively imposes a discount rate of infinity—harvest it now or lose it forever to a competitor) while also setting limits on harvests that a pure market would not itself impose.[17]

The point of all of this is that there are ways to devise effective management policies and strategies that take into account such unreasonable facts of life as uncertainty and greed. It will not be automatic, as the doctrinaire proponents of laissez-faire or the wishful advocates of an unvarying maximum sustained yield would have it. But neither is it beyond the means of human ingenuity or political will, as the ecological doomsayers would have it. There are a number of successful examples of sophisticated yet elegantly simple regulatory mechanisms that have been instituted that embody bioeconomic principles, and there is growing movement in that direction. Fisheries where producers have long resisted limits on the size of the fleet in favor of total annual catch quotas have begun to give way (albeit in some cases, such as Atlantic groundfish, only after catastrophic collapses have woken them up). There are also many admonitory examples, the African elephant most notably, of what happens to policies built on the idealistic hope that mankind will renounce profit and be guided by loftier motives. For some strange reason there are still a considerable number of people who insist upon behaving precisely as people throughout recorded human history have always behaved.

We have passed a bit quickly over one question that probably deserves a fairer hearing, and that has to do with the uncertainty that is an inherent property of many biological populations. There are no guarantees that nature will behave in an orderly, balanced, and self-equilibrating manner; even very simple biological systems can, under the right circumstances, exhibit unpredictable and chaotic fluctuations. That was one of the key arguments for human intervention: Leaving nature to her own devices may not produce the results we want or expect.

But doesn't chaos equally sabotage hopes that man can do any better in getting nature to behave? While some environmentalists are still scorning the ideas of ecological disturbance and chaos as the inventions of "permissive" ecologists who are trying to excuse man's intrusions and exploitations in the natural world, others have seen an opportunity here and have seized on the findings of nature's disorder as proof that the end of Western anthropocentric rationalism is upon us. If nature is not governed by an ultimate order, if it is ultimately uncertain and un- knowable, then man must abandon his arrogant notions of rationally understanding and controlling the world about him.[18] The Heisenberg uncertainty principle—the quantum mechanical principle that the speed and location of a subatomic particle cannot be precisely deter- mined simultaneously—has led to all sorts of cocktail-party philoso- phizing about whether the universe is knowable and whether God plays with dice; now chaos appears to be setting off a second wave.

To scientists all of this is a bit baffling. The starting point for sci- ence was not complete knowability, after all, but complete ignorance. What science has done from the start has been to reduce the uncer- tainties of a world that was at first totally inexplicable. As a practical matter, humans have never been able to predict the natural world with certainty, nor have scientists assumed they could, and the theo- retical limitations imposed by quantum mechanics or chaos theory changes nothing. We now realize that it is theoretically impossible for us ever to predict the exact location of every raindrop in a thunder- storm. But so what? That fact may distress some philosophers of sci- ence, but as a practical matter this has always been impossible—not because Newton's deterministic laws of motion are an insufficient de- scription of a chaotic and quantum mechanical universe but because the number of measurements needed to calculate the deterministic Newtonian trajectory of every raindrop has always been beyond any- thing humans could manage, or ever will be able to manage even with the largest supercomputers. What is being grandly billed as the death of rationalism turns out to be the inconsiderable spectacle of a straw man having the stuffing kicked out of him.

There is a less grandiose argument to be made about the difficulties that ecological disorder poses for human attempts to manage natural sys- tems. It may not be the end of Western scientific rationalism, but it clearly does make the job harder. Yet we have already seen a hint, in the fisheries examples, of how uncertainty can be explicitly incorporated into a management strategy. Recognizing that some fluctuations will always occur and that there will always be surprises, solutions can often be devised to react to those surprises. If for whatever reason—weather, currents, chaos—the number of yellowfin tuna drop, a sensible strategy will note that drop and respond by reducing or halting exploitation until numbers recover. The probabilistic properties of quantum mechanics did not prevent the development of the transistor; indeed, one solid-state device, the tunnel diode, actually exploits the probabilistic nature of the electron's behavior to generate a useful electronic property. Similarly, the chaotic properties of biological populations need not rule out strategies for coping with this fact of life. One of the important things that mathematical analysis in population biology has done, in fact, is to identify what precise factors cause a population to fluctuate, cycle, or behave chaotically. A chaotically fluctuating population is unpredictable, but the conditions that give rise to that chaotic behavior are not.

The ultimate test is the practical one. Simply, can humans identify, understand, and successfully manipulate the factors that control a biological population, and have consistent results to show for it at the end of the day? One of the problems in putting ecological understanding to the test is that most ecosystem studies and experiments are still done on a tiny scale; study areas of a square kilometer are typical, "hardly bigger than the organism itself," says one ecologist, only half-joking.

A notable exception, in fact probably *the* notable exception to date, has been an exhaustive effort that began in the early 1980s to understand everything there was to know about the population biology, community ecology, and management of the red grouse in Scotland and northern England.

Although the red grouse is a free-living species, it is among the most intensively managed wildlife populations anywhere on earth. An estimated four million acres of moorland in Britain are managed primarily for the production of grouse; on at least the most productive estates, revenue earned from renting out the shooting rights to well-heeled sportsmen far surpasses income from sheep farming, forestry, or other competing land uses. Estates that are able to sustain a density of more than 150 grouse per square mile offer what is called "driven" shooting: Shooters stand concealed behind a string of stone butts spread in a line forty yards apart while beaters drive the grouse across the heather moors toward them. For this they pay about a hundred dollars for each "brace," or pair, of birds shot. A day's shooting can bring in fifteen thousand dollars or more to an estate owner; the average Scottish grouse estate let out forty-five days of shooting in 1989.

Where grouse densities are lower, the hunt takes the less lucrative (though, to Americans at least, more recognizable) form of "walked up" shooting or hunting with dogs; sportsmen pay about half as much per brace for these activities. A study of the economics of grouse in Scotland found that the annual shoot of a quarter million birds, which begins August 12 of each year, generates about nine million dollars in direct revenues and at least fifteen million dollars in indirect income to the country (food, lodging, travel, ammunition, supplies). It also generates the equivalent of more than two thousand full-time jobs in a part of the world where employment opportunities are few and far between.[19]

All of which helps explain why a sudden and unprecedented decline in grouse numbers in the mid-1970s set off alarms, and why an intensive research effort was promptly launched to figure out what was going on. (In the hardest-hit region, eastern Scotland, the average grouse bag dropped from about 150 to 10 per square mile from the mid-1970s to the early 1980s. Elsewhere in Scotland and in northern England the decline was not quite so sharp, but overall the loss averaged 40 percent for Britain as a whole.)[20]

From a scientific point of view, grouse were in some ways an ideal problem. A huge wealth of basic data already existed. Estates had kept meticulous records, often going back 150 years, of the number of birds shot each year. With more than three hundred separate, privately owned estates, each employing somewhat different management techniques, there was also a significant amount of practical experience accumulated; trial and error alone had established some basic ecological principles about what works to increase grouse numbers and what does not.

In fact, until the population crash in the 1970s, the management of grouse moors was a remarkable example of sustained, intensive, and successful ecosystem management on an astonishing scale. The heather moorlands that most of us automatically associate with Scotland are in fact largely a nineteenth-century artifact, the direct result

Figure 25. The steep decline in the red grouse population in Scotland. The sale of shooting rights is a major source of income to land owners; the most profitable form, in which grouse are driven by beaters to a line of guns, is possible only when densities exceed sixty birds per square kilometer.

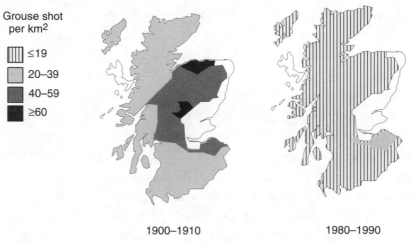

Grouse shot
per km²

▥	≤19
▦	20–39
▨	40–59
■	≥60

1900–1910   1980–1990

Adapted from Hudson, *Grouse in Space and Time,* 18.

of concerted and intentional modification of the landscape with the primary aim of encouraging red grouse. Three thousand years ago much of the area that now consists of heather moorland in Scotland was forest, mainly Scotch pine. Heather, a tough, low-growing ever-green shrub, was confined to bare wind-blown hilltops and the occasional forest clearing where lightning-set fires had done their job. Repeating the pattern of humans everywhere, the Neolithic farmers who appeared on the scene at this time began to burn down the forest to clear land for growing crops and grazing cattle; grazing and more deliberate burning kept the land open. Heather was and is the only thing that survives the harsh winters to provide feed for livestock; grazing and burning thus became tightly bound with the moorlands in a self-perpetuating cycle. As land was burned, the isolated patches of heather spread and linked up to form open moorlands; the moorlands supported cattle, which in turn maintained the moorlands by preventing the regeneration of Scotch pine and other forest species.

Walking across the wild hillsides of the Highlands today, one can often find remains of the ancient stone huts, or shealings, where the cattle herders encamped for the summers before moving down the glens as winter approached. Theirs was a rough, shifting (and, not infrequently, murderous) existence; but they had already begun the process of wholesale ecological change that characterizes the entire region today. The process of forest clearing accelerated rapidly in the late eighteenth and early nineteenth centuries as the industrial revolution fueled demand for meat and wool. The rent-paying small farmers were thrown off the land by the lairds and replaced by much more profitable sheep, whose numbers grew rapidly during this period.

But it was Queen Victoria who really sealed the fate of the great Caledonian Forest. After the unsuccessful Jacobite uprising in 1745, British troops occupied Scotland, the wearing of tartan dress was made a capital offense, and the clan system was ruthlessly broken up. But in 1782 the proscriptions were lifted, and a great sentimental Scottish revival, given a timely boost by Sir Walter Scott's immensely popular romantic novels, began to sweep England. In 1842 Queen Victoria visited Scotland, liked it, and her husband Albert soon thereafter plunked down the cash to buy the twenty-four-thousand acre estate of Balmoral. The other thing that happened about this time was the invention of the breech-loading rifle. Grouse, a minor game species up until this time, was suddenly all the rage, and anybody who wanted to be anybody had to own a Scottish shooting estate.[21]

Gamekeepers, whose job it had been to shoot food for the laird's pot, now were expected to see to it that there were plenty of grouse for the amusement of the new owners, often newly wealthy English industrialists and merchants. Grouse are confined to open moorland. The adults eat virtually nothing but heather; they are the only truly herbivorous moorland bird in the world. Like other ground-nesting birds, red grouse also depend on thick ground cover—heather again in their case—to hide from predators while brooding and rearing their young. "If you haven't got heather, you haven't got grouse," says Peter Hudson, the biologist who was called in by the Game Conservancy to launch its grouse research program.

That was one fact, anyway, that it had not taken a research biologist to discover, and nineteenth-century gamekeepers pursued it with relentless logic. Moors were burned more intensively and extensively than ever before, usually on a rotation of small, thirty-yard-wide patches, to maintain a continuous supply of fresh growing young heather. Sheep grazing also helped to maintain the heather and pre-vent the regrowth of birch scrub and pine trees.

The other fact that common sense dictated was that since foxes and crows eat grouse, if the owner wants grouse, killing a lot of foxes and crows was the way to go. So the hillsides went up in flames every summer, the foxes and crows were slaughtered in staggering numbers each spring, and the grouse increased to staggering numbers each Au-gust, when Parliament would shut down like clockwork and the rul-ing class, joined by everybody else who wished he were a member of the ruling class, decamped from London to reach the Scottish shoot-ing lodges in time for the "glorious twelfth."

Common sense worked remarkably well. Grouse bags remained high year after year (except for a brief break during World War I when, says Hudson, "it wasn't seen to be socially acceptable to be shooting grouse when you should be shooting Germans"); the old adage was to burn the heather hard and kill the foxes hard and pray for good weath-er in July, and the rest was in the lap of the gods. Hudson's job was to find out why common sense stopped working in the mid-1970s.

A careful analysis of the bag records of nearly four hundred shoot-ing estates revealed that there were actually two separate problems going on. In Scotland, bags had simply plummeted. But on many moors in northern England, the average bag remained quite high but was subject to quite extreme cyclic fluctuations. The cycle would re-peat roughly every four years; at the peaks one estate might shoot five thousand birds, at the troughs virtually zero.[22]

Working from Crubenmore, a stone Victorian Gothic shooting lodge located on the twenty-five-thousand-acre estate of John Drys-dale, an early supporter of the research effort, Hudson and his re-search team began a full frontal assault on the problem. They combed square-kilometer sections of English and Scottish moors once a week in search of grouse corpses and examined the remains to determine the cause of death. Predators leave their signature like the criminals in detective stories; it is often possible to tell by the pattern of the in-juries whether it was a fox or harrier that did the deed. To insure that the corpses found on the ground reflected the different causes of death in their true proportions, fifty grouse were caught and fitted with radio-tags and tracked, the cause of death being determined in each case. (One bird was poached and subsequently radio-tracked to the poacher's house eight miles away. The householder denied knowledge of the crime and belligerently refused to believe that the researchers were able to use a radio to find a wayward grouse; finally, he admitted that his son had probably shot the bird and locked it in the gun cupboard, and he would have him drop it off at the gas station when he returned for the weekend. More radio tracking proved necessary when the gas station owner's wife, who had received the bird from the poacher's son, subsequently committed suicide and no one knew the whereabouts of the bird. It was finally tracked to the back of a chest of drawers. The poacher can still be heard in the pub demanding to know who got him in trouble.) The other radio-tagged birds met less dramatic ends in roughly the same proportion as the birds whose corpses were found within the study areas.

The researchers pored over keepers' records of the number of foxes and crows they killed each year. They examined how predation rates varied with grouse density. They looked at changes in land use and trends in other wildlife populations, particularly rabbits, which are another major food source for foxes. They examined dead birds and grouse feces for evidence of internal parasites. They used pointer dogs to locate nesting grouse and then followed the progress of the chicks as they hatched out.

In both Scotland and England the situation turned out to be considerably more complex than either gamekeepers or wildlife biologists had believed, though in both cases what was going on turned out to have a clear and manageable explanation. The mortality studies showed beyond doubt that predators were the primary cause of death and that foxes did the greatest share of the damage. But that still left several open questions. Simply showing that many birds were killed by foxes did not prove that had those birds not been killed, more would have survived and reproduced. A well-accepted theory by many wildlife biologists (shades of Yellowstone's elk managers) had it that the birds' own territorial spacing-behavior acted as a self-regulatory mechanism to keep grouse numbers low. And both in popular lore and in the scientific literature, the belief that predators selectively kill only the weak and old is widely held.

Hudson's team, though, proceeded to meticulously demolish both arguments. Chest muscle size is a strong indicator of health in grouse;

measurements found no difference in muscle size between grouse killed by predators, grouse shot by sportsmen, and grouse that died by colliding with fences. The spacing behavior hypothesis was a much more complex problem. According to this idea, the territorial behavior of grouse in the fall set a limit on how many birds would nest in the spring; if one of these territorial birds was killed over the winter, its place would simply be taken by one of the pool of nonterritorial birds. So by this hypothesis, predation is simply not a determining factor on the ultimate number of grouse. Hudson's group tried a very simple and direct experiment to find out. In the spring they captured grouse from one area, transported them twenty miles or more, and released them into a new area. In every case, even when the release area already had a density of more than 250 birds per square mile, about a quarter of the introduced birds were subsequently found breeding. In other words, there were more available nesting sites than there were birds to occupy them, even on the most densely populated moors.[23]

Empirical evidence all along had suggested that predation was the problem. Rabbit numbers had increased dramatically in the 1960s and 1970s, and at least indirect evidence suggested that fox numbers had, too. The spread of tax-subsidized forestry in Scotland had increased refuges for both crows and foxes, too, often on lands adjacent to grouse moors—lands that once had been grouse moors themselves, where these predators had been controlled by keepers as well. And while English grouse estates employed one keeper per three thousand acres, in Scotland the average was one per twelve thousand acres. A study of two adjacent moors that had closely tracked one another's perfor- mance over the years showed a dramatic decline in grouse numbers on one moor when the keeper fell ill and was absent for several years.

Once grouse numbers fall, some interesting population dynamics all but guarantee that they will stay low, absent vigorous predator con- trol. Hudson's studies found that the predation rate actually *increases* as grouse numbers decline. This is the opposite of what all the classi- cal predator-prey models assume; they are based on the common- sense proposition that as the prey population increases, predators both increase in number as the available food source grows and also be- come more efficient hunters: The higher the density of prey, the easi- er it is to find one for a given degree of effort.

Figure 26. More foxes, fewer grouse: Two adjacent moors in northern England showed very similar trends in grouse population until the keeper on one moor fell ill and ceased to control predators; grouse numbers on that moor plummeted.

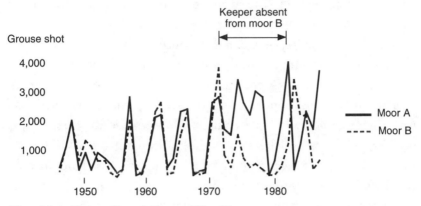

Adapted from Hudson, *Grouse in Space and Time*, 36.

In the case of grouse, however, three factors were working against this. First, predators such as peregrines are highly territorial. Over a given area, the number of grouse killed by peregrines will thus tend to be a constant. And that means that as grouse numbers fall, the proportion of the population killed each winter by peregrines will increase. Second, the effort by keepers to control foxes tends to have much the same effect. With no control, foxes would increase in step with the grouse. But modest control tends to stabilize fox numbers per unit area. Again, the fewer the grouse, the more proportionately are taken. Finally, at high densities, grouse are better able to defend themselves by forming into packs. Once they drop below a certain point they are picked off more readily than they otherwise would have been.

The practical consequence of this is that at the low densities that are now the norm on many Scottish estates, grouse are caught in a "predator trap." This is very similar to the situation we encountered in the fisheries model illustrated in figure 24c, where instabilities can send populations crashing downward once they drop on to the low end of the population curve. As numbers begin to fall, either through a temporary rise in fox numbers or a series of years of bad weather or a disease such as the tick-borne virus known as louping ill, the proportion of the population lost to predators increases, causing a further drop in

population, and so on. To get out of the trap requires intensive predator control to allow grouse numbers to get past the part of the curve
where this so-called inverse density-dependence reigns. Keepers tradi-
tionally left fox control to late spring, but Hudson's studies found that
fox predation reaches its peak in early summer and fall, suggesting the
need for year-round fox control if the grouse are to escape the trap.[24]

Some ecologists and population biologists have been suitably impressed by all of this. "We have now learned more from grouse about
what controls animal populations and how they can be managed than
from any other animals," says Andrew Dobson, a leading population
modeler, who has collaborated with Hudson on some of his research.[25] But in another example of the conspiracy of ignorance on
such issues, not everyone shares his enthusiasm. Keepers don't especially like the idea of having to change their routine or assume responsibility for the results; even some ecologists don't particularly like it,
Hudson says, when he stands up at a scientific meeting and says that
we actually can understand what's going on in an wildlife population.
Least amused of all were some nature lovers who, apparently unhappy
at the prospect that Hudson's work might be used to legitimize the
killing of now-protected raptors, sent Hudson threats to firebomb his
house when he began studying raptor predation of grouse.

There are fewer friends of trichostrongyle worms, which may explain
why Hudson received no death threats for his work in England trying to
determine the cause of the population cycles that were the problem there.
It had been known since the end of the nineteenth century that grouse
are host to this parasitic worm, and one early study even suggested that
crashes in the grouse population might be caused by the worms killing
off large numbers of the birds. But studies in the fifties had seemed to
rule this out; the worms simply did not kill their hosts in sufficient numbers to explain the cyclical crashes. Moreover, there was a growing body
of theoretical conventional wisdom which assumed that because parasites
depend upon their hosts' survival for their own survival, any successful
parasite would have coevolved with its host to a standoff. Population
models confirmed that parasite-induced mortality would actually stabilize the host population rather than cause it to fluctuate, and it is easy to
see why. Every time a parasite kills a host, it is destroying part of its habi-

tat; in a heavily infected population, the loss of one grouse means the loss of many parasites. If the grouse population starts falling, the worm population starts falling even faster, the infestation abates, and the remaining grouse population recovers that much faster.[26]

The whole thing seemed to be a dead end; Hudson thought he would do a quick study simply to eliminate parasitism as a factor. "I remember saying, 'I'm not going to spend the next ten years looking at grouse crap,'" Hudson says. "But that's exactly what I did." The key was precisely the fact that the worms were *not* killing the grouse. What they were doing was weakening them, which showed up months later in smaller clutches of eggs laid and poorer chick survival. Such a time lag is the classic mathematical condition for cycling in a population. The lag allows an infected grouse population to continue to expand before any effect of the parasites on total grouse numbers is felt—the effect only shows up the following year when fewer grouse hatch out. Meanwhile, the moors are becoming loaded with infective larvae that cause the infection rate to increase even after grouse numbers begin to fall. It is the time delay itself that causes the instability: When grouse numbers are falling, worm numbers are rising, and vice versa; the stabilizing tendencies of a parasite can never exert themselves on the host population because the two populations are always out of sync.

In Scotland, where total grouse numbers are much lower, the cycling tends not to occur because the host population is too widely dispersed to sustain a large parasite burden. For trichostrongyles, as with many parasites, transmission is everything; the only way an adult worm can cause the worm population to increase is by producing eggs which are passed in the host's feces and then hatch out into the free-living infective larvae that are eventually consumed by a feeding bird. A sparse population cannot maintain the transmission rate needed to sustain large worm populations.

In effect, cycling is a price of effective predator control—in the absence of predators, grouse can increase to the point that parasites become a problem. But there are some interesting, counterintuitive quirks about the interactions of predators and parasites. A small degree of predation can actually increase the grouse population when parasites are also present in significant numbers. This is because predation, up to a point, actually removes a greater proportion of the worm population than of the grouse population during the part of the cycle where the

Figure 27. Treating grouse for parasites produced dramatic results, eliminating the crashes in the boom-and-bust cycles that characterize grouse populations in northern England.

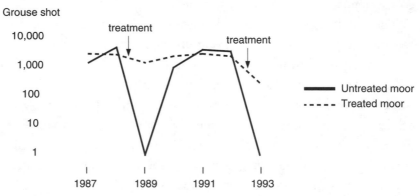

Adapted from *Game Conservancy Review of 1993*, 118.

grouse are heavily infested. The grouse population as a whole thus recovers faster than it otherwise would as it starts to crash under the burden of the peak worm load. The result is basically to lop off the bottom part of each cycle, raising average grouse numbers over time and damping out the cycles (see figure 28). As a result of these findings, a number of moor owners have begun to treat grouse directly with antiworm medication, either by spreading medicated grit or in some cases actually by capturing, dosing, and releasing the birds, with notable success.[27]

Hudson's work is impressive for its thoroughness, scope, and intellectual rigor; but this is not, as the saying goes, rocket science. He works out of a tin shed with a secretary, three field technicians, five post-docs, and three students on a budget of a half-million dollars a year to cover both Scotland and England; his equipment consists of radio tags, cameras, dissecting knives, test tubes to collect grouse feces in, and Land Rovers to drive around in. The practical problems of how animal populations behave and how they can be controlled are eminently solvable when the will exists to solve them.

The heather moors of Scotland and northern England exist today mainly because of grouse shooting. But a number of rare and threatened species of birds are secondary beneficiaries of grouse manage-

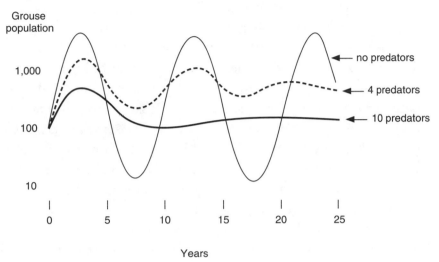

Figure 28. Two cheers for predators: Theoretical models suggest that modest amounts of predation can also even out the boom and bust cycles: When a fox kills a heavily parasitized grouse, the loss to the worm population is proportionately greater than the loss to the grouse population.

Adapted from Hudson, *Grouse in Space and Time,* 176.

ment practices. With much of the area of lowland heather moor lost to development, many species native to these areas have found refuge in the artificially maintained upland moors of Scotland and northern England. Golden plovers, greenshanks, merlin, and several other birds protected by the European Community are ground-nesting moorland residents that have clearly benefited both from the creation and maintenance of heather moorlands in Britain and from the control of foxes and other predators that prey on ground-nesting birds. There is a persuasive correlation between number of grouse or the number of keepers on the one hand and the number of plovers and other such birds on the other. Even a number of rare and endangered predatory birds, which are sometimes illegally persecuted by grouse moor keepers, seem on balance to benefit from grouse management; control of foxes helps ground-nesting hen harriers, and the maintenance of a high density of grouse provides an important source of prey for these raptors.[28]

It is a happy coincidence, to be sure, that what is good for the grouse that can pay their own way is also good for endangered species lacking a direct economic value. On the other hand, nature itself is nothing *but* coincidence. The diversity of life guarantees that some of the landscapes created and maintained for mankind's economic ends will invariably prove to be beneficial (or even crucial) to at least some species as an unintended side effect. The window ledges of skyscrapers have long provided habitat for pigeons and house sparrows; the sudden appearance of hawks on the Hanford nuclear site in Washington State in the 1980s coincided with the erection of high-tension-line towers, which the birds exploited as nesting sites.[29] While unintentional, these benefits are tokens of a largely untapped potential to apply ecological insights in a more purposeful fashion for the benefit of wildlife on lands that are managed primarily for production of a crop or other commodities. The solutions are never perfect, and a million acres of cropland will never substitute for a hundred acres of old-growth eastern hardwoods where the red-cockaded woodpecker is concerned. But the proposition is not all or nothing, nature or wasteland. Even those crassly commercial uses of the land that have recently come in for the special excoriation of environmentalists— clear-cuts, "monocultures" of trees or crops, rapaciously grazing cattle, for that matter even suburban developments—can with ingenuity be made to yield trees *and* owls, row houses *and* rabbits.

The potential importance of such crassly commercial lands to wildlife is manifest in the surprising ability of even highly altered landscapes to support wildlife in the nooks and crannies left—purely unintentionally—on farms, along roadsides, and even in cities. The acreage represented by these waste places is vast. Roads and roadsides in the United States occupy some twenty million acres; in North Dakota, roadsides and railway rights-of-way occupy twice the area of the state's wildlife refuges, game management areas, and federal waterfowl protection areas. Studies in Great Britain found that roadside vegetation serves as a breeding habitat for twenty of fifty native mammals, forty of two hundred birds, all six reptiles, five of six amphibians, and twenty-five of sixty butterflies. Roadside vegetation also serves as corridors linking larger chunks of wildlife habitat; as minimum viable population analysis showed, such corridors can greatly increase the chances of a species' survival over time.[30]

Studies of urban cemeteries have similarly found an astonishing variety of bird life often supported in very small areas. Chicago's urban cemeteries were found to be not only a haven but actually a colonization source for many species otherwise rare in cities, especially cavity-nesting birds such as woodpeckers, flickers, and flycatchers. Rather than being overrun by invading "urban" birds such as pigeons and house sparrows, these cemetery dwellers, quite the contrary, spilled over into adjacent parts of the city. A similar study in which forty-nine urban cemeteries in Boston were combed found more than a thousand nests and identified ninety-five species, including what the authors termed such "surprises" as the great blue heron, sparrow hawk, kingfisher, and bobwhite—this on a total of only seventeen hundred acres.[31]

For the most part, roadsides, urban parks, and cemeteries have not been managed with wildlife particularly in mind; the diversity of life already supported in these nooks and crannies of civilization represents only a fraction of a potential that could be fully realized through planting vegetation that provides food or cover, leaving grass uncut to provide concealment for ground-nesting birds, or other deliberate (and often not very expensive) management steps.

Waste places on farms play such an important role in providing wildlife habitat in many parts of the world that they can literally determine the fate of a species. And again, the cost of managing for wildlife on these acreages is often small or even trivial. In Illinois, as in much of the Midwest, the increasing practice of "clean farming" led to a dramatic decline in farm wildlife from the 1930s to the 1970s. Some of the change in farm practice was driven by overriding economic considerations, as subsistence farming characterized by a mix of crops and livestock gave way to cash grain farming, as tractors replaced horses, and as larger equipment proved incompatible with small fields criss-crossed with fencerows. Hayfields and pastures gave way to soybeans, fencerows were pulled out, crop residues were neatly tilled under. The major effect was to simplify and reduce the heterogeneity of the landscape. From 1939 to 1974, the number of bobwhite dropped by 78 percent and cottontails by 96 percent.

But government subsidies had as much to do with these changes as technology and the basic economics of the market, or perhaps even more. The Soil Bank program of the 1950s encouraged the set-aside of millions of acres of farmland for conservation, but subsequent gov-

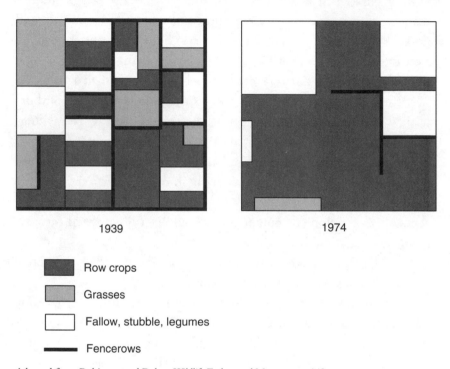

Figure 29. Patterns of agricultural land use have an enormous influence on wildlife populations. Mechanization and government subsidies have led to a much more homogeneous and simplified landscape, to the great detriment of farm wildlife. The diagram shows the changes in land use on one section of Illinois farmland.

1939   1974

Row crops

Grasses

Fallow, stubble, legumes

Fencerows

Adapted from Robinson and Bolen, *Wildlife Ecology and Management,* 149.

ernment programs sent conflicting signals, encouraging maximum production or, at best, idling plots for a single season at a time; the frequent mowing or replanting of cover crops under these programs may actually have done more harm than good, especially to ground-nesting birds. The more recent Conservation Reserve Program, which was established in 1985 and appears to provide just as much economic benefit to U.S. farmers, now takes a much longer view, requiring set-aside lands to be maintained in unmowed cover crops (mainly grass) or wood for at least ten years. Some thirty-four million acres have been enrolled in the program.[32]

Sometimes quite small changes in cultural practices can have dramatic effects on wildlife populations. In Britain, a set-aside program was introduced in 1993 with aims similar to those of the Conservation Reserve Program in the United States—reduce grain production to boost prices and simultaneously provide wildlife and game habitat. Game surveys found, however, that because the government regulations required mowing or cultivating of the set-aside acreages to control weeds, the number of pheasants on farms actually declined: The birds were attracted to the tall cover of grasses or naturally reseeded cereal stands and proceeded to nest there, only to be killed by mowers. Early spring cultivation also was found to kill vast numbers of overwintering sawflies, which form a major part of the diet of pheasant and partridge chicks.

In response to these research findings, the rules for 1994 were changed to allow the use of herbicides to control weeds instead. Studies also found that many of the seeming conflicts between good farming practice and wildlife conservation could be reduced or eliminated by adjusting the timing of mowing or cultivation. Early mowing will eliminate nesting and brooding habitat but will at least avoid enticing the birds to an untimely death; cultivating after mid-May will allow sawflies to emerge unscathed. In the United States, agricultural scientists have recently begun to promote the use of native grasses, as forage crops with a similar end in mind. Conventional hay and pasture grasses, such as timothy, orchardgrass, and bluegrass, grow quickly in the spring and are ready to be mowed just at the time turkey, bobwhite, cottontails, savannah sparrows, and other species begin to nest and brood; many nests are destroyed by farm machinery. These exotic grasses also form very dense stands that wildlife find it difficult to move through and forage in. But most of the native American grasses, all but forgotten for three centuries, grow more slowly and are ready for harvest in mid-July; because they are bunch-type grasses that grow in clumps, they also leave corridors for wildlife to travel through. While the exotics must be grazed or cut down to a few inches to maintain their maximum growth rate, the native "warm-season" grasses are most productive when mowed to fifteen to eighteen inches, thus leaving considerable cover for wildlife even after they are harvested. Farms where as little as 5 percent of the hayfields were replanted with warm-season grasses showed a tenfold increase in wild bird populations.[33]

The widespread adoption of conservation tillage practices, in which crop residues are left on the fields in the fall and the soil is not plowed over each year, has also helped to tip the balance back in favor of wildlife at no cost to farmers. In addition to reducing soil erosion, conservation tillage saves time and fuel by reducing the number of passes a farmer has to make over his fields; the crop residues provide both food and (on spring-fallowed fields) nesting cover.

The great wars over America's forests and rangelands, epitomized by the ongoing litigation over the spotted owl and the recent campaign by national environmental groups to tag the cow as an arch eco-villain, have distracted attention away from research that, intelligently and creatively applied, could go a long way toward reconciling other apparently irreconcilable demands on the land. Logging, if managed as part of a coherent plan across the landscape, is ready-made for maintaining the disturbance processes necessary for supporting a diversity of wildlife. A careful study of breeding bird populations in northern hardwood forests found that a mosaic of even-aged stands of timber supported twice as many species of birds as an extensive stand of uneven-aged, "climax" forest. Different species were adapted to different-aged stands; many species that showed up in the first few years following a clear-cut, such as flickers and some thrushes and warblers, disappeared after ten or fifteen years as the forest matured. But *every* species that could breed in uneven-aged stands was also found in one or more even-aged stands. By clear-cutting in rotation, the mosaic of different even-aged stands can be maintained, to the benefit of both loggers and birds. By contrast, a strict preservationist strategy would eventually lead to a mature, homogeneous, uneven-aged stand and a loss of bird diversity. Some modest compromises in harvesting practice can yield further benefits. Leaving unharvestable stubs standing in clear-cuts provided suitable breeding habitat for cavity nesting birds such as bluebirds and flickers early on. There is no doubt that some birds, especially woodpeckers and many owls, do indeed require old stands to nest in. But old-growth forest is not some ecological nirvana. It is just one of many different habitats that different species of birds have adapted to. A world of nothing but old-growth forest is just as much a biological desert as a world lacking in old-growth.[34]

Detailed studies of the interactions of wildlife, domestic animals,

Figure 30. Rotational clear-cutting can be compatible with successful habitat management for breeding birds. In northern New England hardwood forests, different species were found to be adapted to different-aged stands. No species found nesting in uneven-aged "climax" stands actually required that habitat—all could nest as well in at least one even-aged stand.

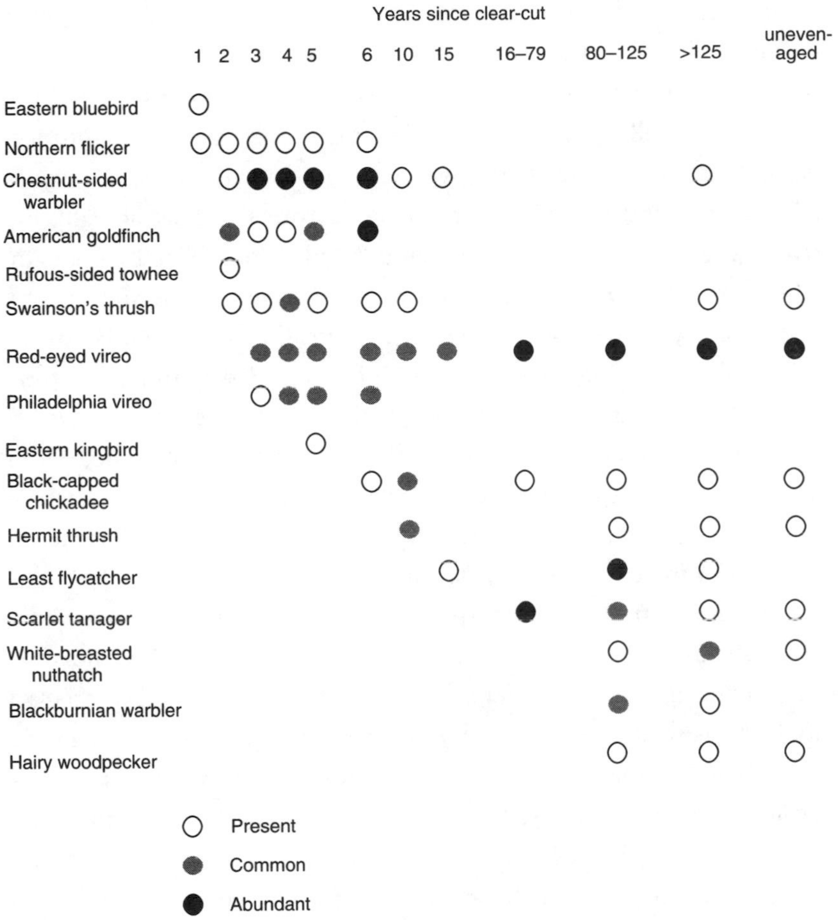

Years since clear-cut

Species	1	2	3	4	5	6	10	15	16–79	80–125	>125	uneven-aged
Eastern bluebird	○											
Northern flicker	○	○	○	○	○	○						
Chestnut-sided warbler		○	●	●	●	●	○	○			○	
American goldfinch	●	○	○	●		●						
Rufous-sided towhee	○											
Swainson's thrush	○	○	●	○		○	○				○	○
Red-eyed vireo		●	●	●		●	●	●	●	●	●	●
Philadelphia vireo		○	●	●		●						
Eastern kingbird						○						
Black-capped chickadee						○	●		○	○	○	○
Hermit thrush							●			○	○	○
Least flycatcher								○		●	○	
Scarlet tanager									●	●	○	○
White-breasted nuthatch										○	●	○
Blackburnian warbler										●	○	
Hairy woodpecker										○	○	○

○ Present

◐ Common

● Abundant

Adapted from DeGraaf, "Breeding Bird Assemblages," 160–61.

and vegetation have demonstrated how even that nemesis of good environmentalists everywhere, the cow, can be managed in a way that benefits wildlife. The usual solution to the problems of overgrazing on western rangelands that preservationists propose is getting rid of cattle. One grandiose scheme even envisions the wholesale replacement of cattle with more ecologically correct bison across the American West. While it is true that cattle have overgrazed many rangelands to the detriment of wildlife species that share these resources (overgrazing, for example, has been shown to destroy the cover that pronghorn fawns need to escape from predators), grazing when done properly can actually create resources for wildlife that would otherwise be unavailable. For example, when cattle were allowed to graze vegetation during spring and early summer and were then removed, the plants subsequently regrew to produce high-quality forage for overwintering elk. Without the initial grazing, the plants grew tough and rank, and the winter stands were of poor overall nutritional quality. The total production of cattle plus elk from this land actually increased as a result of the initial grazing. Moderate grazing by sheep or cattle, which prefer to eat grasses, can also encourage the subsequent growth of shrubby plants favored by browsers such as deer. By moving winter feeding stations for cattle, encouraging the animals to concentrate at various spots, cattle have even been used effectively to create the patchwork pattern of openings favored by bobwhite.[35] The enormous body of knowledge accumulated about domesticated animals' feeding behavior, which includes many practical experiments, is only beginning to be tapped by wildlife ecologists.

The purists still look down their noses at all of this, of course; animal husbandry is for people who go to cow colleges in the Midwest, not something that elite scientists at Harvard should be expected to muck about with. And farms and ranches hardly satisfy the image of nature that fills the romantic daydreams of nature lovers or the portentous theories of those self-declared heirs of Thoreau who fill academic journals with essays on "biophilia" and mankind's innate yearnings for the wild. An ecologist given the choice of studying birds in the tropical rain forests of the Amazon or cows on a farm in Iowa is rarely going to choose the latter.

On the other hand, those who would save nature might find it prudent to work with the material they have instead of so sedulously lamenting what they have not.

NINE

Reinventing the Wild

Vacant lots, railroad sidings, and the suburbs of Chicago do not rank high among the places where ecologists choose to do their fieldwork. They have not figured in any fund-raising appeals by preservationists out to save the wilderness, protect the earth's biodiversity, and halt the heedless destruction of the environment. They have inspired no known wildlife documentaries, bumper stickers, folk songs, or counterfeit speeches by Native American chiefs. Choked with weeds, derelict, abandoned, littered with trash mounds, rutted with motorcycle tracks, they are literally the last places on earth that nature lovers or ecologists would normally care to spend their time.

Yet beneath the all-too-obvious signs of human disturbance on these forsaken corners of nature lay an ecological gold mine waiting to be discovered. And that discovery, when it finally came, almost too late, launched one of the remarkable success stories of ecosystem restoration. Through a combination of historical detective work, sharp scientific insight, and no-holds-barred experimentation, a lost ecosystem was literally rediscovered and resurrected—something that could never have been accomplished through preservation alone.

Ecological restoration is the ultimate test of man's ability to under-

227

stand what makes an ecosystem tick. It may also prove the means by which we come to embrace the legitimacy and even the necessity of humans as active participants in nature, shaping and guiding the natural world.

The lost ecosystem that lay buried in a Chicago junkyard once stretched across thirty million acres of the Midwest. Where the prairies ended and before the forests began, vast open groves of oak woodlands dominated the landscape. Early settlers called them barrens, scattering timber, oak openings, prairie groves, or flats; the term favored by scientists today is oak savanna. The original savannas were exactly halfway between deep forest and wide-open prairie in their composition and form. Trees were spaced at graceful intervals, often as few as four per acre. In between, a rich carpet of prairie grasses and wildflowers covered the ground. Other low-lying plants, some more characteristic of the deep woods, some still prairielike, clustered around the half-shade at the base of the trees. The feeling was parklike and spacious.

The oak savannas that grew alongside the tallgrass prairies shared their rich, fertile soils. And so, like the prairies themselves, they were the first lands to be plowed under by the early settlers. The oak savanna quickly vanished. All that was spared were odd corners of fields cut off by roads or railways and odd bits of land near cities that had ironically been spared the plow by their urban location.[1]

When researchers finally began looking in these spots, they found among the trash and the tangle of weeds some remarkable and rare plants that had all but vanished from the region. Some equally rare animals that depended on those plants also began cropping up in these unexpected places. A railroad edge in northeastern Illinois harbored the silvery blue butterfly, a species that was once reported as common throughout the region but which had been spotted only twice in the past four decades—in one spot in 1951 and another in 1962.[2]

Other remnants of the lost savanna lands began turning up. Forests choked with underbrush and dark with the heavy shade cast by a solid canopy of tall oaks showed telltale signs that they were not what they seemed to be. The oaks carried wide crowns and large, spreading lower limbs, proof that they had spent their formative years in a sun-filled opening, not a dense and dark closed forest. Botanists who had been

Figure 31. Oak savannas—both broad expanses (shaded areas) and scattered stands (dots)—once covered thirty million acres in the eastern and midwestern United States.

Reprinted from Haney and Apfelbaum, "Characterization of Oak Savannas," fig. 1.

on the lookout for extremely rare and endangered prairie plants began finding the odd scattered specimen in these woods, too. They were not forests, after all. They were the degraded remnants of savannas.

By the 1980s, careful surveys had uncovered a little over one hundred remnants of this once vast ecosystem across the Midwest, a total of about six thousand acres—or about one–five thousandth of its original extent.[3] Still, by far the best specimens were alongside railroad tracks. The best single example of a surviving tallgrass savanna, believed to

closely resemble in appearance and structure the savannas as they existed before 1820, was located in a Chicago suburb next to the railroad.

Railroad rights-of-way were obviously protected from agricultural
development, but there was another factor at work that explained this
strange affinity between remnant ecosystems and trains. Until 1945
the railroads used coal-burning, and before that wood-burning, loco-
motives, and sparks frequently ignited the nearby vegetation. In much
of the rest of the Midwest and certainly in most of its woodlands, fire
had been suppressed by the arriving settlers, and the oaks grew to
form a closed canopy. Woody shrubs and trees that are easily destroyed by fire invaded, displacing the understory of deep-rooted
herbaceous prairie plants. Eventually the invaders formed their own
solid understory, which blocked off oak regeneration. Across much of
the oak savanna region, shade-tolerant (and fire-susceptible) sugar
maples are today taking over the forests altogether. In some well-stud-
ied systems, like the East Woods of the Morton Arboretum in Illinois,
the biological diversity of the woods has plummeted; all that is left
growing up from the forest floor today are seedling maples, seedling
ashes, sumac, and a few other woody species.[4]

Over the years, even many professional foresters had failed to recognize what was happening; they classified these lands as forests and
managed them as such. The best-preserved savanna remnants found
today within such "forests" are where mowed bridle paths or grazing
by cattle duplicated some of the effects of fire; the worst are where the
forests were "preserved" from the ravages of man.

Like fire, grazing and mowing selectively remove woody species
that invest much of their energy and growth above ground, while
opening up the ground to sunlight and favoring the prairie grasses and
wildflowers that resprout from roots after being cut or burned. But
grazing and mowing were no more a part of a deliberate policy of
landscape management than were sparks shot out by passing locomo-
tives. They were little more than lucky happenstance that inadvertently saved what managers had no idea was even being lost. A
publication by the Cook County Forest Preserve District in the 1920s
shows spacious, open groves with tablecloths spread beneath the trees
for picnics. Although fire had been eliminated decades before with
the arrival of settlers, grazing had kept the savanna relatively open in

the intervening time. But with the establishment of the forest preserve, the authorities evicted the cattle, and the woods quickly filled
in. "To transverse some of the same ground today," says Steve Packard
of the Nature Conservancy, who has been a leader in the savanna
restoration effort, "would require an armored vehicle, or dynamite.
Tackling it with merely a machete would be slow going."[5]

The role of fire in maintaining both prairie and savanna against the encroachment by invading trees and woody shrubs is now well known. It
was also well known to early writers and naturalists who described the
region. But such were the effects of Clements's ideas of climatic determinism and Smokey Bear's public relations efforts that the knowledge
was effectively lost, if not suppressed, and had to be rediscovered.

*Figure 32. Tallgrass savanna, then and now: Before European settlement, periodic
fires maintained an open canopy of bur oaks with hundreds of species of herbaceous
plants growing below. Without fire, other tree species quickly invade, displacing the
low-lying herbs and eventually forming a closed canopy that chokes off regeneration of the oaks as well. Restoration involves mechanical clearing of overgrown
brush and the reintroduction of fire.*

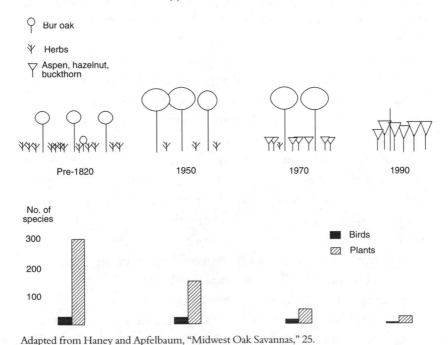

Adapted from Haney and Apfelbaum, "Midwest Oak Savannas," 25.

Workers who began studying oak savannas in the 1980s soon found a wealth of evidence on both the original extent of these lost ecosystems and the pattern of fires that had created them. Old land-survey records gave at least a rough idea of the location and extent of the savannas. A number of early naturalists noted that savannas tended to be found on sites that were in some way sheltered from the full force of the vast fires that surged across the open prairies. They were found far more often on the east sides of rivers and lakes than on the west sides, the water acting as a natural firebreak that sheltered the land as flames were driven eastward by the prevailing winds. Savannas also tended to occur in areas of broken terrain or on sandy soils where the vegetation was not lush enough to fuel an intense fire. Here the fires burned less often and at a lower intensity than on the open prairie; hot enough to kill off woody shrubs and many oak seedlings but not quite hot enough to eliminate the fire-resistant mature oaks that from time to time got a foothold.

Much of this process was accurately described as early as 1863 by the botanist Henry Engelmann (after whom the eponymous spruce is named). Other clues, left in the structure of the forests themselves, completed the story. A typical stand of degraded savanna is populated by several groups of oaks, each group of a single age class. Apparently, fires normally burned through the savannas nearly every year. Oak seedlings emerged and started to grow after each fire, only to be killed off in the next inferno. But once or twice every century or two, a series of wet years would disrupt this pattern. Seedlings would go unburned for ten or fifteen years, long enough to reach a diameter of an inch or so. At that size oaks become relatively resistant to burning. These periodic reprieves allowed a new generation of young trees to gain a foothold and grow to maturity. A precarious, tenuous balance maintained the savannas. Without fire they would be closed forest, without the rare but vital cessation of fire they would be open prairie.[6]

It was obvious to researchers studying the oak savannas that without active management, preservation of the remnants they were unearthing would be futile; soon there would not even be remnants of savanna recognizable within the rapidly changing forests. Many of these savanna fragments had already lost their character through "preservation"—that was precisely the problem. What they needed was less "protection" and more management.

There was little to go on, however, for constructing a management strategy: a general description of what savannas looked like in the nineteenth century, a general knowledge of prairie plant species, and a general understanding that burning was part of the process that made a savanna a savanna. But what ecological theory, historical evidence, or botanical knowledge could not supply, experimentation just possibly could. Significantly, the first major savanna restoration effort, which was led by Steve Packard, began almost as an accident.

Packard's work started not as an effort to resurrect or even rediscover some long-lost ecosystem. It was rather a much more modest project to bring back to health a small patch of tallgrass *prairie* that had survived within one of the forest preserves that stretched from within Chicago itself to the northern suburbs. Prairie restoration has become a routine, even a commercial business these days. Seed mixes containing prairie grasses and wildflowers are readily available; for the rarer plants, Packard and his group of volunteers collected seeds from odd spots of remnant prairie. The prairie patches in the forest preserve were small, a few acres at most, and the plan was to expand them by clearing out surrounding brush and sowing prairie plants on the cleared ground.

Clearing out the overgrown ash, elm, and cottonwood was a straightforward enough decision (although not without controversy itself: many visitors and even some of Packard's own volunteers from the local Sierra Club vigorously protested cutting down the trees at first). But the problem was what to do about the old oaks that grew scattered among the thickets. How far should they let the prairie fires they planned to set as part of the restoration effort burn into the "forest"? Intrigued by the idea of restoring the picture they had read about of prairie plants growing right up to scattered oaks, they decided to let the fires burn as far as they would go. That turned out not to be very far. In the forests of Yellowstone and other parts of the West, years of fire suppression had led to the accumulation of huge fuel loads of dead timber. But on the prairies and savannas, fire is fueled by the annual growth of grasses and herbs that each fall die and dry to a thick bed of tinder. In Packard's woods, fire suppression had eliminated this source of fuel altogether, as the prairie grasses and herbs were replaced by woody thickets. Dry prairie grass forms a mat of concentrated tinder a foot or two thick; an overgrown thicket contains much less fuel, and it is spread out over five to ten feet of vertical space.

The raging grass fires the restorers set stopped dead when they reached the thicket. Finally, a more aggressive effort at cutting and burning did the trick, carrying the flames to the base of the trees.[7] But even after seeding the burnt and cleared ground below the oaks with prairie plants, a no-man's land remained around each tree, where neither prairie nor forest herbs grew well. This seemed to contradict the picture of the oak savannas that both historical and theoretical evidence had painted. The prairie grasses stopped short of the oaks, leaving bare ground that was rapidly invaded by thistles, dandelions, and other exotic weeds.

At one site, grasses did grow right up to the base of the trees, a finding that caused momentary elation, until Packard realized that the grasses consisted of three totally unfamiliar species—none of which were ones that he had included in his seed mix. He sadly concluded that they were alien interlopers.

What had appeared to be a failure, however, was actually an experimental discovery of remarkable significance. Indeed, it was a discovery that has become something of a landmark in establishing ecological restoration as both an end and a means. Putting together a functioning ecosystem is the ultimate test of our understanding of what ingredients and interconnections are required to make an ecosystem work; but at the same time, *trying* to put together a functioning ecosystem may be the only way to truly learn what those ingredients and interconnections are. Packard found that the three mystery grasses were not aliens but rather some rare and unfamiliar natives—wedge grass, wood reed, and Virginia wild rye. On closer examination other "oddball" plants began showing up among the thistles and dandelions growing in the partial shade of the oaks—tinker's weed, Solomon's seals, hazelnuts. They shared a number of characteristics. Unlike open-prairie plants, which are long-lived perennials that require full sun to become established, these plants that thrived in the partial shade of the oaks were more "fugitive" in their character. They were annuals or biennials or clambering vines, traits that allowed them to move rapidly to exploit the more irregular colonization opportunities created by the erratic burning patterns that fashioned the savannas in the first place. While the prairie plants produced light, wind-borne seeds, these "oddball" species yielded up fruits, nuts, and berries, precisely what one would expect for plants that can use such forest-edge animals as turkeys, squirrels, and deer to spread their seeds.

Further historical research found that many of these species had in fact been identified in 1846 by one nineteenth-century botanizing physician who lived in the area and published his observations in a local journal called the *Prairie Farmer:* 118 plants were listed by the good doctor as characteristic of "barrens." Seed-hunting expeditions to the shady margins of railroad rights-of-way, bridle paths, mowed picnic groves, or other spots selected for having 10 to 80 percent canopy turned up more likely specimens that were sown under the oaks. Within three years, hundreds of thousands of rare and uncommon grasses and wildflowers were flourishing beneath and between the oaks.[8]

Packard's pioneering work has inspired efforts to restore other types of lost oak savanna, with equally remarkable results. Unlike the tallgrass savannas, which grow on soils long coveted for farmland, the sand savannas of much of the upper Midwest have poor soils and have tended to be preserved in larger blocks, albeit in the degraded form of closed forests. But probably because of their poor soils, they have proved less susceptible to invasion by exotics and have preserved more of their original savanna species either in dormant seeds or tiny wisps of vegetation that have hung on as the forest has grown dark and dense around them. Some eighty thousand acres of dense forest, much of it in eight-to-ten-thousand-acre parcels, are now being returned to savanna by the reintroduction of fire. The very rare Mead's milkweed, a plant on the federal endangered species list, doubled in population following a vigorous series of controlled burns on the Shawnee National Forest in southern Illinois; a number of the plants flowered for the first time in several years following the burn. At the Moquah Barrens on the Chequamegon National Forest in Wisconsin, the rare ternate grape-fern, a plant known from only two other sites in northwestern Wisconsin, likewise showed a stunning increase following the reintroduction of fire to what managers are now forthrightly calling these "fire-starved" forests.[9]

Restoration has always been viewed with a certain amount of aloof disdain by ecologists. At best it's landscaping; at worst it's nothing but glorified civil engineering. In any volume devoted to restoration, there are plenty of papers about concrete anti-erosion mats and the right way to excavate dirt with heavy machinery.

Success stories, such as the oak savanna work, are slowly chipping away at this image of restoration as something only for bulldozer operators. But beyond the practical successes, the power of restoration as an experimental technique, one that can resolve fundamental questions about community ecology, is beginning to make ecologists sit up and take notice. Packard has referred to his work as "research by restoration"; he said that at first "we weren't picking up on what the savanna was trying to tell us." The only real way to find out which plants are part of the oak savanna ecosystem is to plant them. By modifying the landscape and sowing seeds, Packard's team "asked" the natural system for the answer.

Ecologists are used to piecing together clues from whatever combination of circumstances they happen to stumble across in nature, which is rather like trying to figure out what the volume control on a radio does by observing the behavior of various radios one finds in the neighborhood and noting where the volume control is set on each at the time. After looking at enough radios, it might be possible to make a plausible case that the volume control adjusts the loudness, though it would be impossible to be certain; an equally plausible theory might be that when the knob is turned up high the radio plays rock music, but when it is low it plays easy listening or classical. Being allowed to do the "experiment"—giving the knob a turn oneself—would settle the matter in short order. Restoration is a way to do controlled experiments on natural systems that on ethical, legal, and practical grounds would otherwise be impossible.

In such an enterprise, the failures can be as instructive as the successes. In fact, the failures can often be more instructive because they serve to separate the processes or components that matter vitally to an ecosystem from those that do not matter. They can point out what is missing from our understanding of what makes an ecosystem work; in the context of the earlier discussion of what controls populations, failures serve to identify keystone species or vital ecosystem "services" that other species depend upon.

Indeed, the rediscovery in the 1940s of the essential role played by fire in maintaining the conditions that prairie plants need to grow was the direct result of one such failure. The very first restoration project that aimed to reproduce a native ecosystem, as opposed to merely "reclaiming" eroded agricultural lands or forests, began in the fall of 1935 when a team of workers from the Depression-era Civilian Conservation Corps began digging up sod at the University of Wisconsin Arboretum. The project was Aldo Leopold's, and his plan was to replace the old farm fields with a replica of tallgrass prairie. So the sod was dug, the seeds were sown, and the artificial prairie looked more like the lawn in a suburban subdivision than like a prairie: Bluegrass reinvaded and dominated the prairie grasses. Years of failure finally led to a classic series of experiments in the 1940s that attempted to discover what went wrong. Experimental plots in the arboretum's prairie were burned at different times of year and at different intervals. The result was the first published studies of the ecological role of fire in prairies. The research also marked the turning point in prairie restoration efforts at the University of Wisconsin and elsewhere.[10]

Other failures have been equally illuminating. Descriptive studies going back to the last century established that many plants carry fungi in or on their roots, and that the fungi tend to be especially abundant in nutrient-poor soils. But their function and ecological role was poorly understood. It took restoration experiments to do what description could not. Repeated failures to reestablish a forest on a severely degraded site in the Klamath Mountains of southern Oregon that had been clear-cut in the 1960s was one such experiment that pointed to the pivotal role played by these soil microorganisms. The soil within the clear-cut was found to be severely depleted in the root fungi. The original loss of trees was compounded by the failure of replanted seedlings; each failure caused a further loss of soil fungi in a process that spiraled downward over twenty years. When new trees were planted and inoculated with less than half a cup of soil taken from a healthy tree plantation, growth rates doubled and survival rates for the newly planted seedlings increased 50 percent. Other similar experiences—oaks and pines planted on soils that have not previously harbored fungi-bearing plants die or fail to grow well unless inoculated—have helped to establish the role that the fungi play in increasing nutrient uptake, fighting off root diseases, and in physically altering the soils so that they hold water and nutrients better.[11]

Restoration experiments are a way to figure out how natural ecosystems work; they are also a way to figure out what went wrong in natural systems that are no longer working properly. Eugene Morton, an expert on tropical birds at the National Zoological Park, knew from earlier studies that forty-two species of birds had disappeared from Barro Canal Island, a sanctuary in the Panama Canal maintained by the Smithsonian Tropical Research Institute and the Panamanian government. Most had vanished for the straightforward reason that the northeastern half of the six-square-mile island had been open ground at the time the island was formed in 1913 by the digging of the Panama Canal and Gutan Lake; they were nonforest species that lost their habitat as the forest matured and took over the island. But the disappearance of fourteen of the birds could not be so readily explained. Some researchers chalked the loss up to E. O. Wilson's biogeographic theory: The area of the island itself rigidly determined the number of species that would exist on it. The small size of Barro Canal Island had simply doomed a certain number of birds.

But of course that was no explanation at all. Morton wanted to know precisely what had caused these forest birds to vanish. That was clearly a more sensible approach than the fatalistic one implied by island biogeography; for one thing, it might point out specific steps that could be taken to halt the loss of the same or other species elsewhere in the tropics or even reintroduce them. The alternative offered by biogeographic theory, as we have seen, was simply to blame it all on the loss of tropical forest.

Trying to find out what caused a vanished bird to vanish is, to go back to our radio analogy, a bit like trying to determine the effect of the volume control by examining radios that are missing the speaker. So Morton set out to reintroduce two of the missing species, the song wren and the white-breasted wood wren, both common on the mainland, and follow their progress. "I did not expect this reintroduction to be successful," he explained; "what I wanted was to find out what had caused their demise . . . by observing my introduced population as it became extinct."[12]

The white-breasted wood wrens chose to settle not in the mature forest but in small patches of second growth that remained along the shore and in cleared areas created by the fall of large trees. That alone suggested that the cause of their demise was quite similar to that which had doomed the twenty-eight other nonforest species which could not survive in the island's maturing forests. The bird had been misclassified as a forest species.

The song wren was more of a mystery, however. One theory, that it had been outcompeted by a species known as the antbird, seemed plausible on the basis of the sort of descriptive studies that ecologists normally rely on for such things: Since the disappearance of the song wren, antbird populations had become considerably more abundant on the island. But Morton's reintroduced song wrens settled at sites that bore no relation, one way or the other, to the distribution of antbirds. Competition seemed an unlikely explanation.

The song wrens proceeded to nest and bear young. But in a little over two years, all but a single bird of the original seven pairs released were gone. Most had been killed by predators. And it soon became clear why. Song wrens use their nests both for breeding and as a regular home that they return to every night. Their nests are cleverly fashioned to resemble the clumps of debris that get washed downstream in high water and caught in the crotch of a tree; the birds build nests along streams and even orient the nests downstream so that they more closely resemble the originals. It is all a remarkable evolutionary adaptation to the problem of hiding from night-prowling predators. The trouble on Barro Canal Island is that there are few streams. Moreover, the birds apparently mistook trails cut through the woods for streams and built most of their nests right along the trails. Instead of looking like one of countless piles of junk, their nests now stood out—and stood out right on the paths already heavily used by coatis and other predators. The apparently trivial alteration of the habitat involved in cutting trails proved fatal to the song wren. "While island biogeographic theory may predict overall numbers of species that may become extinct," Morton concluded in a tactful phrase heavy on conditionals, "it does not reveal the underlying causes of extinction for any one species." Pilot reintroductions, however, can. The most interesting thing about Morton's experiment is that it was *designed* to fail. The best way to learn how an ecosystem works is to try to make one—and not quite succeed.[13]

Of course, even many large-scale restoration projects that were not intended to fail have also failed. That has often prompted criticism from environmentalists that restoration is too costly and too uncertain in its results and that even when it succeeds, the end product is never a 100-percent faithful reproduction of the original. Deals by which developers agree to create new wetlands to replace ones they have drained and paved over to build highways or shopping malls on top of have come in for particular scorn. "Most mitigation stories read like horror stories," one state environmental official told *Science* magazine. Recreated marshes dry up and vanish; key species are missing; holes are blasted in solid rock to create vast "ponds" to fill up the required restoration area, since water is easier to "restore" than the complex assemblage of vegetation that fringe the water in a true wetland. Although prairie restoration is fairly cheap—$125 an acre for the initial site preparation and seeding plus $12 to $18 an acre per year to maintain a three-year burning rotation—some restoration efforts are proving astronomically expensive. A plan to restore the floodplain of the Kissimmee River, which feeds the Everglades, and to restore the natural meander to the river, which had been dredged out into a nice straight channel by the U.S. Army Corps of Engineers in the 1960s, is estimated to cost close to half a billion dollars, earning it the epithet of "environmental pork barrel" by some critics.[14]

Yet many of the failures reflect not bad science but bad management. The belief that a site can simply be restored and then left to run on autopilot has actually been reinforced by many environmentalists who support restoration but who simply see it as a way to add to the stockpile of "protected" land. They view it still as a fight against developers and rapers of the land, a way to save land that would otherwise be "irretrievably lost to conservation."[15] This approach may on occasion work. Clear-cut areas of tropical forests do indeed exhibit some "self-healing" processes, as do other disturbances where an adjacent recolonization source remains intact. The Gogol Valley of Papua New Guinea was rated an environmental disaster area after clear-cutting; eighteen months later the regrowth by secondary tree species was so dense that it was impossible for a person to walk through, and after ten years primary forest species occupied 70 percent of the area.[16]

But these are the exceptions. Restoration is usually but the first step in an ongoing process. Restoration is never finished. The fact that even the best restored sites are never 100-percent faithful copies or require tinkering and adjustment to make them work or continuing management to keep them working is no more than a restatement of all of the realities of nature we have encountered in this book. Perfect restoration is an impossibility for precisely the same reason perfect preservation is an impossibility. A restored population will be different from the "original" for the same reason that the "original" is different from another "original" elsewhere in space or the same original at a different moment in time. Even if they look the same, they will never have the same exact age-population structure or genetic make-up. Some reintroductions of species will fail or produce unexpected results, for the same reason that otherwise identical South Pacific islands often harbor different assemblages of birds. The luck of the draw appears to have as much to do with it as anything else. On some islands one species just happened to arrive first and excluded certain others; on other islands a different species took advantage of a shift in the winds or weather or a falling tree or a bad year for some parasite and elbowed its way in.[17]

To damn restored ecosystems for their failure to be "self-sustaining" is a special absurdity; it is to demand of restoration a feat that nature itself is incapable of performing. Practicing restoration forces us to confront these ambiguities about nature, as disappointing as they may at first be to our cherished dreams of perfection and order. Restoration is a hands-on drill, a practical demonstration of the vagaries and randomness and impermanence of nature, imperfections we might otherwise try to deny with our mere museumgoer's acquaintance with her. A visitor to the Everglades might nurse a vision of ideal nature as a place where no trace of man should ever intrude; a restorer trying to bring back a dwindling butterfly population or fight off an invasion of Australian pines takes a more sober view of the reality.

Restoration is also a step toward viewing ecological problems from a broader perspective than we are used to. There is little point in trying to save the Mead's milkweed if there is no suitable habitat for the Mead's milkweed to be saved in. Trying to turn the landscape upside down to hack out or cobble together a habitat for one endangered species or other may actually be harder work than reassembling an entire functioning ecological community that supplies the habitat by virtue of landscape-wide processes.[18]

The act of restoration brings us face to face with the stuff that ecosystems are made of. A doctor does not lose his capacity for humanity or love or his ability to admire beauty by the fact of his having dissected a corpse; but neither is he likely to become a Christian Scientist as a result of the experience. To the extent that restoration efforts make us realize that restoration is "never done," that is only a virtue: Restoration may be the means to reacquaint us with our responsibilities to the natural world, responsibilities that in the name of aesthetics or religion or even "ecology" we have tried so hard to renounce.

CONCLUSION

Nature on
Human Terms

Our love of nature has been everything but true. It has been the refined and self-congratulatory love of the aesthete, at first; the desperate love of the sinner looking for peace or redemption or a miraculous cure; the sensuous but self-absorbed love of the libertine; at times even the cynical and manipulative love of the political organizer looking for a propaganda coup. We expect nature to be a thing of beauty, a place of harmony and peace, a cure for our ailments, or a slogan in the war against the military-industrial-technological complex. As long as we don't wake up, nature obliges, satisfying the fantasies of our dreams.

"Human kind cannot bear very much reality," wrote T. S. Eliot; when myths and stories have filled our minds for so long, they become an investment that is most easily protected by buying more of the same. Nature has been an impenetrable mystery for so long that the doses of reality have been small, infrequent, and unburdensome. But as ecology at last becomes a science and begins to illuminate and explain and even master nature, the shocks have become greater and harder to shrug off. The mystic turn that the environmental movement has taken in recent years is perhaps a sign that the reality is becoming too much even for dreamers to bear.

But there are other reasons why we are so reluctant to face up to the realities of nature. If nature is beauty or the embodiment of self-regulating harmony or, better yet, the unknowable part and particle of God himself, then our job is humble and simple. But if nature is comprehensible and manageable, we suddenly have serious responsibilities—not just to see that nature does what it ought to but, infinitely harder, to figure out what that "ought to" is. "I slept and dreamed that life was beauty. / I woke—and found that life was duty."[1] It is not just mystics who prefer to dream.

Ecological science has much to say about how to keep to the course we set for nature. The careful studies of how predators and prey and parasites and hosts interact, how nutrients cycle, how competitors fill their niches, and how disturbance forms habitat can help us grow Kirtland's warblers or wheat, red-cockaded woodpeckers or tallgrass savanna.

It has far less to say about what course to set in the first place. Some great minds and many not so great minds have labored long and hard on this question, with no convincing or enduring result. Aldo Leopold, a great champion of human stewardship and management, was one of the great minds who struggled with the question of what, after all, *is* good stewardship and good management. He spoke of the "beauty" and "integrity" of biotic communities, of reinforcing the links between man and the biota and the soil; in the end all he had really said was that he knew it when he saw it. Much more recently there have been many sober and laborious efforts to scientifically define "ecosystem health"; a conference sponsored by the Environmental Protection Agency devoted solely to this question attracted many papers, filled with soaring flights of rhetoric. But even a squinty-eyed logistician with a rusty shotgun might have brought them to earth, revealing them on closer inspection for what they were, the plainest of tautologies. A healthy ecosystem, they said, is an ecosystem that is, well, healthy. Or, according to the few papers that got down to details, one that is "natural." "To gain consensus on a measure of ecological health," wrote one of the contributors, "[ecologists] must assume that an ecosystem somehow behaves as though it has a goal or an optimal state. . . . I see no alternative to it. If we do not accept the idea of a goal or accept at least the possibility, we are open to the accusation that ecologists are arrogant with regard to nature and can manipulate its processes for the will of humankind without risk of ultimate failure."[2]

And so we are back to square one, to ideas that simply do not stand up to the realities of a biological world that is ever changing in answer to the vagaries of climate, the perversity of chaos, the dynamics of fire and flood, and the long, long influence of man himself as a part of it all. Some who cling to the old ideas about balance and order and purpose in nature do so because they can find no handhold on the rough terrain they have been thrust upon and fear that what they really are on is a slippery slope. If it is permissible to cut down trees, set fires, kill predators, and release new species, what, then, is impermissible? "Hands off" is a simple rule to apply in practice, if for no other reason than that it is based on frank human conduct rather than subtle biological complications. Its disadvantage is that it has nothing to do with the realities of nature.

Some researchers have tried to use stability as the measure of whether we're treating nature right, but many others who have looked closely are dubious. Even the most "natural" and "undisturbed" systems are variously stable, unstable, or somewhere in between, and they have an annoying habit of changing over time for no clear reason. An extensive survey identified forty-nine studies that tracked biological populations over a long enough time to even out short-term demographic fluctuations; it found a continuum of stability with no clear dividing line between stable and unstable populations. Only parasites, as a group, exhibited uniformly little variation in their numbers over time, a finding that is unfortunately of rather limited utility. "Attempts to determine the status or stability of recovering ecosystems may be difficult, or even impossible," the researchers concluded.[3]

Campaigners on behalf of global biodiversity nonetheless continue to invoke stability both as the paramount scientific measure of ecosystem health and as the prime scientific argument for preserving the rain forests; in doing so, they are doubly wrong. Stability is not only an inadequate measure of how an ecosystem is doing; worse, it doesn't even support the case for diversity. Diverse systems in fact are unlikely to be any more stable than less diverse ones. Biodiversity proponents have recently made much of experiments conducted in the "Ecotron," an enclosed grasslands community put together at Imperial College in London; these and similar experiments elsewhere showed that communities that contain a greater variety of plant species are more productive, and more resilient in the face of drought, than simpler ones. But as many ecologists have been quick to point out, there are plenty of examples that show just the opposite. A monoculture of alien eucalyptus trees is far more productive than the native California scrubland it invades, apparently because its deep roots can reach down to underground water inaccessible to the native species. Agricultural systems generally produce more pounds of plant matter per acre than more complex native plant communities. And many monocultures are exceedingly stable, the grasses of a salt marsh, for example. If the case for protecting a tropical rain forest rests on its stability or productivity, an equal case could be made for an Iowa farm. In any event, the fundamental finding by mathematical ecologist Robert May about chaos in ecological systems remains unrefuted: More complex systems are actually less stable, not more stable, than simple ones. The natural tendency of all biological systems is to fall apart and simplify. The pressures of competition and evolution are fighting a never-ending battle against these forces of mathematical entropy. Those who would draw a sweeping connection between the stability of an experimental grassland community in the face of a single episode of drought and the stability of all life on the planet for eons to come as a case for preserving the tropical rain forests are playing a semantic game; these two sorts of "stability" have nothing in common. Stability, in the long run, has more to do with evolution than with diversity; it carries no brief for one management policy over another.[4]

A more promising route might be to look at ecosystem functions, or "services," in deciding whether we're doing the right thing. The cycling of water and nutrients, the stability of the soil, the maintenance of disturbance processes are surely all measures of whether an ecosystem is "working." Whether it is a sufficient definition is another matter. Only a few keystone species typically play a crucial role in mediating these processes; they often don't include the ones we seem to care so much about, like spotted owls or Florida panthers or whooping cranes.

But perhaps that is the real point, after all. Why do we try so hard to make our desires into scientific imperatives? Why do we look to science to vindicate our all-too-human aspirations? If we would save an endangered species or maintain a vignette of an ancient landscape or fill a hillside with grouse or raise food and timber to feed and house ourselves, science can help us attain those goals and even reconcile some of them one with another. Science is a tool, a means to an end. It can tell us if we are holding true to the direction we meant to travel in. But it cannot set the course for us. We are trying so hard to find an objective, scientific standard that produces the "right" answer; why not save a step, since that "right" answer is ultimately no less than the sum of many things that have little if anything to do with science. From the beginning to the end the goals we must seek in nature are human goals, goals that reflect an imperfect mix of morality and commerce, aesthetics and need, stewardship and politics. We might as well admit it and get on with the job. Having renounced the irresponsibility of living a pipe dream, we cannot duck the responsibility that comes with embracing reality. Part of facing up to the realities and complexity of nature is admitting that any approach we take will be incomplete, imperfect, provisional, experimental—a compromise based on many competing objectives and a good deal of uncertainty about the result. The important thing is to try. When we face difficult problems in our personal lives, most of us don't look to a sociology textbook, expecting to find the answer lying there; we bring to bear the sum of our experience, knowledge, and ethical convictions. Mistakes and disappointments are inevitable. To do nothing because we cannot know the future with certainty is a stance that we seem to have no trouble rejecting as absurd in every field but ecosystem management.

The very act of trying holds out hope not just for nature but for ourselves. We have, in enshrining nature, alienated ourselves from her. Our relationship is that of the voyeur, at best. Environmentalism has bequeathed us with a paralyzing sense of species guilt that has left us believing that the only proper way to approach nature is not at all. "Ironically, such a perspective turns us all—hiker, birder, and strip miner alike—not into members of the community but into users and consumers of the natural landscape," writes William Jordan of the University of Wisconsin Arboretum. "It is largely non-participatory, and engages only a fraction of human interests and skills." And so it is ultimately self-defeating. We are asked to adopt a new ethic toward nature, to love and revere her, but never touch her.

What a contrast is the spirit of the restoration projects at Jordan's institution. Where the arboretum once found its biggest problem was fighting a futile war against "overuse" by the visiting public, now it cannot get enough volunteers to help out on all the restoration projects it hopes to carry out. A vast cadre of enthusiastic volunteer preservationists has already joined Packard's restoration efforts in the Chicago area. Participation in such projects "liberates us from our position as observers of the community into the role of citizenship," Jordan says.

Perhaps the best model for us to follow is that of the gardener, who, as Frederick Turner has written, "handles nature with respect but without self-abnegation." He brings the full scope of human aptitudes to bear on the landscape, aesthetic, scientific, utilitarian, even moral; he knows that what he is fashioning will reflect his creativity and wisdom; but he knows in the end that the effort is a joint one.[5]

However important mathematical and theoretical ecology will ultimately prove to the effort, still we must start, and starting means overcoming not so much scientific ignorance as the cultural taboos that remain from a century or more of nature worship. "The best advice . . . is to try," write two scientists who have much experience in ecological restoration. "One does not have to be a scientist, or even have a high school diploma, in order to experiment. All it takes is common sense—perhaps backed up by a little intuition."[6]

NOTES

Chapter 1. "Good Poetry, Bad Science"

1. Cronon, *Changes in the Land,* 142–45.
2. "Is Bambi Hogging the Forest?" *Washington Post,* December 1, 1992.
3. Westman, "Managing for Biodiversity," 29; Hudson, *Grouse in Space and Time,* 46; "Rain Forests Seen as Shaped by Human Hand," *New York Times,* July 27, 1992.
4. Williamson, "Balancing Act," 26.
5. Gore, *Earth in Balance,* 2; NRDC example quoted in Kaufman, "How Nature Really Works," 17–18; Miller, "Promoting Ecological Awareness"; Massachusetts Society for the Prevention of Cruelty to Animals, *Animals, People, and the MSPCA,* 10.
6. Botkin, *Discordant Harmonies,* 1, 5.
7. Peter Chesson, quoted in Kaufman, "How Nature Really Works," 18.
8. Brower quoted in Hamilton, "Enduring Wilderness."
9. McLaughlin, "Ecosystem Management in Rondeau," 6.
10. Maryland Cooperative Extension Service, "Deer in Our Forests."
11. Stephen Smith, quoted in McLaughlin, "Ecosystem Management in Rondeau," 7.
12. Cronon, *Changes in the Land,* 50–51; Romme and Despain, "Yellowstone Fires of 1988."
13. Jordan, Gilpin, and Aber, eds., *Restoration Ecology,* 332–33; Pielou, *After the Ice Age,* 299.
14. Letters, *Harper's,* December 1991, 4.
15. Mlot, "Isle Royale: End of an Era?"
16. Jorgensen, *Guide to New England's Landscape,* 188, 191–95; Pollan, *Second Nature,* 209–11, 237.

17. Cronon, *Changes in the Land,* 112–14.
18. Jorgensen, *Guide to New England's Landscape,* 191.
19. See Pollan, *Second Nature,* 213. The forest was purchased in 1883 by the Calhoun family, whose property adjoins the tract, specifically to protect it from logging; it remained in the family until 1967 when they deeded it to the Nature Conservancy.
20. Quoted in Pollan, *Second Nature,* 236–37.
21. Westman, "Managing for Biodiversity," 29.
22. Jordan, Gilpin, and Aber, eds., *Restoration Ecology,* 333.
23. Haney and Apfelbaum, "Structure and Dynamics of Oak Savannas," 24–25; Haney and Apfelbaum, "Characterization of Oak Savannas," 2.
24. Caldicott, *If You Love This Planet,* 15; Worster, *Nature's Economy,* ix.
25. Gore, *Earth in Balance,* 50.
26. John Harper, in Jordan, Gilpin, and Aber, eds., *Restoration Ecology,* 38–39.
27. Worster, *Nature's Economy,* ix–x.
28. Ibid., 240–42.
29. Taylor, "Disagreeing on the Basics," 32. For a discussion of the idea of wilderness as a modern cultural "taboo" and the use and limitations of this idea, see Pollan, *Second Nature,* 214–25.
30. Vicki Miller of "ARK II," a Canadian animal-rights and environmental organization, quoted in Mowat, *Rescue the Earth!* 118; Singer, *Animal Liberation,* 226.
31. See, for example, Worster, *Nature's Economy,* 230–32.
32. Mowat, *Rescue the Earth!* 248–65; Gore, *Earth in Balance,* 260. As additional authority for this view, Mowat cites a woman he sat next to on an airplane one time (he didn't catch her name), who told him: "When the womb of our Earth mother is being hurt, women feel it inside themselves" (p. 247).
33. Berman, *Reenchantment of the World,* 15–18, 20–21; Fox, *Coming of the Cosmic Christ,* 1–2; Gore, *Earth in Balance,* 12, 367.
34. McKibben, "End of Nature," 70, 73, 104.
35. Katz, "Call of the Wild."
36. McKibben, "End of Nature," 74, 76.
37. Nash, *Wilderness and the American Mind,* 238–49.
38. Dick DeGraaf, quoted in Williamson, "Balancing Act," 28.
39. Leopold, *Sand County Almanac,* vii; McKibben, "End of Nature," 104. There is a vast literature of denunciations of science by academic humanists; most of it focuses on the supposedly "reductionist" and "mechanistic" approach of modern science, usually blamed upon Bacon and Newton and especially upon Newton's metaphor of the universe as a clockwork. Many of these critics combine an antipathy for materialism and capitalism in society with a personal distaste for mathematics. See, for example, Merchant, *Death of Nature;* Merchant, *Ecological Revolutions;*

Evernden, *Natural Alien;* Worster, *Nature's Economy;* Oelschlaeger, *Idea of Wilderness;* Berman, *Reenchantment of the Earth;* Daly, *Gyn/Ecology.*

Chapter 2. The Cult of the Wild

1. Cronon, *Changes in the Land,* 5.
2. Rees, "The Taste for Mountain Scenery," 306.
3. Botkin, *Discordant Harmonies,* 85–86; Albanese, *Nature Religion in America,* 34–35; Nash, *Wilderness and the American Mind,* 26, 29, 36.
4. Nash, *Wilderness and the American Mind,* 44; Rees, "The Taste for Mountain Scenery," 306–7.
5. Rees, "The Taste for Mountain Scenery," 307.
6. Elliott, "Dead Trees & Fake Hermits," 18, 20; Johnson, *Principles of Gardening,* 226–27.
7. Nash, *Wilderness and the American Mind,* 47; Worster, *Nature's Economy,* 81–83; Rees, "The Taste for Mountain Scenery," 308–10.
8. Oelschlaeger, *Idea of Wilderness,* 34.
9. For a discussion of environmental conspiracy theories and the search for lost traditions, see Bramwell, *Ecology in the 20th Century,* 34–36.
10. Roszak, *Voice of the Earth,* 50, 338–39; Murray, "Little Green Lie." Many slightly different versions of the fictitious speech are in circulation; the example quoted here comes from Fox, *Inhumane Society,* 136. The complete account of how Perry's screenplay was misrepresented by the environmental movement as the authentic words of Chief Seattle can be found in Wilson, "What Chief Seattle Said." The article also contains the full text of the 1887 newspaper account of Seattle's actual 1855 speech, in which he thanks the whites for their "just" offer and agrees to settle peacefully on the reservation. Even this version of the speech may be a somewhat wishful reconstruction of the chief's actual words. Although most scholars accept this account as authentic, the lapse of thirty years and the distinctly Victorian mannerisms in the published speech raise some questions about the accuracy of the reporter's memory.

    Modern generalizations about Indian attitudes toward nature are often a matter of wishful thinking; Indian nature religion is much more complicated than those who seek simple ecological lessons like to admit. There are pitfalls everywhere. The anthropologist A. Irving Hallowell, in the 1950s, once asked an old Ojibwa man, "Are all the stones we see about here alive?" The man thought for a long time. "No!" he finally replied. Then perhaps fearing he had disappointed his interviewer, he added, "But *some* are." (See Albanese, *Nature Religion in America,* 20.)
11. White, "Historical Roots of our Ecologic Crisis," 1205; Oelschlaeger, *Idea of Wilderness,* 33, 42, 70.
12. Quoted in Oelschlaeger, *Idea of Wilderness,* 65–66.

13. Oelschlaeger, *Idea of Wilderness,* 70, 72; White, "Historical Roots of our Ecologic Crisis," 1206; Petrarch quoted in Nash, *Wilderness and the American Mind,* 19–20.

14. Joseph Caryl, quoted in Albanese, *Nature Religion in America,* 39–40. As authority for a law that gave legal possession of lands to Indians only if they "subdued" the land through tillage, the Massachusetts General Court cited Psalms 115:16 ("The heavens belong to the Lord, but the earth He gave over to man") as well as the several passages from Genesis exhorting man to fill the earth and master it. See Cronon, *Changes in the Land,* 63.

15. Nash, *Wilderness and the American Mind,* 13–14.

16. Albanese, *Nature Religion in America,* 43–45.

17. Emerson and Thoreau, *"Nature" and "Walking,"* 94–95, 99–100.

18. Oelschlaeger, *Idea of Wilderness,* 138; Thoreau, *Walden,* 331, 338; Emerson and Thoreau, *"Nature" and "Walking,"* 71–91; Emerson, "Thoreau," 240; Stevenson, "Henry David Thoreau," 667.

19. Hutchinson, *Granite Songster,* 32–33.

20. Furnas, *The Americans,* 142–43, 332–33.

21. Albanese, *Nature Religion in America,* 130–32, 140–42; Furnas, *The Americans,* 441–42.

22. Graham, *Defence of the Graham System,* 8–10; Graham, *Lecture to Young Men,* iv, 11–15, 17–25, 70–74.

23. Emerson and Thoreau, *"Nature" and "Walking,"* 53, 63–64; Worster, *Nature's Economy,* 86–87; Alcott, *Concord Days,* 42.

24. Muir, *Story of My Boyhood,* 184–86; Muir, *Thousand Mile Walk,* 1–2.

25. Muir, *Mountains of California,* 64–65; Albanese, *Nature Religion in America,* 97–100; Nash, *Wilderness and the American Mind,* 125; Oelschlaeger, *Idea of Wilderness,* 185–88; Worster, *Wealth of Nature,* 195.

26. Letter to Jeanne Carr, 1870, quoted in Albanese, *Nature Religion in America,* 100–101.

27. Albanese, *Nature Religion in America,* 104.

28. Mowat, *Rescue the Earth!* 12–15, 108–9.

29. Mardon, "Wilderness Ethics"; Wilson, *Diversity of Life,* 350.

Chapter 3. Nazis, Planners, Eugenicists, and Other Ecologists

1. *Boston Daily Advertiser,* July 17, 19, 21, 1869, quoted in Murray, *Adventures in the Wilderness,* 40–41 (introduction).

2. Nash, *Wilderness and the American Mind,* 98–100.

3. Patrick Abercrombie, quoted in Lowe and Goyder, *Environmental Groups,* 15–18; William Lethaby, quoted in Bramwell, *Ecology in the 20th Century,* 79–82.

4. Murray, *Words Fitly Spoken,* 370.

5. Warde Fowler, quoted in Worster, *Nature's Economy,* 15–16.

6. Pollard et al., *Hedges,* 209–20.

7. Eliot's article is reprinted in Worster, ed., *American Environmentalism,* 177–82.

8. Lowe and Goyder, *Environmental Groups,* 20–22, 138.

9. Bramwell, *Ecology in the 20th Century,* 118, 161–74, 178.

10. Seton, *Birch Bark Roll,* ix–x, xxii–xxiii; Bramwell, *Ecology in the 20th Century,* 105–8; Rosenthal, *Character Factory,* 159, 244–52.

11. Bramwell, *Ecology in the 20th Century,* 199–200.

12. Runte, *Public Lands,* 15–16; Miller, "Nationalism as Theory of Nature," 88, 94; Nash, *Wilderness and the American Mind,* 73.

13. Quoted in Goldman, *Rendezvous with Destiny,* 33.

14. Pinchot, *Breaking New Ground,* 26, 85–86.

15. Pinchot, *Fight for Conservation,* 88; Pinchot, *Breaking New Ground,* 190–91, 235.

16. Pinchot, *Breaking New Ground,* 27–29, 265–66, 273; Botkin, *Discordant Harmonies,* 33–34, 54.

17. "Thinking Big, Permanent & Inviolate," *Wild Forest Review,* January/February 1994, 8.

18. Tobey, *Saving the Prairies,* 24, 30.

19. Barrington Moore, quoted in Worster, *Nature's Economy,* 203.

20. Tobey, *Saving the Prairies,* 32–33; Wheeler, *Philosophical Biology,* 219–20.

21. The quotation, and the discussion of Haeckel and his influence, are drawn from Bramwell, *Ecology in the 20th Century,* 39–55.

22. Tansley, "Use and Abuse of Vegetational Concepts," 292.

23. Clements, *Plant Succession,* 6, 63, 106. The description of Clements's concept of succession also draws on the excellent discussions in Tobey, *Saving the Prairies,* 72–74, and Worster, *Nature's Economy,* 208–15.

24. Quoted in Tobey, *Saving the Prairies,* 209–10.

25. Bramwell, *Ecology in the 20th Century,* 88–91.

26. Worster, *Nature's Economy,* 326–32; Bramwell, *Ecology in the 20th Century,* 64–66.

27. Wheeler quoted in Worster, *Nature's Economy,* 320–25.

28. Gleason, "Further Views on Succession," 305–7, 310–12, 317, 324.

29. Tobey, *Saving the Prairies,* 219, 221.

30. Worster, *Wealth of Nature,* 150–52, 178.

31. Quoted in Mowat, *Rescue the Earth!* 105.

32. Oelschlaeger, *Idea of Wilderness,* 3–4, 58; Theodore Roszak, quoted in Evernden, *Natural Alien,* 5; Merchant, *Death of Nature,* 293.

Chapter 4. Disorderly Conduct

1. Veblen, "*Nothofagus* Forests," 38–40, 50.

2. Knight, "Vegetation Mosaic," 73–74; Ahlgren, "Effects of Fires on Forests," 195; Wright and Bailey, *Fire Ecology,* 255.

3. Jorgensen, *Guide to New England's Landscape,* 185–86; National Science Foundation, "Ecological Consequences of Hurricane Andrew," 1; Davis, "Stability of Forest Communities," 148; Pickett and White, eds., *Ecology of Natural Disturbance,* 4; Pickett and Thompson, "Patch Dynamics and Nature Reserves," 29–33.

4. Reice, "Nonequilibrium Determinants of Community Structure," 427.

5. Runkle, "Disturbance in Temperate Forests," 32. The clearing of New England's forests for agriculture and the subsequent abandonment of many of those fields in the nineteenth century was an unintended experiment that proved this point. These clear-cut areas were rapidly colonized by white pines, which, prior to European settlement, naturally grew only on burned-over land or on rocky, sandy, or exposed sites that could not support the more sensitive but shade-tolerant hardwood species.

6. Wiens, "Vertebrate Responses to Environmental Patchiness," 187; Pickett and White, eds., *Ecology of Natural Disturbance,* 80.

7. Sousa, "Intertidal Disturbance and Patch Dynamics," 116–19, 122.

8. Little, "Effects of Fire on Forests: Northeastern U. S.," 232; Canham and Marks, "Response of Woody Plants to Disturbance," 199–203, 214; Christensen, "Shrubland Fire Regimes," 94–95; Ahlgren, "Effects of Fires on Forests," 200–204.

9. Bendell, "Effects of Fire on Birds and Mammals," 87, 104, 123; Wright and Bailey, *Fire Ecology,* 60–63.

10. Pyne, *Fire in America,* 143.

11. Little, "Effects of Fire on Forests: Northeastern U. S.," 229.

12. Wright, "Landscape Development, Forest Fires, and Wilderness Management," 492; Dodge, "Forest Fuel Accumulation," 139.

13. Thompson and Smith, "Forest Primeval," 262–64; Vogl, "Effects of Fire on Grasslands," 139, 179.

14. Wright and Bailey, *Fire Ecology,* 55, 60–63; Botkin, "Stability and Disturbance," 8–9.

15. Bendell, "Effects of Fire on Birds and Mammals," 74–76.

16. Karr and Freemark, "Disturbance and Vertebrates," 155–56.

17. Davis, "Climatic Instability," 269; Pielou, *After the Ice Age,* 8.

18. Botkin, "Stability and Disturbance," 4; Pielou, *After the Ice Age,* 269–75, 301–10; Jorgensen, *Guide to New England's Landscape,* 168–70.

19. Davis, "Stability of Forest Communities," 132–33.

20. According to Lorimer, "Presettlement Forest of Northeastern Maine," for example, the low frequency of catastrophic fires (once every 800 years) and hurricanes (1,150 years) has allowed the conifer forests of northern Maine to reach a steady-state climax in accordance with classical forest succession theory. Bormann and Likens, "Catastrophic Disturbance and Steady-State," make a similar argument for northern hardwood forests.

For an effective presentation of the climatic counterargument, see Webb, "Vegetational Change in Eastern North America," 505.

21. Pielou, *After the Ice Age,* 185–89, 217–22, 251.
22. Pielou, *After the Ice Age,* 182, 202.
23. Reice, "Nonequilibrium Determinants of Community Structure," 432–34.
24. Gleason, "Individualistic Concept of Plant Association," 93–95, 105.
25. Colinvaux, *Why Big Fierce Animals Are Rare,* 63–72; Whittaker, *Communities and Ecosystems,* 34–38; Whittaker, "Gradient Analysis of Vegetation," 229.
26. Davis, "Climatic Instability," 270–75, 283.
27. Davis, "Stability of Forest Communities," 151–52; Webb, "Vegetational Change in Eastern North America," 502–4.
28. Botkin, *Discordant Harmonies,* 44–47; Elton, *Animal Ecology and Evolution,* 16.
29. The discovery that even simple ecological models could give rise to chaos was made in 1974 by the mathematical ecologist Robert M. May, a finding that had a revolutionary impact on ecology and many other fields of science as well, including the study of turbulence in physics. (See May, "Simple Models with Complicated Dynamics," and May, "Stable Points, Stable Cycles, and Chaos.") "To see mathematical ecology informing theoretical physics is a pleasing inversion of the usual order of things," May observes (May, ed., *Theoretical Ecology,* 17).
30. May, ed., *Theoretical Ecology,* 7–17; May and Seger, "Ideas in Ecology," 262.
31. Hastings and Higgins, "Persistence of Transients in Ecological Models."
32. Stone, "Chaos in Simple Ecological Models," 620.
33. May, *Stability and Complexity,* 130.
34. Rosenzweig, "A Tool to Study Population Interactions?" 194–200; Cockburn, *Evolutionary Ecology,* 126–27; Paine, "Food Web Complexity."
35. Elton, *Animal Ecology and Evolution,* 17.
36. Colinvaux, *Why Big Fierce Animals are Rare,* 199–206. For a typical presentation of the traditional argument that complexity equals stability, see Wilson and Bossert, *Primer of Population Biology,* 138–42.
37. Goel, Maitra, and Montroll, *Nonlinear Models of Interacting Populations,* 113; May, ed., *Theoretical Ecology,* 103.

Chapter 5. Footprints in the Jungle

1. Quoted in Day, "The Indian as an Ecological Factor," 329.
2. Pyne, *Fire in America,* 46–47; Botkin, *Discordant Harmonies,* 53; Martin, "Fire and Forest Structure," 39; Day, "The Indian as an Ecological Factor," 334–35, 337.

3. Maxwell, "Use and Abuse of Forests by Virginia Indians," 82; Day, "The Indian as an Ecological Factor," 331, 329, 334–35.

4. Quoted in Bromley, "Forest Types of Southern New England," 64.

5. Quoted in Maxwell, "Use and Abuse of Forests by Virginia Indians," 93.

6. Little, "Effects of Fire on Forests: Northeastern U.S.," 227.

7. Barrett and Arno, "Indian Fires in the Northern Rockies."

8. William Wood—the year was 1639—quoted in Thompson and Smith, "Forest Primeval," 259.

9. Pyne, *Fire in America,* 46–47.

10. Ibid., 71–75; Day, "The Indian as an Ecological Factor," 330; Weatherford, *Native Roots,* 41–43; Barrett, "Indian Fires in Western Montana," 36–37; Stewart, "Fire as the First Great Force," 118–19.

11. Cronon, *Changes in the Land,* 48; Day, "The Indian as an Ecological Factor," 332–33; Pyne, *Fire in America,* 46–47.

12. "Voices in the Forest: An Interview with Bob Zybach," *Evergreen Magazine,* March-April 1994; Lewis and Clark, *Journals,* 95; Watts, *Reading the Landscape,* 37–39.

13. Cronon, *Changes in the Land,* 50–51

14. Jorgensen, *Guide to New England's Landscape,* 202–3.

15. Spurr and Barnes, *Forest Ecology,* 347.

16. There are still some dissenters. Some ecologists argue that Indian-set fires were mostly small, localized, and of limited ecological significance—at most creating small grassy clearings in the immediate vicinity of villages and campsites. See, for example, Russell, "Indian-set Fires in Northeastern U.S."

17. Pyne, *Fire in America,* 75–76, 84–85.

18. Sauer, "The Agency of Man on Earth," 55; Blainey, *Triumph of the Nomads,* 76.

19. "Rain Forests Seen As Shaped by Human Hand," *New York Times,* July 27, 1993.

20. Vogl, "Effects of Fire on Grasslands," 145.

21. Lemon, "Effects of Fire on African Grassland"; Goudie, *Human Impact,* 46, 33; Adams and McShane, *Myth of Wild Africa,* 43–48.

22. Adams and McShane, *Myth of Wild Africa,* 35–36.

23. Pielou, *After the Ice Age,* 254–57.

24. Steadman and Olson, "Bird Remains on Henderson Island."

25. Maxwell, "Use and Abuse of Forests by Virginia Indians," 96–98.

26. Goudie, *Human Impact,* 58.

27. White, "Historical Roots of Our Ecologic Crisis," 1203.

28. Goudie, *Human Impact,* 37, 56; Dimbleby, "Legacy of Prehistoric Man," 280–81; Miller and Watson, "Heather Moorland: A Man-made Ecosystem," 145–47.

29. Groppali, "Breeding Birds in Tree Rows and Hedges," 153–54; Farina, "Bird Fauna in Changing Agricultural Landscape," 162–63; Bunce and Hallam, "Ecological Significance of Linear Features."

30. Goudie, *Human Impact,* 103–4; Holloway, "Nurturing Nature," 102; U.S. Congress, *Harmful Non-Indigenous Species,* 75.

31. Heywood, "Invasions by Terrestrial Plants," 41; Kalkhoven, "Survival of Populations," 84.

32. Bidwell and Falconer, *History of Agriculture in Northern U.S.,* 84–87; Harper, "Changes in the Forest Area of New England," 443, 447; Jorgensen, *Guide to New England's Landscape,* 213; Thomson, *Changing Face of New England,* 46.

33. Crosby, *Ecological Imperialism,* 155–56; Thomson, *Changing Face of New England,* 47.

34. U.S. Congress, *Harmful Non-Indigenous Species,* 79–92; Jorgensen, *Guide to New England's Landscape,* 214; Mooney and Drake, "Biological Invasions," 491.

35. Goudie, *Human Impact,* 59; Bidwell and Falconer, *History of Agriculture in Northern U.S.,* 159; di Castri, "History of Biological Invasions," 12.

36. Jean de Crèvecoeur, quoted in Crosby, *Ecological Imperialism,* 189–90.

37. William Hudson, quoted in Crosby, *Ecological Imperialism,* 178.

38. National Research Council, *Wild and Free-Roaming Horses and Burros,* 13, 42; U.S. Congress, *Wild Horses and Burros,* 1–2, 51, 57.

39. Hester, "National Park Service Experience with Exotic Species"; U.S. Congress, *Harmful Non-Indigenous Species,* 73–75.

40. Seegmiller and Ohmart, *Ecological Relationships of Feral Burros and Bighorn Sheep,* 6, 44–52; U.S. Congress, *Wild Horses and Burros,* 49–53.

41. Mark Hay and Orrin H. Pilkey, quoted in "Horses of Coast Islands, A Regional Symbol, Harm the Environment," *New York Times,* July 27, 1993.

42. Seegmiller and Ohmart, *Ecological Relationships of Feral Burros and Bighorn Sheep,* 6, 91; U.S. Congress, *Wild Horses and Burros,* 73; National Research Council, *Wild and Free-Roaming Horses and Burros,* 11–13.

43. Holm et al., *Geographical Atlas of World Weeds,* viii; Holm et al., *World's Worst Weeds,* 84–86.

44. Dimbleby, "Legacy of Prehistoric Man," 281.

45. di Castri, "History of Biological Invasions," 12; King, *Weeds of the World,* 14.

46. The coevolutionary origins of domesticated animals are discussed at much greater length in my book, Budiansky, *Covenant of the Wild.*

47. Usher, "Biological Invasions of Nature Reserves," 126–27; Westman, "Managing for Biodiversity," 30; Macdonald et al., "Wildlife Conservation and Invasion of Nature Reserves," 236; Rummel and Roughgarden, "Invasion-Structured and Coevolution-Structured Communities."

48. Westman, "Managing for Biodiversity," 31.

49. Macdonald et al., "Wildlife Conservation and Invasion of Nature Reserves," 240–45, 228–29.
50. Brown, "Invasions by Invertebrates," 105–6.

Chapter 6. The Science, but Mostly the Politics, of "Natural Management"

1. Brussard, "Role of Ecology in Biological Conservation," 10; Brussard, "Future of Yellowstone."
2. Interview with John Varley, September 1992. See also Despain et al., *Wildlife in Transition*, 27, 112, where Park Service officials also refer to the "politically attractive" aspects of this "experimental" policy.
3. Houston, "Ecosystems of National Parks," 648.
4. Bonnicksen, "Fire Gods and Federal Policy," 67.
5. This synthesis of the five reasons why natural management fails draws upon Brussard, "Role of Ecology in Biological Conservation"; Brussard, "Nature in Myth and Reality"; Botkin, *Discordant Harmonies*, 195–97; Pickett and Thompson, "Patch Dynamics and Nature Reserves"; and White and Bratton, "After Preservation."
6. Leopold, *Game Management*, 21.
7. Cahalane, "Wildlife Surpluses in the National Parks."
8. The conference report, "Management of National Parks and Equivalent Areas," First World Conference on National Parks, Seattle, July 1962, is quoted in Leopold et al., "Wildlife Management in National Parks," 30–31.
9. Leopold et al., "Wildlife Management in National Parks," 32, 34, 40, 43.
10. National Research Council, *Science and the National Parks*, 39.
11. Ibid., 53–55.
12. The 1977 report (Durward L. Allen and A. Starker Leopold, *A Review and Recommendations Relative to the NPS Science Program: Memorandum Report to Director*, Washington, D.C.: National Park Service, 1977) and the 1989 report (National Parks and Conservation Association, *National Parks: From Vignettes to a Global View. Commission on Research and Resource Management Policy in the National Park System*, Washington, D.C.: NPCA, 1989, also known as the "Gordon commission" report) are quoted in National Research Council, *Science and the National Parks*, 45, 50.
13. Christensen et al., "Interpreting the Yellowstone Fires of 1988," 680, 685.
14. Strong, *Trip to Yellowstone*, 104–6.
15. Cahalane, "Predator Control in National Parks," 230–32, 235–36.
16. Leopold et al., "Wildlife Management in National Parks," 39–40; Kay, "Yellowstone's Northern Elk Herd," 2–6.
17. This statement is from an unpublished report (Glen F. Cole, *Elk and the Primary Purpose of Yellowstone National Park*, mimeographed report,

Yellowstone National Park, 1968, pp. 2–3), quoted in Kay, "Yellowstone's Northern Elk Herd," 8.

18. In a 1971 article in *Science,* a Yellowstone park biologist begins thus: "The primary purpose of the National Park Service in administering natural areas is to maintain an area's ecosystem in as nearly pristine conditions as possible. This means that ecological processes, including plant succession *and the natural regulation of animal numbers, should be permitted to proceed as they did under pristine conditions."* (Houston, "Ecosystems of National Parks," 648; emphasis added.)

19. U.S. Congress, *Control of Elk Population,* 19–20.

20. See, for example, Houston, "History of Northern Yellowstone Elk," 578, nn. 1, 2, 4.

21. Cole, "Ecological Rationale for Natural or Artificial Regulation," 419.

22. Yellowstone National Park, *Wolves for Yellowstone,* vol. IV: 1-158, 1-255; Kay, "Yellowstone's Northern Elk Herd," 24.

23. Kay, "Yellowstone's Northern Elk Herd," 60–63, 82–83, 116, 121–22, 206, 236, 249–50.

24. Kay, "Aboriginal Overkill."

25. Kay, "Abundance of Wolves in Yellowstone," 14–15.

26. Kay, "Too Many Elk in Yellowstone," 40.

27. Yellowstone National Park, *Wolves for Yellowstone,* vol. IV: 4-108.

28. Ibid., vol. IV: 4-57. A discussion of wolf predation rates on pp. 4-49 and 4-50 offers no evidence for preferring one figure over the other; rather it notes that actual wolf kill rates are variable and not well established. Other models have used considerably higher kill rates, as high as twenty-five per wolf per year.

29. "Scientists Fight over Who's Faithful to Yellowstone," *Los Angeles Times,* November 22, 1993.

30. Botkin, *Discordant Harmonies,* 16–19; Bonner, "Crying Wolf over Elephants," 52–53.

31. Pickett and Thompson, "Patch Dynamics and Nature Reserves," 31, 34.

32. Pennisi, "Conservation's Ecocentrics."

33. Ehrlich and Wilson, "Biodiversity Studies," 761.

34. Bongaarts, "Population Policy Options," 774.

35. Sedjo, *World's Forests,* 6–7; Huston, "Biological Diversity, Soils, and Economics"; Bonner, "Crying Wolf over Elephants," 30; Macdonald et al., "Wildlife Conservation and Invasion of Nature Reserves," 215.

Chapter 7. Waiting for Newton

1. Brussard, "Persistence of Small Populations," 41–42.

2. Goodman, "Ecological Expertise," 328, 330, 332.

3. Leopold, *Game Management,* 4–5, 9, 13; Robinson and Bolen, *Wildlife Ecology and Management,* 9, 14, 251; Worster, *Nature's Economy,* 262–70.

4. Robinson and Bolen, *Wildlife Ecology and Management,* 262.

5. Clutton-Brock and Albon, "Trial and Error in the Highlands," 11; Leopold et al., "Overpopulated Deer Ranges."

6. Goodman, "Ecological Expertise," 352.

7. Wilson, *Diversity of Life,* 280.

8. Address to the Opening Session of the United Nations Commission on Sustainable Development, June 14, 1993.

9. Heywood and Stuart, "Species Extinctions in Tropical Forests," 93–100, summarizes the field evidence for mass extinctions. The authors note that documented extinction rates of birds and mammals have increased from one every four years to one per year; if other organisms show a like propensity to extinction, the total extinction rate would be at most about two thousand per year. "Despite extensive enquiries," they conclude, "we have been unable to obtain conclusive evidence that massive extinctions have taken place in recent times."

10. Ehrlich and Wilson, "Biodiversity Studies," 759; Wilson, "Toward Renewed Reverence for Life," 72; Wilson, *Diversity of Life,* 276, 280; "Species Loss: Crisis or False Alarm?" *New York Times,* 20 August 1991; Mann, "Extinction: Are Ecologists Crying Wolf?" 737.

11. Edward O. Wilson, "Before Skies Become Entirely Barren of Birds; Mass Extinctions Grow," Letters, *New York Times,* 25 May 1993; Connor and McCoy, "Statistics and Biology of the Species-Area Relationship," 801–3. Connor and McCoy observed that in a "completely unrelated discipline," the same formula has been used to relate brain weight with body weight of various organisms, and z values consistently fall within the 0.2 to 0.4 range, too. Apparently, any data set characterized by a wide range in the independent variable (area, in the case of the species-area curve) and a small range in the dependent variable (species) that fits a power relationship of the form $S = CA^z$ fairly well has this property. They conclude that the species-area connection may be a "correlation . . . without a functional relationship."

12. Heywood and Stuart, "Species Extinctions in Tropical Forests," 105. See also Simberloff, "Do Species-Area Curves Predict Extinction?" 76–79, and Budiansky, "Extinction or Miscalculation?"

13. Quoted in Simberloff, "Do Species-Area Curves Predict Extinction?" 75. When asked, McMahon said he was in fact unaware of island-biogeographical theory when he invented this scene for his novel.

14. Brown, "Conservation of Neotropical Environments," 380; see also Brown and Brown, "Habitat Alteration and Species Loss in Brazilian Forests," 126–28.

15. Simberloff quoted in Heywood and Stuart, "Species Extinctions in Tropical Forests," 104. The politics surrounding extinction predictions have become rather ugly within the field of conservation biology. Perhaps because alarming statistics have proved so successful a public relations tool, many ecologists find themselves reluctant to criticize them too loudly. Heywood, in an interview with me for an article on the subject that appeared in *U.S. News & World Report* ("The Doomsday Myths," 13 December 1993), stated that biologists "are much more skeptical in private" about the very high extinction figures used by Wilson but "are very cautious about expressing their views [publicly] because they don't want to be seen rocking the boat. This is the fear it might damage 'the cause.' "

16. The Endangered Species Act has become the cause célèbre of a conservative movement that sees the "takings clause" of the Constitution as the magic bullet that will slay government regulation. The argument is that by placing an economic cost on private landowners, government regulations act as an unconstitutional "taking" of private property by the government without compensation. A certain skepticism is thus in order as to the motives of those libertarians who crank out pamphlets urging that the act be "improved." On the other hand, they make a telling criticism when they point out the perverse incentives of the act: Instead of rewarding landowners for preserving the habitat of an endangered species, the act turns endangered species into a liability for a landowner who may be ordered to cease farming or logging his land or forbidden to develop it. In a number of documented cases, landowners who suspect their land harbors endangered species have taken swift action to eliminate the habitat in question by mowing or clear-cutting. At the same time, the act penalizes landowners who have carefully managed their land for wildlife values. For example, one North Carolina landowner who cut his timber on a long, eighty-year rotation with the aim of maintaining old-growth habitat has now been forbidden to cut any of his older stands, which have become prime habitat for endangered red-cockaded woodpeckers. His response is unsurprising: He now plans to clear-cut all of his remaining timber on a forty-year rotation to insure that no more of his land ever becomes woodpecker habitat. See Lambert and Smith, *Endangered Species Act: Time for a Change,* 36–37; Mannix, "Origin of Endangered Species."

17. Lambert and Smith, *Endangered Species Act: Time for a Change,* 10–12.

18. Shaffer, *Beyond the Endangered Species Act,* 8–9.

19. Taubes, "Dubious Battle to Save Sea Turtle," 614.

20. Lynn Llewellyn, quoted in Mann and Plummer, "The Butterfly Problem," 55. See also Rohlf, "Reasons the Endangered Species Act Doesn't Work," 275.

21. May, "How Many Species Inhabit the Earth?" 44, 46; Ehrlich and Wilson, "Biodiversity Studies," 759.

22. Robinson and Bolen, *Wildlife Ecology and Management,* 212–15; Fiedler and Ahouse, "Hierarchies of Cause," 38–39

23. Soulé, ed., *Viable Populations for Conservation,* 1. The description of population viability analysis in these and the following paragraphs draws upon Shaffer, "Minimum Population Sizes for Species Conservation"; Shaffer, "Coping with Uncertainty"; Gilpin and Soulé, "Processes of Species Extinction"; Soulé and Simberloff, "Design of Nature Reserves"; Goodman, "Demography of Chance Extinction"; and Goodman, "Design and Maintenance of Biological Reserves."

24. Pimm, *Balance of Nature?* 32, 54; Belovsky, "Extinction Models and Mammalian Persistence," 43–49.

25. Shaffer, "Coping with Uncertainty," 77, 81; Goodman, "How Do Any Species Persist?" 61.

26. Pickett, Parker, and Fiedler, "New Paradigm in Ecology," 84.

27. Caro and Laurenson, "Ecological and Genetic Factors in Conservation"; Lande, "Genetics and Demography in Biological Conservation." Caro and Laurenson point out that despite the demonstrably extreme inbreeding of wild and captive cheetahs, the decline of the species cannot be attributed to any genetic defects. High mortality rates in the wild are almost completely due to predation of cheetah cubs by lions; reproductive failures in captivity were found to arise from poor management and maternal neglect and cannibalism, not genetic factors.

28. Goodman, "Design and Maintenance of Biological Reserves," 226; Goodman, "How Do Any Species Persist?" 61; Brussard, "Minimum Viable Populations," 23, 25; Shaffer, "Population Viability Analysis," 40.

29. Prendergast et al., "Diversity Hotspots and Conservation Strategies."

30. Ehrlich's other favorite metaphor drawn from pulp science fiction is the phrase "only a madman would give a loaded gun to an idiot child," which he invokes as a warning against practically every new technology that comes along, including, in one memorable instance, cold fusion. While other scientists were ridiculing the whole concept of cold fusion as scientific nonsense (as it turned out to be), Ehrlich was fretting that its supposed promise of unlimited energy would only further compound mankind's woes.

31. Soulé and Simberloff, "Design of Nature Reserves," 35.

32. Robinson and Bolen, *Wildlife Ecology and Management,* 22–23.

33. Pimm, *Balance of Nature?* 280–93.

34. Note that this is a more precise statement than the blanket assertion that complex systems are more stable than simple ones, which we dismissed back in chapter 4.

35. Pimm, *Balance of Nature?* 347–56.

Chapter 8. Bioeconomy

1. "Top Scientists Warn Humans Are Making the Earth Unlivable," *Atlanta Constitution,* November 19, 1992; address by Al Gore to the Opening Session of the United Nations Commission on Sustainable Development, June 15, 1993; U.S. Congress, *World Food Production,* 55.
2. Ehrlich and Ehrlich, *Population Explosion,* 19, 23.
3. Brown et al., *State of the World 1994,* 191, 197.
4. Macdonald, "Wildlife Conservation and Invasion of Nature Reserves," Table 9.1.
5. Jared Diamond, in Jordan, Gilpin, and Aber, eds., *Restoration Ecology,* 330.
6. Jordan, Gilpin, and Aber, eds., *Restoration Ecology,* 39–42.
7. Clark, "Bioeconomics," 401–2. Although many continue to blame the collapse of the anchoveta fishery on an incursion of tropical water that interferes with upwelling of nutrient-rich water—an anomaly known as "El Niño"—the population crash was actually well under way before the 1973 El Niño occurred.
8. Ludwig, Hilborn, and Walters, "Uncertainty, Resource Exploitation, and Conservation," 17; interview with Brian Gorman, National Marine Fisheries Service.
9. Ludwig, Hilborn, and Walters, "Uncertainty, Resource Exploitation, and Conservation," 36.
10. "Trashing the Northern Rockies," *Wild Forest Review,* March 1994, 18–21.
11. Clark, "Bioeconomics," 417. I am greatly indebted to Clark's essay for the examples of bioeconomic analysis here and in the following paragraphs.
12. Ibid., 402.
13. Ibid., 413.
14. See, for example, the chapter on fisheries management in Getz and Haight, *Population Harvesting,* 135–224.
15. "A Puzzle for Zimbabwe: Too Many Elephants," *New York Times,* November 14, 1989; "Where Elephants Roam, a Plea for Understanding," *New York Times,* August 9, 1989; Bonner, "Crying Wolf over Elephants."
16. This view was expressed to me, in an interview, by Terry Anderson of the Political Economy Research Center, a leading libertarian-environmental think tank.
17. Clark, "Bioeconomics," 398–99; May, "Economics of Extinction"; Lande, Engen, and Saether, "Optimal Harvesting."
18. See, for example, "Chaos Theory Seeps into Ecology Debate, Stirring Up a Tempest," *Wall Street Journal,* July 11, 1994.
19. *Game Conservancy Review of 1990,* 151; Hudson, *Grouse in Space and Time,* 6, 216; "Shooters Help the Shot," *Economist,* August 15, 1992, 80.

20. Hudson, *Grouse in Space and Time,* 16, 56.
21. Miller and Watson, "Heather Moorland: A Man-made Ecosystem," 146, 153; Lister-Kaye, "Securing a Future for the Highlands," 70.
22. Hudson, *Grouse in Space and Time,* 16, 138.
23. Ibid., 75–79, 109–12.
24. Ibid., 79, 84, 95–96.
25. Quoted in Ridley, "Grouse for Better or Worse," 34.
26. Hudson, *Grouse in Space and Time,* 142. See also Anderson and May, "Regulation and Stability of Host-Parasite Interactions. I."
27. May and Anderson, "Regulation and Stability of Host-Parasite Interactions. II"; Hudson, *Grouse in Space and Time,* 161–77; *Game Conservancy Review of 1993,* 117–19.
28. Hudson, *Grouse in Space and Time,* 46–55.
29. Fitzner and Newell, "Hawk Nesting on the Hanford Site," 125.
30. Bennett, "Roads, Roadsides and Wildlife Conservation," 100–104.
31. Lussenhop, "Urban Cemeteries as Bird Refuges," 457, 460; Thomas and Dixon, "Cemetery Ecology," 108.
32. Robinson and Bolen, *Wildlife Ecology and Management,* 147–50, 171–72; Council for Agricultural Science and Technology, *Ecological Impacts,* 5–11.
33. *Game Conservancy Review of 1993,* 60–70; Latshaw, "Native Warm Season Grasses."
34. DeGraaf, "Breeding Bird Assemblages," 157–62.
35. Robinson and Bolen, *Wildlife Ecology and Management,* 186–95.

Chapter 9. Reinventing the Wild

1. Nuzzo, "Midwest Oak Savanna," 6–11; Haney and Apfelbaum, "Structure and Dynamics of Oak Savannas"; Haney and Apfelbaum, "Characterization of Oak Savannas."
2. Packard, "Rediscovering the Tallgrass Savanna," 57, 63.
3. Interview with Alan Haney, University of Wisconsin, September 1994; Nuzzo, "Midwest Oak Savanna," 11.
4. Haney and Apfelbaum, "Structure and Dynamics of Oak Savannas," 24; Burger et al., eds., *Oak Woods Management Workshop,* 21, 42.
5. Packard, "A Few Oddball Species," 30, 33.
6. Engelmann, "Prairies, Flats, and Barrens," 389–91; Anderson, "Presettlement Forests of Illinois," 9–11; Alan Haney interview.
7. Packard, "Rediscovering the Tallgrass Savanna," 55–56, 63.
8. Packard, "A Few Oddball Species," 32–38.
9. Stritch, "Landscape-scale Restoration," 74–75; Alan Haney interview.
10. Jordan, Gilpin, and Aber, eds., *Restoration Ecology,* 3–9, 257–61; Jordan, "Restoration Practice and Ecological Theory," 20.

11. Jordan, Gilpin, and Aber, eds., *Restoration Ecology,* 208–16; Perry and Amaranthus, "Plant-Soil Bootstrap."

12. Morton, "Reintroduction as a Method of Studying Ecology," 167–68.

13. Ibid., 169–71.

14. Roberts, "Wetlands Trading," 1890; Holloway, "Nurturing Nature," 102; Brumback, "Restoring Florida's Everglades," 352–55.

15. Berger, ed., *Environmental Restoration,* xv–xxiii.

16. Hamilton, "Restoration of Degraded Tropical Forests," 118–19.

17. Simberloff, "Reconstructing the Ambiguous," 37–40; Jordan, Gilpin, and Aber, eds., *Restoration Ecology,* 154–55, 331–33.

18. Simberloff, "Reconstructing the Ambiguous," 44.

Conclusion: Nature on Human Terms

1. The quotation is Ellen Sturgis Hooper's poem, "Beauty and Duty."

2. Bruce Hanon, in Costanza, Norton, and Haskell, eds., *Ecosystem Health,* 214.

3. Inouye, "Variation in Undisturbed Populations," 43, 48.

4. Baskin, "How Much Does Diversity Matter?"; Cherfas, "How Many Species Do We Need?"

5. Jordan, " 'Sunflower Forest' "; Aber and Jordan, "Restoration Ecology"; Jordan, "Shaping the Land, Transforming the Human Spirit."

6. Perry and Amaranthus, "Plant–Soil Bootstrap," 100.

A BRIEF GUIDE
TO THE SOURCES

For those interested in pursuing any of the topics in this book in greater depth, I offer here a brief guide to the sources. Full citations to the works mentioned below can be found in the Bibliography, which follows.

The history and philosophy of nature is a relatively new field of academic study, too young to have developed much of a sense of irony or skepticism. It is dominated by humorless and heavy-handed polemics bemoaning the psychological, economic, and social failings of a society that is destroying the planet. One of the better treatments is still one of the first, Roderick Nash's exhaustively researched *Wilderness and the American Mind,* which saves the polemics for the end and offers a detailed and rich account of the origins and growth of the idea of wilderness along the way. Oelschlaeger, *Idea of Wilderness,* is also a work of serious scholarship that contains many valuable examples, though it is laden with gratuitous and unsubstantiated opinions about saving the planet. Bramwell, *Ecology in the Twentieth Century,* is heavy going but is almost unique for its skeptical tone and its sharp analysis of the link between nature worship and fascism. Albanese, *Nature Religion in America,* contains an interesting discussion of the various nineteenth-century health and nature fads, as does (briefly) Furnas, *The Americans.* Tobey, *Saving the Prairies,* has more than most people will want to know about the history and sociology of the American school of plant ecology but contains useful discussions of the rise and fall of Clements's ideas of plant succession and climatic determinism.

The definitive political history of the American environmental movement written from a perspective other than that of cheerleading has yet to appear in print. A useful collection of primary sources is found in Worster, ed., *American Environmentalism;* readers can draw their own conclusions.

The classic study of the effect the New England Indians had on their environment is Day, "The Indian as an Ecological Factor." Virtually every writer on the subject in the four decades since this article appeared has closely followed Day's approach. Other useful articles that discuss the role of the Indian in nature are Hawes, "New England Forests in Retrospect"; Maxwell, "Use and Abuse of Forests by Virginia Indians"; Martin, "Fire and Forest Structure"; Thompson and Smith, "The Forest Primeval"; and Barrett, "Indian Fires in Western Montana." An excellent overview of the effect that man, including primitive man, has had on his environment is Goudie, *Human Impact.* Alfred Crosby's *Ecological Imperialism* and *The Columbian Exchange* focus on the introduction of exotic species and the role that agriculture played in the European conquest of the New World; they are somewhat uneven works, in a ponderous style, but well worth the effort. Cronon, *Changes in the Land,* is limited to New England but is a much more readable work as well as being a model of dispassionate scholarship that brings together history and ecology. Bidwell and Falconer, *History of Agriculture in the Northern United States,* and Russell, *A Long Deep Furrow: Three Centuries of Farming in New England,* are good overviews for those interested in delving more deeply into this aspect of North America's ecological history.

Among the better introductory texts and popularizations of modern ecology, forestry, and population biology that the nonspecialist will find useful are Whittaker, *Communities and Ecosystems;* Cockburn, *Introduction to Evolutionary Ecology;* Spurr and Barnes, *Forest Ecology;* Colinvaux, *Why Big Fierce Animals Are Rare;* and Botkin, *Discordant Harmonies.* Those with a mathematical inclination will want to tackle May, ed., *Theoretical Ecology.*

An excellent and concise introduction to fire ecology is Cooper, "Ecology of Fire." The exhaustive treatment, from both a scientific and cultural perspective, is Pyne, *Fire in America*. Pickett and White, eds., *Ecology of Natural Disturbance*, is a collection of technical, yet still for the most part quite accessible, papers on this important topic.

A series of articles on the management of Yellowstone National Park appeared in *BioScience*, November 1989, in the wake of the 1988 Yellowstone fires. They are an excellent and up-to-date introduction to the controversies surrounding the Park Service's policies. Keiter and Boyce, eds., *Greater Yellowstone Ecosystem*, is another good collection of technical perspectives on these issues. Kay, "Yellowstone's Northern Elk Herd," is the definitive indictment of the "natural regulation" hypothesis; Despain et al., *Wildlife in Transition* and Houston, *The Northern Yellowstone Elk*, offer the Park Service's viewpoint.

For a solid, up-to-date introduction to contemporary issues in ecosystem management, a good place to begin is the textbook by Robinson and Bolen, *Wildlife Ecology and Management*. Though it leans heavily toward a worldview that some ecologists find out of date, with an emphasis on managing game for hunters, it is well written and clear and, in its details if not in its larger perspective, reflects the latest research. Two excellent perspectives on the shortcomings of the Endangered Species Act, one from an environmental organization and one from a libertarian think tank, are Shaffer, *Beyond the Endangered Species Act*, and Lambert and Smith, *The Endangered Species Act: Time for a Change*. Mann and Plummer, *Noah's Choice*, explores the convoluted politics of endangered species with some excellent reporting on what goes on inside the Fish and Wildlife Service.

Edward O. Wilson's collected agitprop for biodiversity, *Diversity of Life*, is itself the best testimony to the limited utility of the species-area relation in management decisions. The collection of papers in *Tropical Deforestation and Species Extinction*, especially those by Simberloff, Heywood and Stuart, and Brown and Brown, will come as an eye-opening revelation to those who have assumed that dire warnings of global extinction rates are based on scientific fact. Those who want to delve more deeply into the controversy over extinction rates will want to consult Brown, "Conservation of Neotropical Environments"; Connor and McCoy, "Statistics and Biology of the Species-Area Relationship"; Heywood et al., "Uncertainties in Extinction Rates"; and Budiansky, "Extinction or Miscalculation?"

Population-viability analysis has spawned a huge literature, most of it steeped in mathematical complexities that the general reader will find unrewarding; the best summary of the concept, with a good discussion of its implications, is Shaffer, "Coping with Uncertainty." The other chapters found in the same volume (Soulé, ed., *Viable Populations for Conservation*) are also generally helpful, although some are quite technical.

The search for more general laws of natural systems is an enormously complex subject, and a neophyte plunging into the literature is likely to find himself hopelessly confused by the seemingly contradictory and incomplete theories and the ongoing academic battles over what evidence supports which ideas. The only attempt that I am aware of to synthesize all of this messy and confusing business for anything remotely resembling a nonspecialist audience is Pimm, *Balance of Nature?* a messy, confusing, and extremely frustrating book that heroically tackles an impossible subject and perhaps all too faithfully reflects the current diversity of opinion. For those who stick with it, it is full of surprising insights.

Several works offer a tentative vision of putting together a unified conservation strategy: Brussard, "How Many Are Too Few?"; White and Bratton, "After Preservation"; Soulé and Simberloff, "Design of Nature Reserves"; and Falk, "Theory of Integrated Conservation Strategies."

An excellent introduction to the economics of managed populations is contained in Clark, "Bioeconomics." Although mathematically rigorous, it is still readable and valuable to those who skip over the equations. Hudson, *Grouse in Space and Time,* tells the entire story of the scientific campaign to understand and manage red grouse in Scotland, a model of its kind.

One of the best overviews of restoration ecology is the aptly named *Restoration Ecology,* edited by Jordan, Gilpin, and Aber. Jordan has also written a brilliant essay, " 'Sunflower Forest,' " that advances the imaginative and inspiring notion that restoration ecology may be both the means to solve the world's ecological problems and a way to break down the artificial and debilitating separation of man from nature that has so paralyzed us in our approach to the natural world.

BIBLIOGRAPHY

Aber, John D., and William R. Jordan III. "Restoration Ecology: An Environmental Middle Ground." *BioScience* 35 (1985): 399.

Adams, Jonathan S., and Thomas O. McShane. *The Myth of Wild Africa: Conservation Without Illusion.* New York: W. W. Norton, 1992.

Ahlgren, C. E. "Effects of Fires on Temperate Forests: North Central United States." In *Fire and Ecosystems,* edited by T. T. Kozlowski and C. E. Ahlgren. New York: Academic Press, 1974.

Albanese, Catherine L. *Nature Religion in America: From the Algonkian Indians to the New Age.* Chicago: University of Chicago Press, 1990.

Alcott, A. Bronson. *Concord Days.* Boston: Roberts Brothers, 1872.

Altherr, Thomas L. " 'Chaplain to the Hunters': Henry David Thoreau's Ambivalence Toward Hunting." *American Literature* 56 (1984): 345–61.

Anderson, R. M., and R. M. May. "Regulation and Stability of Host-Parasite Population Interactions. I. Regulatory Processes." *Journal of Animal Ecology* 47 (1978): 219–47.

Anderson, Roger C. "Presettlement Forests of Illinois." In *Proceedings of the Oak Woods Management Workshop,* edited by George V. Burger, John E. Ebinger, and Gerould S. Wilhelm. Charleston: Eastern Illinois University, 1991.

Bakker, Jan Pouwel. *Nature Management by Grazing and Cutting.* Boston: Kluwer Academic Publishers,1989.

Baldassarre, G. A., et al. "Dynamics and Quality of Waste Corn Available to Post-breeding Waterfowl in Texas." *Wildlife Society Bulletin* 11 (1983): 25–31.

Baldwin, A. Dwight, Judith de Luce, and Carl Pletsch, eds. *Beyond Preservation: Restoring and Inventing Landscapes.* Minneapolis: University of Minnesota Press, 1993.

Barrett, Stephen W. "Indian Fires in the Pre-settlement Forests of Western Montana." In *Proceedings of the Fire History Workshop,* October 20–24, 1980, Tucson, Arizona. General Technical Report RM-81. Fort Collins, Colo.: Rocky Mountain Forest and Range Experiment Station, U.S. Forest Service, 1980.

Barrett, Stephen W., and Stephen F. Arno. "Indian Fires as an Ecological Influence in the Northern Rockies." *Journal of Forestry* 80 (1982): 647–51.

Baskin, Yvonne. "Ecologists Dare to Ask: How Much Does Diversity Matter?" *Science* 264 (1994): 202–3.

Belovsky, Gary E. "Extinction Models and Mammalian Persistence." In *Viable Populations for Conservation,* edited by Michael E. Soulé. Cambridge: Cambridge University Press, 1987.

Belsky, A. Joy, and Charles D. Canham. "Forest Gaps and Isolated Savanna Trees." *BioScience* 44 (1994): 77–84.

Bendell, J. F. "Effects of Fire on Birds and Mammals." In *Fire and Ecosystems,* edited by T. T. Kozlowski and C. E. Ahlgren. New York: Academic Press, 1974.

Bennett, A. F. "Roads, Roadsides and Wildlife Conservation: A Review." In *Nature Conservation 2: The Role of Corridors,* edited by Denis A. Saunders and Richard J. Hobbs. Chipping Norton, Australia: Surrey Beatty & Sons, 1991.

Berger, John, ed. *Environmental Restoration: Science and Strategies for Restoring the Earth.* Washington, D.C.: Island Press, 1990.

Berman, Morris. *The Reenchantment of the World.* Ithaca, N.Y.: Cornell University Press, 1981.

Bidwell, Percy W., and John I. Falconer. *History of Agriculture in the Northern United States, 1620–1860.* Publication 358. Washington, D.C.: Carnegie Institution of Washington, 1925.

Blainey, Geoffrey. *Triumph of the Nomads: A History of Ancient Australia.* South Melbourne: Macmillan,1975.

Bongaarts, John. "Population Policy Options in the Developing World." *Science* 263 (1994): 771–76.

Bonner, Raymond. "Crying Wolf over Elephants." *New York Times Magazine,* February 7, 1993.

Bonnicksen, Thomas M. "Restoration Ecology: Philosophy, Goals, and Ethics." *Environmental Professional* 10 (1982): 25–35.

———. "Fire Gods and Federal Policy." *American Forests,* July-August 1989.

Bormann, F. Herbert and Gene E. Likens. "Catastrophic Disturbance and Steady-State in Northern Hardwood Forests." *American Scientist* 67 (1979): 660–69.

Botkin, Daniel B. "Life and Death of a Forest: The Computer as an Aid to

Understanding." In *Ecosystem Modeling in Theory and Practice,* edited by C. A. S. Hall and J. W. Day, Jr. New York: Wiley, 1977.

_____. "A Grandfather Clock Down the Staircase: Stability and Disturbance in Natural Ecosystems." In *Forests: Fresh Perspectives from Ecosystem Analysis,* edited by Richard H. Waring. Proceedings of the fortieth Biology Colloquium. Corvallis: Oregon State University Press, 1979.

_____. *Discordant Harmonies.* New York: Oxford University Press, 1990.

Bradshaw, A. D. "The Restoration of Ecosystems." *Journal of Applied Ecology* 20 (1983): 1–17.

Bramwell, Anna. *Ecology in the Twentieth Century: A History.* New Haven: Yale University Press, 1989.

Braun, E. Lucy. *The Deciduous Forests of Eastern North America.* New York: Hafner Publishing, 1964.

British Ecological Society. *Large Scale Ecology and Conservation Biology.* Thirty-fifth Symposium of the British Ecological Society, 1993. Edited by Peter J. Edwards, Robert M. May, and Nigel R. Webb. Oxford: Blackwell, 1994.

Bromley, Stanley W. "The Original Forest Types of Southern New England." *Ecological Monographs* 5 (1935): 61–89.

Brown, J. K. "Fire Cycles and Community Dynamics in Lodgepole Pine Forests." In *Management of Lodgepole Pine Ecosystems,* edited by D. M. Baumgartner. Pullman: Washington State University Cooperative Extension Service, 1975.

Brown, James H. "Patterns, Modes and Extents of Invasions by Invertebrates." In *Biological Invasions: A Global Perspective,* edited by J. A. Drake et al. SCOPE Report 37. New York: John Wiley & Sons, 1989.

Brown, Keith S., Jr. "Conservation of Neotropical Environments: Insects as Indicators." In *The Conservation of Insects and Their Habitats,* edited by N. M. Collins and J. A. Thomas. R.E.S. Symposium XV. London: Academic Press, 1991.

Brown, Keith S., Jr., and G. G. Brown. "Habitat Alteration and Species Loss in Brazilian Forests." In *Tropical Deforestation and Species Extinction,* edited by T. C. Whitmore and J. A. Sayer. London: Chapman & Hall, 1992.

Brown, Lester R., et al. *State of the World 1994.* New York: W. W. Norton, 1994.

Brumback, Barbara C. "Restoring Florida's Everglades: A Strategic Planning Approach." In *Environmental Restoration: Science and Strategies for Restoring the Earth,* edited by John Berger. Washington, D.C.: Island Press, 1990.

Brussard, Peter F. "Minimum Viable Populations: How Many are Too Few?" *Restoration & Management Notes* 3 (1985): 21–25.

_____. "The Likelihood of Persistence of Small Populations of Large Animals and its Implications for Cryptozoology." *Cryptozoology* 5 (1986): 38–46.

_____. "Nature in Myth and Reality." Review of *Discordant Harmonies,* by Daniel B. Botkin. *Conservation Biology* 5 (1991): 571–72.

_____. "The Role of Ecology in Biological Conservation." *Ecological Applications* 1 (1991): 6–12.

_____. "The Future of Yellowstone." Review of *The Greater Yellowstone Ecosystem,* edited by Robert B. Keiter and Mark S. Boyce. *Science* 255 (1992): 1148–49.

Brussard, Peter F., and Michael E. Gilpin. "Demographic and Genetic Problems of Small Populations." In *Conservation Biology and the Black-Footed Ferret,* edited by Ulysses S. Seal et al. New Haven: Yale University Press, 1989.

Buckley, G. P., ed. *Biological Habitat Reconstruction.* London: Belhaven Press, 1989.

Budiansky, Stephen. *The Covenant of the Wild: Why Animals Chose Domestication.* New York: William Morrow, 1992.

_____. "Extinction or Miscalculation?" *Nature* 370 (1994): 105.

Bunce, R. G. H., and C. J. Hallam. "The Ecological Significance of Linear Features in Agricultural Landscapes in Britain." In *Landscape Ecology and Agroecosystems,* edited by R. G. H. Bunce, L. Ryzkowski, and M. G. Paoletti. Boca Raton, Fla.: Lewis Publishers, 1993.

Burch, William R., Jr. *Daydreams and Nightmares: A Sociological Essay on the American Environment.* New York: Harper & Row, 1971.

Burger, George V., John E. Ebinger, and Gerould S. Wilhelm, eds. *Proceedings of the Oak Woods Management Workshop.* Charleston, Ill.: Eastern Illinois University, 1991.

Cahalane, Victor H. "The Evolution of Predator Control Policy in the National Parks." *Journal of Wildlife Management* 3 (1939): 229–37.

_____. "Wildlife Surpluses in the National Parks." *Transactions of the North American Wildlife and Natural Resources Conference* 6 (1941): 355–61.

Cairns, John, Jr., ed. *The Recovery Process in Damaged Ecosystems.* Ann Arbor, Mich.: Ann Arbor Science, 1980.

_____. *Rehabilitating Damaged Ecosystems.* 2 vols. Boca Raton, Fla.: CRC Press, 1988.

Caldicott, Helen. *If You Love This Planet: A Plan to Heal the Earth.* New York: W. W. Norton, 1992.

Canham, Charles D., and P. L. Marks. "The Response of Woody Plants to Disturbance: Patterns of Establishment and Growth." In *The Ecology of Natural Disturbance and Patch Dynamics,* edited by S. T. A. Pickett and P. S. White. Orlando, Fla.: Academic Press, 1985.

Caro, T. M., and M. Karen Laurenson. "Ecological and Genetic Factors in Conservation: A Cautionary Tale." *Science* 263 (1994): 485–86.

Cauley, Darrell L., and James R. Schinner. "The Cincinnati Raccoons." *Natural History,* November 1982, pp. 58–60.

Chadwick, George F. *The Park and the Town.* London: Architectural Press, 1966.

Cherfas, Jeremy. "How Many Species Do We Need?" *New Scientist,* August 6, 1994, pp. 36–40.

Christensen, Norman L. "Shrubland Fire Regimes and Their Evolutionary Consequences." In *The Ecology of Natural Disturbance and Patch Dynamics,* edited by S. T. A. Pickett and P. S. White. Orlando, Fla.: Academic Press, 1985.

Christensen, Norman L., et al. "Interpreting the Yellowstone Fires of 1988." *BioScience* 39 (1989): 678–85.

Clark, Andrew Hill. *The Invasion of New Zealand by People, Plants and Animals.* New Brunswick, N.J.: Rutgers University Press, 1949.

Clark, Colin W. "Bioeconomics." In *Theoretical Ecology: Principles and Applications,* 2nd ed., edited by Robert M. May. Oxford: Blackwell Scientific, 1981.

————. *Bioeconomic Modeling and Fisheries Management.* New York: Wiley-Interscience, 1985.

Clements, Frederic C. *Plant Succession, An Analysis of the Development of Vegetation.* Publication 242. Washington, D.C.: Carnegie Institution of Washington, 1916.

Clutton-Brock, T. H., and S. D. Albon. "Trial and Error in the Highlands." *Nature* 358 (1992): 11–12.

Cockburn, Andrew. *An Introduction to Evolutionary Ecology.* Oxford: Blackwell Scientific Publications, 1991.

Cole, Glen F. "An Ecological Rationale for the Natural or Artificial Regulation of Native Ungulates in Parks." *Transactions of the North American Wildlife and Natural Resources Conference* 36 (1971): 417–25.

Colinvaux, Paul. *Why Big Fierce Animals Are Rare: An Ecologist's Perspective.* Princeton, N.J. Princeton University Press, 1978.

"Confidence in the Past." *Yellowstone Science,* Fall 1992, pp. 10–15.

Connor, Edward F., and Earl D. McCoy. "The Statistics and Biology of the Species-Area Relationship." *American Naturalist* 113 (1979): 791–833.

Cooper, Charles F. "The Ecology of Fire." *Scientific American,* April 1961, pp. 150–60.

Costanza, Robert, Bryan G. Norton, and Benjamin D. Haskell, eds. *Ecosystem Health: New Goals for Environmental Management.* Washington, D.C.: Island Press, 1992.

Council for Agricultural Science and Technology. *Ecological Impacts of Federal Conservation and Cropland Reduction Programs.* Task Force Report no. 117. Ames, Iowa: CAST, 1990.

Crawley, Michael J., ed. *Natural Enemies: The Population Biology of Predators, Parasites and Disease.* Oxford: Blackwell Scientific Publications, 1992.

Cronon, William. *Changes in the Land: Indians, Colonists, and the Ecology of New England.* New York: Hill and Wang, 1983.

Crosby, Alfred W. *The Columbian Exchange: Biological and Cultural Conse-quences of 1492.* Westport, Conn.: Greenwood, 1972.

———. *Ecological Imperialism: The Biological Expansion of Europe, 900–1900.* Cambridge: Cambridge University Press, 1986.

Curtis, J. T., and M. L. Partch. "Effect of Fire on the Competition Between Blue Grass and Certain Native Prairie Plants." *American Midland Naturalist* 39 (1948): 437–43.

Daly, Mary. *Gyn/Ecology: The Metaethics of Radical Feminism.* Boston: Beacon Press, 1990.

Davis, Margaret Bryan. "Quaternary History and the Stability of Forest Communities." In *Forest Succession: Concepts and Application,* edited by Darrell C. West, Herman H. Shugart, and Daniel B. Botkin. New York: Spinger-Verlag, 1981.

———. "Climatic Instability, Time Lags, and Community Disequilibrium." In *Community Ecology,* edited by J. Diamond and T. J. Case. New York: Harper & Row, 1984.

Day, Gordon M. "The Indian as an Ecological Factor in the Northeastern Forest." *Ecology* 34 (1953): 329–46.

DeGraaf, Richard M. "Breeding Bird Assemblages in Managed Northern Hardwood Forests in New England." In *Wildlife and Habitats in Managed Landscapes,* edited by Jon E. Rodiek and Eric G. Bolen. Washington, D.C.: Island Press, 1991.

Despain, Don G., et al. *Wildlife in Transition: Man and Nature on Yellowstone's Northern Range.* Boulder, Colo.: Robert Rinehart, 1986.

Di Castri, Francesco. "History of Biological Invasions with Special Emphasis on the Old World." In *Biological Invasions: A Global Perspective,* edited by J. A. Drake et al. SCOPE 37. New York: John Wiley & Sons, 1989.

Dimbleby, G. W. "The Legacy of Prehistoric Man." In *Conservation in Practice,* edited by A. Warren and F. B. Goldsmith. London: Wiley, 1974.

Dodge, Marvin. "Forest Fuel Accumulation—a Growing Problem." *Science* 177 (1972): 139–42.

Dottavio, F. Dominic, Peter F. Brussard, and John D. McCrone, eds. *Protecting Biological Diversity in the National Parks: Workshop Recommendations.* Transactions and Proceedings Series no. 9. Washington, D.C.: U.S. Department of the Interior, National Park Service, 1990.

Ehrard, Jean. *L'idée de nature en France dans la première moitié du XVIIIe siècle.* Geneva: Slatkine, 1981.

Ehrlich, Paul R., and Anne H. Ehrlich. *The Population Explosion.* New York: Simon & Schuster, 1990.

Ehrlich, Paul R., and Edward O. Wilson. "Biodiversity Studies: Science and Policy." *Science* 253 (1991): 758–62.

Elfring, Chris. "Yellowstone: Fire Storm over Fire Management." *Bio-Science* 39 (1989): 667–72.

Elliott, Charles. "Dead Trees & Fake Hermits." *Horticulture,* January 1994, pp. 17–22.

Elton, Charles. *Animal Ecology and Evolution.* Oxford: Clarendon Press, 1930.

Emerson, Ralph Waldo. "Thoreau." *The Atlantic,* August 1862, pp. 239–49.

Emerson, Ralph Waldo, and Henry David Thoreau. *Nature/Ralph Waldo Emerson. Walking/Henry David Thoreau.* The Concord Library. Boston: Beacon Press, 1991.

Encyclopedia of American Forest and Conservation History. 2 vols. New York: Macmillan, 1983.

Engelmann, Henry. "Remarks upon the Causes Producing the Different Characters of Vegetation Known as Prairie, Flats, and Barrens in Southern Illinois, with Special Reference to Observations Made in Perry and Jackson Counties." *American Journal of Science and Arts* 36, 2nd series (1863): 384–96.

Evernden, Neil. *The Natural Alien.* 2nd ed. Toronto: University of Toronto Press, 1993.

Fahey, T. J., and Dennis H. Knight. "Lodgepole Pine Ecosystems." *Bio-Science* 36 (1986): 610–17.

Falk, Donald A. "The Theory of Integrated Conservation Strategies for Biological Diversity." In *Ecosystem Management: Rare Species and Significant Habitats,* edited by Richard S. Mitchell, Charles J. Sheviak, and Donald J. Leopold. Proceedings of the Fifteenth Annual Natural Areas Conference. Bulletin no. 471, New York State Museum, Albany, N.Y., 1990.

Farina, A. "Bird Fauna in the Changing Agricultural Landscape." In *Landscape Ecology and Agroecosystems,* edited by R. G. H. Bunce, L. Ryzkowski, and M. G. Paoletti. Boca Raton, Fla.: Lewis Publishers, 1993.

Fiedler, Peggy L., and Jeremy J. Ahouse. "Hierarchies of Cause: Toward an Understanding of Rarity in Vascular Plant Species." In *Conservation Biology: The Theory and Practice of Nature Conservation , Preservation, and Management,* edited by Peggy L. Fiedler and Subodh K. Jain. New York: Chapman and Hall, 1992.

Filonov, Constantine. "Predator-Prey Problems in Nature Reserves of the Eastern Part of the RSFSR." *Journal of Wildlife Management* 44 (1980): 389–96.

Fitzner, Richard E., and Robert L. Newell. "Ferruginous Hawk Nesting on the U.S. DOE Hanford Site: A Recent Invasion Following Introduction of Transmission Lines." In *Issues and Technology in the Management of Impacted Wildlife: Proceedings of a National Symposium, Glenwood Springs, Col-*

orado, February 6–8, 1989, edited by Peter R. Davis, et al. Boulder, Colo.: Thorne Ecological Institute, 1989.

Fox, Matthew. *The Coming of the Cosmic Christ: The Healing of Mother Earth and the Birth of a Global Renaissance.* San Francisco: Harper & Row, 1988.

Fox, Michael W. *Inhumane Society: The American Ways of Exploiting Animals.* New York: St. Martin's Press, 1990.

Frazer, Sir James George. *The Worship of Nature.* New York: AMS Press, 1976.

Furnas, J. C. *The Americans: A Social History of the United States, 1857–1914.* New York: Putnam, 1969.

The Game Conservancy. *The Game Conservancy Review of 1990.* Edited by Charles Nodder. Fordingbridge, U.K.: The Game Conservancy, 1991.

_____. *The Game Conservancy Review of 1993.* Edited by Julian Murray-Evans. Fordingbridge, U.K.: The Game Conservancy, 1994.

Gara, R. I., et al. "Influence of Fires, Fungi, and Mountain Pine Beetles on Development of a Lodgepole Pine Forest in South-Central Oregon." In *Management of Lodgepole Pine Ecosystems,* edited by D. M. Baumgartner. Pullman: Washington State University Cooperative Extension Service, 1975.

Geis, Aeired. "Effects of Urbanization and Type of Urban Development on Bird Populations." In *A Symposium on Wildlife in an Urbanizing Environment,* edited by John H. Noyes and Donald R. Progulske. Planning and Resource Development Series no. 28, Holdsworth Natural Resources Unit. Amherst: Massachusetts Cooperative Extension Service, 1974.

General Accounting Office. *Wildlife Management: Many Issues Unresolved in Yellowstone Bison-Cattle Brucellosis Conflict.* GAO/RCED-93-2. Washington, D.C.: GPO, 1992.

Getz, Wayne M., and Robert G. Haight. *Population Harvesting: Demographic Models of Fish, Forest, and Animal Resources.* Monographs in Population Biology 27. Princeton, N.J.: Princeton University Press, 1989.

Gilpin, Michael E., and Michael E. Soulé. "Minimum Viable Populations: Processes of Species Extinction." In *Conservation Biology: The Science of Scarcity and Diversity,* edited by Michael E. Soulé. Sunderland, Mass.: Sinauer, 1986.

Gimingham, C. H. "Conservation: European Heathlands." In *Heathlands and Related Shrubs,* edited by R. L. Spect. Amsterdam: Elsevier Scientific, 1981.

Gimingham, C. H., and I. T. de Smidt. "Heaths and Natural and Semi-natural Vegetation." In *Man's Impact on Vegetation,* edited by W. Holzner, M. J. A. Werger, and I. Ikusima. The Hague: Junk, 1983.

Gleason, Henry A. "Further Views on the Succession Concept." *Ecology* 8 (1927): 299–326.

_____. "The Individualistic Concept of the Plant Association." *American Midland Naturalist* 21 (1939): 92–110.

Gleason, Henry A., and Arthur Cronquist. *The Natural Geography of Plants.* New York: Columbia University Press, 1964.

Goel, N. S., S. C. Maitra, and E. W. Montroll. *On the Volterra and Other Nonlinear Models of Interacting Populations.* Reviews of Modern Physics Monographs. New York: Academic Press, 1971.

Goldman, Eric F. *Rendezvous with Destiny.* New York: Knopf, 1953.

Goodman, Daniel. "Ecological Expertise." In *Boundaries of Analysis: An Inquiry into the Tocks Island Dam Controversy,* edited by Harold A. Feiveson et al. Cambridge, Mass.: Ballinger, 1976.

_____. "Consideration of Stochastic Demography in the Design and Maintenance of Biological Reserves." *Natural Resource Modeling* 1 (1987): 205–34.

_____. "How Do Any Species Persist?" *Conservation Biology* 1 (1987): 59–62.

_____. "The Demography of Chance Extinction." In *Viable Populations for Conservation,* edited by Michael E. Soulé. Cambridge: Cambridge University Press, 1987.

Gore, Al. *Earth in the Balance: Ecology and the Human Spirit.* Boston: Houghton Mifflin, 1992.

Goudie, Andrew. *The Human Impact: Man's Role in Environmental Change.* 3rd ed. Cambridge, Mass.: MIT Press, 1990.

Graham, Sylvester. *A Defence of the Graham System of Living.* New York: W. Applegate, 1835.

_____. *A Lecture to Young Men.* New York: Arno Press, 1974. Reprint.

Greer, David M. "Urban Waterfowl Population: Ecological Evaluation of Management and Planning." *Environmental Management* 6 (1982): 217–29.

Grizzle, Raymond E. "Environmentalism Should Include Human Ecological Needs." *BioScience* 44 (1994): 263–68.

Groppali, Riccardo. "Breeding Birds in Traditional Tree Rows and Hedges in the Central Po Valley (Province of Cremona, Northern Italy)." In *Landscape Ecology and Agroecosystems,* edited by R. G. H. Bunce, L. Ryzkowski, and M. G. Paoletti. Boca Raton, Fla.: Lewis Publishers, 1993.

Gruell, G. E., and L. L. Loope. *Relationships Among Aspen, Fire, and Ungulate Browsing in Jackson Hole, Wyoming.* U.S. Forest Service Special Publication. Jackson, Wyo.: USFS, 1974.

Hallam, Thomas G., and Simon A. Levin, eds. *Mathematical Ecology: An Introduction.* Berlin: Springer-Verlag, 1986.

Hamilton, Bruce. "An Enduring Wilderness?" *Sierra,* September/October 1994, 46–50.

Hamilton, Lawrence S. "Restoration of Degraded Tropical Forests." In *Environmental Restoration: Science and Strategies for Restoring the Earth,* edited by John Berger. Washington, D.C.: Island Press, 1990.

Haney, Alan, and Steven I. Apfelbaum. "Structure and Dynamics of Midwest Oak Savannas." In *Management of Dynamic Ecosystems,* edited by J. M. Sweeney. West Lafayette, Ind.: Wildlife Society, 1990.

———. "Characterization of Midwestern Oak Savannas." Paper presented at the Oak Savanna Conference, Northeastern Illinois University, March 3, 1993.

Harper, John L. "After Description." In *The Plant Community as a Working Mechanism,* edited by E. I. Newman. Special Publication no. 1 of the British Ecological Society. Oxford: Blackwell, 1982.

Harper, Roland M. "Changes in the Forest Area of New England in Three Centuries." *Journal of Forestry* 16 (1918): 442–52.

Hastings, Alan, and Kevin Higgins. "Persistence of Transients in Spatially Structured Ecological Models." *Science* 263 (1994): 1133–36.

Hawes, Austin F. "New England Forests in Retrospect." *Journal of Forestry* 21 (1923): 209–24.

Hester, F. Eugene. "The U.S. National Park Service Experience with Exotic Species." *Natural Areas Journal* 11, no. 3 (1991): 127–28.

Heusmann, H. W., and Richard G. Burrell. "Park Mallards." In *A Symposium on Wildlife in an Urbanizing Environment,* edited by John H. Noyes and Donald R. Progulske. Planning and Resource Development Series no. 28, Holdsworth Natural Resources Unit. Amherst: Massachusetts Cooperative Extension Service, 1974.

Heywood, Vernon H. "Patterns, Extents and Modes of Invasions by Terrestrial Plants." In *Biological Invasions: A Global Perspective,* edited by J. A. Drake et al. SCOPE Report 37. New York: John Wiley & Sons, 1989.

Heywood, Vernon H., and S. N. Stuart. "Species Extinctions in Tropical Forests." In *Tropical Deforestation and Species Extinction,* edited by T. C. Whitmore and J. A. Sayer. London: Chapman & Hall, 1992.

Heywood, Vernon H., et al. "Uncertainties in Extinction Rates." *Nature* 368 (1994): 105.

Hobbs, Richard J., and Denis A. Saunders, eds. *Reintegrating Fragmented Landscapes: Towards Sustainable Production and Nature Conservation.* New York: Springer-Verlag, 1993.

Hoffman, Cliff O., and Jack L. Gottschang. "Numbers, Distributions, and Movements of a Raccoon Population in a Suburban Residential Community." *Journal of Mammalogy* 58 (1977): 623–36.

Holland, Marjorie M., Paul G. Risser, and Robert J. Naiman, eds. *Ecotones: The Role of Landscape Boundaries in the Management and Restoration of Changing Environments.* New York: Chapman & Hall, 1991.

Holloway, Marguerite. "Nurturing Nature." *Scientific American,* April 1994, pp. 98–108.

Holm, LeRoy, et al. *The World's Worst Weeds.* Honolulu: University Press of Hawaii, 1977.

——. *A Geographical Atlas of World Weeds.* New York: John Wiley & Sons, 1979.

Houston, Douglas B. "Ecosystems of National Parks." *Science* 172 (1971): 648–51.

——. "A Comment on the History of the Northern Yellowstone Elk." *BioScience* 25 (1975): 578–79.

——. *The Northern Yellowstone Elk: Ecology and Management.* New York: Macmillan, 1982.

Hudson, Peter. *Grouse in Space and Time.* Fordingbridge, U.K.: The Game Conservancy, 1992.

Huston, Michael. "Biological Diversity, Soils, and Economics." *Science* 262 (1993): 1676–80.

Hutchinson, A. B. *The Granite Songster; Comprising the Songs of the Hutchinson Family.* New York: Charles Holt, 1847.

Inouye, David W. "Variation in Undisturbed Plant and Animal Populations and its Implications for Studies of Recovering Ecosystems." In *Rehabilitating Damaged Ecosystems,* vol. 2, edited by John Cairns, Jr. Boca Raton, Fla.: CRC Press, 1988.

Jacob, Merle. "Sustainable Development and Deep Ecology: An Analysis of Competing Traditions." *Environmental Management* 18 (1994): 477–88.

Janzen, Daniel H. *Guanacaste National Park: Tropical Ecological and Cultural Restoration.* San José, Costa Rica: Editorial Universidad Estatal a Distancia, 1986.

Johnson, Edward A. *Fire and Vegetation Dynamics: Studies from the North American Boreal Forest.* Cambridge: Cambridge University Press, 1992.

Johnson, Hugh. *The Principles of Gardening.* New York: Simon & Schuster, 1979.

Jordan, William R., III. "Restoration and the Dilemma of Human Use." *Restoration and Management Notes* 4 (1986): 50.

——. "Just a Few Oddball Species: Restoration Practice and Ecological Theory." In *Biological Habitat Reconstruction,* edited by G. P. Buckley. London: Belhaven Press, 1989.

——. "Restoration: Shaping the Land, Transforming the Human Spirit." In *Helping Nature Heal,* edited by Richard Nilsen. Berkeley, Calif.: Ten Speed Press, 1991.

——. " 'Sunflower Forest': Ecological Restoration as the Basis for a New Environmental Paradigm." In *Beyond Preservation: Restoring and Inventing Landscapes,* edited by A. Dwight Baldwin, Judith de Luce, and Carl Pletsch. Minneapolis: University of Minnesota Press, 1993.

Jordan, William R., III, Michael E. Gilpin, and John D. Aber, eds. *Restoration Ecology: A Synthetic Approach to Ecological Research.* Cambridge: Cambridge University Press, 1987.

Jorgensen, Neil. *A Guide to New England's Landscape.* Chester, Conn.: Globe Pequot Press, 1977.

Kalkhoven, J. T. R. "Survival of Populations and the Scale of the Fragmented Agricultural Landscape." In *Landscape Ecology and Agroecosystems,* edited by R. G. H. Bunce, L. Ryzkowski, and M. G. Paoletti. Boca Raton, Fla.: Lewis Publishers, 1993.

Karr, James R., and Kathryn E. Freemark. "Disturbance and Vertebrates: An Integrative Perspective." In *The Ecology of Natural Disturbance and Patch Dynamics,* edited by S. T. A. Pickett and P. S. White. Orlando, Fla.: Academic Press, 1985.

Katz, Eric. "The Call of the Wild: The Struggle Against Domination and the Technological Fix of Nature." *Environmental Ethics* 14, no. 3 (1992): 265–73.

Kaufman, Wallace. "How Nature Really Works." *American Forests,* March 1993.

Kay, Charles E. "Too Many Elk in Yellowstone?" Review of *Wildlife in Transition: Man and Nature on Yellowstone's Northern Range,* by Don Despain et al. *Western Wildlands,* Fall 1987, 39–44.

_____. "Yellowstone's Northern Elk Herd: A Critical Evaluation of the 'Natural Regulation' Paradigm." Ph.D. diss., Utah State University, 1990.

_____. "An Alternative Interpretation of the Historical Evidence Relating to the Abundance of Wolves in the Yellowstone Ecosystem." Paper presented at Second North American Symposium on Wolves: Their Status, Biology, and Management. University of Alberta, Edmonton, August 25–27, 1992.

_____. "Aboriginal Overkill: The Role of Native Americans in Structuring Western Ecosystems." *Human Nature* 5 (1994): 359–98.

Keiter, Robert B., and Mark S. Boyce, eds. *The Greater Yellowstone Ecosystem.* New Haven: Yale University Press, 1991.

King, Lawrence J. *Weeds of the World: Biology and Control.* New York: Interscience, 1966.

Knight, Dennis H. "Parasites, Lightning, and the Vegetation Mosaic in Wilderness Landscapes." In *Landscape Heterogeneity and Disturbance,* edited by Monica Goigel Turner. New York: Springer-Verlag, 1987.

Knight, Dennis. H., and Linda. L. Wallace. "The Yellowstone Fires: Issues in Landscape Ecology." *BioScience* 39 (1989): 700–706.

Lambert, Thomas, and Robert J. Smith. *The Endangered Species Act: Time for a Change.* Center for the Study of American Business Policy Study 119. St. Louis: Washington University, 1994.

Lande, Russell. "Genetics and Demography in Biological Conservation." *Science* 241 (1988): 1455–60.

Lande, Russell, Steinar Engen, and Bernt-Erik Saether. "Optimal Harvesting, Economic Discounting and Extinction Risk in Fluctuating Populations." *Nature* 372 (1994): 88–90.

Latshaw, Rick. "Native Warm Season Grasses." *Frederick County (Md.) Forest Conservancy District Board Newsletter,* April 1994, pp. 2–3.

Lemon, Paul C. "Effects of Fire on an African Plateau Grassland." *Ecology* 49 (1968): 316–22.

Leopold, Aldo. *Game Management.* New York: Charles Scribner's Sons, 1933.

———. *A Sand County Almanac.* New York: Oxford University Press, 1949.

———. *The River of the Mother of God and Other Essays.* Madison: University of Wisconsin Press, 1991.

Leopold, Aldo, et al. "A Survey of Overpopulated Deer Ranges in the United States." *Journal of Wildlife Management* 11 (1947): 162–77.

Leopold, A. Starker, et al. "Wildlife Management in the National Parks." *Transactions of the North American Wildlife and Natural Resources Conference* 28 (1963): 28–45.

Lewis, M. A., and J. D. Murray. "Modelling Territoriality and Wolf-Deer Interactions." *Nature* 366 (1993): 738–40.

Lewis, Merriwether, and William Clark. *The Journals of Lewis and Clark.* Edited by Frank Bergon. New York: Penguin Books, 1989.

Lister-Kaye, John. "Securing a Future for the Highlands." *The Field,* June 1994, 68–72.

Little, Silas. "Effects of Fire on Temperate Forests: Northeastern United States." In *Fire and Ecosystems,* edited by T. T. Kozlowski and C. E. Ahlgren. New York: Academic Press, 1974.

Loope, L. L., and G. E. Gruell. "The Ecological Role of Fire in the Jackson Hole Area, Northwestern Wyoming." *Quaternary Research* 3 (1973): 425–443.

Lorimer, Craig G. "The Presettlement Forest and Natural Disturbance Cycle of Northeastern Maine." *Ecology* 58 (1977): 139–48.

Loucks, O. L. "Evolution of Diversity, Efficiency, and Community Stability," *American Zoologist* 10 (1970): 17–25.

Lowe, Philip, and Jane Goyder. *Environmental Groups in Politics.* The Resource Management Series 6. London: Allen & Unwin, 1983.

Lubchenco, J., et al. "The Sustainable Biosphere Initiative: An Ecological Research Agenda." *Ecology* 72 (1991): 371–412.

Ludwig, Donald, Ray Hilborn, and Carl Walters. "Uncertainty, Resource Exploitation, and Conservation: Lessons from History." *Science* 260 (1993): 17–36.

Lussenhop, John. "Urban Cemeteries as Bird Refuges." *Condor* 79 (1978): 456–61.

McDade, Lucinda, et al., eds. *La Selva: Ecology and Natural History of a Neotropical Rainforest.* Chicago: University of Chicago Press, 1994.

Macdonald, Ian A. W., et al. "Wildlife Conservation and the Invasion of Nature Reserves by Introduced Species: A Global Perspective." In *Biological Invasions: A Global Perspective,* edited by J. A. Drake et al. SCOPE Report 37. New York: John Wiley and Sons, 1989.

McIntosh, R. P. *The Background of Ecology.* Cambridge: Cambridge University Press, 1985.

Mack, Richard N. "Temperate Grasslands Vulnerable to Plant Invasions: Characteristics and Consequences." In *Biological Invasions: A Global Perspective,* edited by J. A. Drake et al. SCOPE Report 37. New York: John Wiley & Sons, 1989.

McKibben, Bill. "Reflections: The End of Nature." *New Yorker,* September 11, 1989, pp. 47–105.

McLaughlin, Christopher. "Ecosystem Management in Rondeau Provincial Park." *Alternatives* 19, no. 4 (1993): 6–7.

McNab, J. "Wildlife Management as Scientific Experimentation." *Wildlife Society Bulletin* 11 (1983): 397–401.

McNeilly, Tom. "Evolutionary Lessons from Degraded Ecosystems." In *Restoration Ecology: A Synthetic Approach to Ecological Research,* edited by William R. Jordan III, Michael E. Gilpin, and John D. Aber. Cambridge: Cambridge University Press, 1987.

Maguire, Lynn A. "Using Decision Analysis to Manage Endangered Species Populations." *Journal of Environmental Management* 22 (1986): 345–60.

Mann, Charles C. "Extinction: Are Ecologists Crying Wolf?" *Science* 253 (1991): 736–38.

Mann, Charles C., and Mark L. Plummer. "The Butterfly Problem." *Atlantic,* January 1992, pp. 47–70.

———. *Noah's Choice: The Future of Endangered Species.* New York: Knopf, 1995.

Mannix, Brian. "The Origin of Endangered Species and the Descent of Man (with Apologies to Mr. Darwin)." *American Enterprise,* November-December 1992, pp. 57–63.

Mardon, Mark. Review of *Wilderness Ethics: Preserving the Spirit of Wilderness,* by Laura and Guy Waterman. *Sierra,* November/December 1993, p. 106.

Martin, Calvin. "Fire and Forest Structure in the Aboriginal Eastern Forest." *Indian Historian* 6, no. 4 (1973): 38–42, 54.

Maryland Cooperative Extension Service. "Deer in Our Forests." *Branching Out,* Spring 1994, pp. 1–2.

Massachusetts Society for the Prevention of Cruelty to Animals. *Animals, People, and the MSPCA: 125 Years of Progress.* Boston: MSPCA, 1993.

Maxwell, Hu. "The Use and Abuse of Forests by the Virginia Indians." *William and Mary Quarterly* 19, 1st series (October 1910): 73–104.

May, Robert M. *Stability and Complexity in Model Ecosystems.* Princeton, N.J.: Princeton University Press, 1973.

_____. "Biological Populations with Nonoverlapping Generations: Stable Points, Stable Cycles and Chaos." *Science* 186 (1974): 645–47.

_____. "Simple Mathematical Models with Very Complicated Dynamics." *Nature* 261 (1976): 459–67.

_____. "How Many Species Inhabit the Earth?" *Scientific American,* October 1992, pp. 42–48.

_____. "The Economics of Extinction." *Nature* 372 (1994): 42–43.

May, Robert M., ed. *Theoretical Ecology: Principles and Applications.* 2nd ed. Oxford: Blackwell Scientific, 1981.

May, R. M., and R. M. Anderson. "Regulation and Stability of Host-Parasite Population Interactions. II. Destabilising Processes." *Journal of Animal Ecology* 47 (1978): 249–67.

May, Robert M., and Jon Seeger. "Ideas in Ecology." *American Scientist* 74 (1986): 256–67.

Mech, L. David. "How Delicate Is the Balance of Nature?" *National Wildlife,* February-March 1985, pp. 54–58.

Mech, L. David, Thomas J. Meier, and John W. Burch. "Denali Park Wolf Studies: Implications for Yellowstone." *Transactions of the North American Wildlife and Natural Resources Conference* 56 (1991): 86–90.

Merchant, Carolyn. *The Death of Nature: Women, Ecology, and the Scientific Revolution.* New York: Harper & Row, 1989.

_____. *Ecological Revolutions: Nature, Gender, and Science in New England.* Chapel Hill: University of North Carolina Press, 1989.

Miller, G. R., and A. Watson. "Heather Moorland: A Man-made Ecosystem." In *Conservation in Practice,* edited by A. Warren and F. B. Goldsmith. London: Wiley, 1974.

Miller, Ralph N. "American Nationalism as a Theory of Nature." *William & Mary Quarterly* 12, 3rd series (1955): 74–95.

Miller, Susan A. "Promoting Ecological Awareness." *Childhood Education,* Annual Theme Issue 1992: 330–31.

Mlot, Christine. "Isle Royale: End of an Era?" *Science* 261 (1993): 1115.

Moffat, Anne Simon. "Theoretical Ecology: Winning Its Spurs in the Real World." *Science* 263 (1994): 1090–92.

Mooney, H. A., and J. A. Drake. "Biological Invasions: A SCOPE Program Overview." In *Biological Invasions: A Global Perspective,* edited by J. A. Drake et al. SCOPE Report 37. New York: John Wiley & Sons, 1989.

Mooney, Harold A., et al., eds. *Ecosystem Experiments.* SCOPE Report 45. New York: John Wiley & Sons, 1991.

Morton, Eugene S. "Reintroduction as a Method of Studying Bird Behavior and Ecology." In *Restoration Ecology: A Synthetic Approach to Ecological Research,* edited by William R. Jordan III, Michael E. Gilpin, and John D. Aber. Cambridge: Cambridge University Press, 1987.

Mowat, Farley. *Rescue the Earth! Conversations with the Green Crusaders.* Toronto: McClelland & Stewart, 1990.

Muir, John. *The Mountains of California.* New York: The Century Co., 1911.

_____. *A Thousand-Mile Walk to the Gulf.* Boston: Houghton Mifflin, 1916.

_____. *The Story of My Boyhood and Youth.* Madison: University of Wisconsin Press, 1965.

Murray, Mary. "The Little Green Lie." *Reader's Digest,* July 1993, pp. 100–104.

Murray, William H. H. *Words Fitly Spoken.* Boston: Lee and Shepard, 1872.

_____. *Adventures in the Wilderness.* Syracuse: Syracuse University Press, 1970. Reprint.

Nash, Roderick. *Wilderness and the American Mind.* 3rd ed. New Haven: Yale University Press, 1982.

National Park Service and USDA Soil Conservation Service. *Native Plants for Parks.* D-425. Washington, D.C.: GPO, 1989.

National Research Council. *Wild and Free-Roaming Horses and Burros: Final Report.* Washington, D.C.: National Academy Press, 1982.

_____. *Science and the National Parks.* Washington, D.C.: National Academy Press, 1992.

National Science Foundation. "NSF Funds Research on Ecological Consequences of Hurricane Andrew." Press Release NSF PR 93–6, January 12, 1993.

Naveh, Zev. *Landscape Ecology: Theory and Application.* 2nd ed. New York: Springer-Verlag, 1993.

Nilsen, Richard, ed. *Helping Nature Heal.* Berkeley, Calif.: Ten Speed Press, 1991.

"NPCA Adjacent Lands Survey: No Park Is an Island." *National Parks and Conservation Magazine,* March-April 1979.

Nuzzo, Victoria A. "Extent and Status of Midwest Oak Savanna: Presettlement and 1985." *Natural Areas Journal* 6, no. 2 (1986): 6–36.

Oates, David. *Earth Rising: Ecological Belief in an Age of Science.* Corvallis: Oregon State University Press, 1989.

Oelschlaeger, Max. *The Idea of Wilderness: From Prehistory to the Age of Ecology.* New Haven: Yale University Press, 1991.

Packard, Stephen. "Just a Few Oddball Species: Restoration and the Rediscovery of the Tallgrass Savanna." In *Helping Nature Heal,* edited by Richard Nilsen. Berkeley, Calif.: Ten Speed Press, 1991.

———. "Rediscovering the Tallgrass Savanna of Illinois." In *Proceedings of the Oak Woods Management Workshop,* edited by George V. Burger, John E. Ebinger, and Gerould S. Wilhelm. Charleston.: Eastern Illinois University, 1991.

Paine, R. T. "Food Web Complexity and Species Diversity." *American Naturalist* 100 (1966): 65–74.

Paquet, Paul C. "Winter Spatial Relationships of Wolves and Coyotes in Riding Mountain National Park, Manitoba." *Journal of Mammalogy* 72 (1992): 397–401.

Pennisi, Elizabeth. "Conservation's Ecocentrics." *Science News* 144 (1993): 168–70.

———. "Filling in the Gaps: Computer Mapping Finds Unprotected Species." *Science News* 144 (1993): 248–51.

Perry, David A., and Michael P. Amaranthus. "The Plant-Soil Bootstrap: Microorganisms and Reclamation of Degraded Ecosystems." In *Environmental Restoration: Science and Strategies for Restoring the Earth,* edited by John Berger. Washington, D.C.: Island Press, 1990.

Peterson, Rolf O. *Ecological Studies of Wolves on Isle Royale: Annual Report 1991–1992.* Houghton: Michigan Technological University, School of Forestry and Wood Products, 1992.

Pickett, S. T. A., and J. N. Thompson. "Patch Dynamics and the Design of Nature Reserves." *Biological Conservation* 13 (1978): 27–37.

Pickett, S. T. A., and P. S. White, eds. *The Ecology of Natural Disturbance and Patch Dynamics.* Orlando, Fla.: Academic Press, 1985.

Pickett, Stewart T. A., V. Thomas Parker, and Peggy L. Fiedler. "The New Paradigm in Ecology: Implications of Conservation Above the Species Level." In *Conservation Biology: The Theory and Practice of Nature Conservation , Preservation, and Management,* edited by Peggy L. Fiedler and Subodh K. Jain. New York: Chapman & Hall, 1992.

Pielou, E. C. *After the Ice Age: The Return of Life to Glaciated North America.* Chicago: University of Chicago Press, 1991.

Pierpont, Jon. *Cold Water Melodies.* Boston: Theodore Abbot, 1842.

Pimm, Stuart L. *The Balance of Nature? Ecological Issues in the Conservation of Species and Communities.* Chicago: University of Chicago Press, 1992.

Pinchot, Gifford. *Breaking New Ground.* New York: Harcourt, Brace, 1947.

———. *The Fight for Conservation.* Seattle: University of Washington Press, 1967.

Pollan, Michael. *Second Nature.* New York: Atlantic Monthly Press, 1991.

Pollard, E., et al. *Hedges.* The New Naturalist Series. New York: Taplinger, 1975; London: Collins, 1974.

Poole, Robert W. *An Introduction to Quantitative Ecology*. New York: Mc-Graw-Hill, 1974.

Porter, Roy. "Field of Dreams." Review of *The Wealth of Nature: Ecological History and Ecological Imagination*, by Donald Worster. *New Republic*, July 5, 1993, pp. 33–36.

Prendergast, J. R., et al. "Rare Species, the Coincidence of Diversity Hotspots and Conservation Strategies." *Nature* 365 (1993): 335–37.

Pyne, Stephen J. *Fire in America: A Cultural History of Wildland and Rural Fire*. Princeton, N.J.: Princeton University Press, 1982.

Rees, Ronald. "The Taste for Mountain Scenery." *History Today* 25 (1975): 305–12.

Reice, Seth R. "Nonequilibrium Determinants of Biological Community Structure." *American Scientist* 82 (1994): 424–35.

Remillard, Marguerite Madden, et al. "Disturbance by Beaver (*Castor canadensis* Kuhl) and Increased Landscape Heterogeneity." In *Landscape Heterogeneity and Disturbance*, edited by Monica Goigel Turner. New York: Springer-Verlag, 1987.

Reuther, Rosemary Radford. *Sexism and God-Talk: Toward a Feminist Theology*. Boston: Beacon Press, 1983.

Ridley, Matt. "Grouse for Better or Worse." *Country Life*, July 30, 1992, pp. 34–35.

Roberts, Leslie. "Hard Choices Ahead for Biodiversity." *Science* 241 (1988): 1759–61.

_____. "Bringing Vanished Ecosystems Back to Life." *Science* 260 (1993): 1891.

_____. "Wetlands Trading Is a Loser's Game, Say Ecologists." *Science* 260 (1993): 1890–92.

Robinson, William L., and Eric G. Bolen. *Wildlife Ecology and Management*. New York: Macmillan, 1984.

Rodiek, Jon E., and Eric G. Bolen, eds. *Wildlife and Habitats in Managed Landscapes*. Washington, D.C.: Island Press, 1991.

Rohlf, Daniel J. "Six Biological Reasons the Endangered Species Act Doesn't Work—and What to Do About It." *Conservation Biology* 5 (1991): 273–82.

Romans, Robert C., ed. *Geobotany II*. Proceedings of the Geobotany Conference, held March 1, 1980. New York: Plenum, 1981.

Romme, William H. "Fire and Landscape Diversity in Subalpine Forests of Yellowstone National Park." *Ecological Monographs* 52 (1982): 199–221.

Romme, William H., and Don G. Despain, "Historical Perspective on the Yellowstone Fires of 1988." *BioScience* 39 (1989): 695–99.

Rosenthal, Michael. *The Character Factory: Baden-Powell's Boy Scouts and the Imperatives of Empire*. New York: Pantheon, 1986.

Rosenzweig, Michael L. "Restoration Ecology: A Tool to Study Population Interactions?" In *Restoration Ecology*, edited by William R. Jordan III, Michael E. Gilpin, and John D. Aber. Cambridge: Cambridge University Press, 1987.

Roszak, Theodore. "Beyond the Reality Principle." *Sierra*, March-April 1993.

————. *The Voice of the Earth: An Exploration of Ecopsychology.* New York: Touchstone, 1993.

Roughgarden, Jonathan, Robert M. May, and Simon A. Levin, eds. *Perspectives in Ecological Theory.* Princeton, N.J.: Princeton University Press, 1989.

Rummel, J., and Jonathan Roughgarden. "Some Differences Between Invasion-Structured and Coevolution-Structured Competitive Communities: A Preliminary Theoretical Analysis." *Oikos* 41 (1983): 477–86.

Runkle, James R. "Disturbance Regimes in Temperate Forests." In *The Ecology of Natural Disturbance and Patch Dynamics*, edited by S. T. A. Pickett and P. S. White. Orlando, Fla.: Academic Press, 1985.

Runte, Alfred. *Public Lands, Public Heritage: The National Forest Idea.* Niwot, Colo.: R. Rinehart, in cooperation with the Buffalo Bill Historical Center, 1991.

Russell, Emily W. B. "Indian-set Fires in the Forests of the Northeastern United States." *Ecology* 64 (1983): 78–88.

Russell, Howard S. *A Long Deep Furrow: Three Centuries of Farming in New England.* Hanover, N.H.: Dartmouth University Press, 1976.

Sauer, Carl O. "The Agency of Man on the Earth." In *Man's Role in Changing the Face of the Earth*, edited by William L. Thomas. Chicago: University of Chicago Press, 1956.

————. *Agricultural Origins and Dispersals.* 2nd ed. Cambridge, Mass.: MIT Press, 1969.

Schullery, Paul. "The Fires and Fire Policy." *BioScience* 39 (1989): 686–94.

Scott, Jane. *Field and Forest: A Guide to Native Landscapes for Gardeners and Naturalists.* New York: Walker, 1992.

Scott, J. Michael, et al. "Gap Analysis: A Geographical Approach to Protection of Biological Diversity." *Wildlife Monographs* 123 (1993): 1–41.

Sedjo, Roger A. *The World's Forests: Conflicting Signals.* Washington, D.C.: Competitive Enterprise Institute, February 1995.

Seegmiller, Rick F., and Robert D. Ohmart. *Ecological Relationships of Feral Burros and Desert Bighorn Sheep.* Supplement to the *Journal of Wildlife Management.* Washington, D.C.: Wildlife Society, 1981.

Seton, Ernest Thompson. *The Birch Bark Roll of Woodcraft.* 20th ed. New York: Brieger Press, 1925.

Shaffer, Mark L. "Minimum Population Sizes for Species Conservation." *BioScience* 31 (1981): 131–34.

———. "Determining Minimum Viable Population Sizes for the Grizzly Bear." *International Conference on Bear Research and Management* 5 (1983): 133–39.

———. "Minimum Viable Populations: Coping with Uncertainty." In *Viable Populations for Conservation,* edited by Michael E. Soulé. Cambridge: Cambridge University Press, 1987.

———. "Population Viability Analysis." *Conservation Biology* 4 (1990): 39–40.

———. *Beyond the Endangered Species Act: Conservation in the 21st Century.* Washington, D.C.: Wilderness Society, 1992.

———. *Keeping the Grizzly Bear in the American West: A Strategy for Real Recovery.* Washington, D.C.: Wilderness Society, 1992.

Sheail, John. "The Legacy of Historical Times." In *Conservation in Practice,* edited by A. Warren and F. B. Goldsmith. London: Wiley, 1974.

Simberloff, Daniel. "Reconstructing the Ambiguous: Can Island Ecosystems be Restored?" In *Ecological Restoration of New Zealand Islands,* edited by D. R. Towns, C. H. Daugherty, and I. A. E. Atkinson. Papers presented at Conference on Ecological Restoration of New Zealand Islands, University of Auckland, 20–24 November 1989. Conservation Sciences Publication no. 2. Wellington, New Zealand: Department of Conservation, 1990.

———. "Do Species-Area Curves Predict Extinction in Fragmented Forest?" In *Tropical Deforestation and Species Extinction,* edited by T. C. Whitmore and J. A. Sayer. London: Chapman & Hall, 1992.

Singer, Francis J., et al. "Drought, Fires and Large Mammals." *BioScience* 39 (1989): 716–22.

Singer, Peter. *Animal Liberation.* 2nd ed. New York: New York Review, 1990.

Soulé, Michael E. "What Is Conservation Biology?" *BioScience* 35 (1985): 727–34.

———. "Conservation: Tactics for a Constant Crisis." *Science* 253 (1991): 744–50.

———. "Land Use Planning and Wildlife Maintenance: Guidelines for Conserving Wildlife in Urban Landscape." *APA Journal* 57 (1991): 313–23.

———, ed. *Conservation Biology: Science of Scarcity and Diversity.* Sunderland, Mass.: Sinauer, 1986.

———, ed. *Viable Populations for Conservation.* Cambridge: Cambridge University Press, 1987.

Soulé, Michael E., and Daniel Simberloff. "What Do Genetics and Ecology Tell Us About the Design of Nature Reserves?" *Biological Conservation* 35 (1986): 19–40.

Soulé, Michael E., and B. Wilcox, eds. *Conservation Biology. An Evolutionary-Ecological Perspective.* Sunderland, Mass.: Sinauer, 1980.

Sousa, Wayne P. "Intertidal Disturbance and Patch Dynamics." In *The Ecology of Natural Disturbance and Patch Dynamics,* edited by S. T. A. Pickett and P. S. White. Orlando, Fla.: Academic Press, 1985.

Spurr, Stephen H., and Burton V. Barnes. *Forest Ecology.* 3rd ed. New York: Wiley, 1980.

Steadman, David W., and Storrs L. Olson. "Bird Remains from an Archeological Site on Henderson Island, South Pacific: Man-Caused Extinctions on an 'Uninhabited Island.'" *Proceedings of the National Academy of Science* 82 (1985): 6191.

Stevenson, Robert L. "Henry David Thoreau: His Character and Opinions." *Cornhill Magazine* 41 (June 1880): 665–82.

Stewart, Omer C. "Fire as the First Great Force Employed by Man." In *Man's Role in Changing the Face of the Earth,* edited by William L. Thomas. Chicago: University of Chicago Press, 1956.

Stone, Lewi. "Period-doubling Reversals and Chaos in Simple Ecological Models." *Nature* 365 (1993): 617–20.

Stritch, Lawrence R. "Landscape-scale Restoration of Barrens-Woodland Within the Oak-Hickory Forest Mosaic." *Restoration & Management Notes* 8 (1990): 73–77.

Strong, W. E. *A Trip to the Yellowstone National Park in July, August, and September, 1875.* Norman: University of Oklahoma Press, 1968.

Sullivan, Arthur L., and Mark L. Shaffer. "Biogeography of the Megazoo." *Science* 189 (1975): 13–17.

Sweeney, James M., ed. *Management of Dynamic Ecosystems.* West Lafayette, Ind.: Wildlife Society, North Central Section, 1990.

Tansley, Arthur G. "The Use and Abuse of Vegetational Concepts and Terms." *Ecology* 16 (1935): 292.

_____. "Frederic Edward Clements." *Journal of Ecology* 34 (1946): 194–96.

Taubes, Gary. "A Dubious Battle to Save the Kemp's Ridley Sea Turtle." *Science* 256 (1992): 614–16.

Taylor, D. L. "Some Ecological Implications of Forest Fire Control in Yellowstone National Park, Wyoming." *Ecology* 54 (1973): 1394–96.

_____. "Forest Fires in Yellowstone National Park." *Journal of Forest History* 18 (1974): 69–77.

Taylor, Duncan M. "Disagreeing on the Basics: Environmental Debates Reflect Competing World Views." *Alternatives* 18, no. 3 (1992): 26–33.

Thirsk, Joan, ed. *The Agrarian History of England and Wales.* Vol. 4, *1540–1640.* London: Cambridge University Press, 1967.

Thomas, Jack Ward, and Ronald A. Dixon. "Cemetery Ecology." In *A Symposium on Wildlife in an Urbanizing Environment,* edited by John H. Noyes and Donald R. Progulske. Planning and Resource Development Series no. 28, Holdsworth Natural Resources Unit. Amherst: Massachusetts Cooperative Extension Service, 1974.

Thomas, William L., ed. *Man's Role in Changing the Face of the Earth.* Chicago: University of Chicago Press, 1956.

Thompson, Daniel Q., and Ralph H. Smith. "The Forest Primeval in the Northeast—a Great Myth?" *Proceedings of the Annual Tall Timbers Fire Ecology Conference* 10 (1970): 255–65.

Thompson, Janette R. *Prairies, Forests, and Wetlands: The Restoration of Natural Landscape Communities in Iowa.* Iowa City: University of Iowa Press, 1992.

Thomson, Betty Flanders. *The Changing Face of New England.* New York: Macmillan, 1958.

Thoreau, Henry David. *A Week on the Concord and Merrimack Rivers; Walden; The Maine Woods; Cape Cod.* Edited by Robert F. Sayre. New York: Library of America, 1985.

Tobey, Ronald C. *Saving the Prairies: The Life Cycle of the Founding School of American Plant Ecology, 1895–1955.* Berkeley: University of California Press, 1981.

Towns, D. R., C. H. Daugherty, and I. A. E. Atkinson, eds. *Ecological Restoration of New Zealand Islands.* Papers presented at Conference on Ecological Restoration of New Zealand Islands, University of Auckland, 20–24 November 1989. Conservation Sciences Publication no. 2. Wellington: Department of Conservation, 1990.

U.S. Congress. Office of Technology Assessment. *Harmful Non-Indigenous Species in the United States.* OTA-F-566. Washington, D.C.: GPO, 1993.

———. Senate. Committee on Appropriations. *Control of Elk Population, Yellowstone National Park: Hearing Before a Subcommittee of the Committee on Appropriations. Ninetieth Congress. First Session.* Washington, D.C., 1967.

———. Subcommittee on Agriculture, Rural Development, and Related Agencies. *World Food Production: Hearing Before a Subcommittee of the Committee on Appropriations. United States Senate. One Hundred Third Congress. Second Session.* Senate Hearing 103–487. Washington, D.C., 1994.

———. Subcommittee on the Department of the Interior and Related Agencies. *Wild Horses and Burros: Hearing Before a Subcommittee of the Committee on Appropriations. United States Senate. One Hundred Second Congress. First Session.* Senate Hearing 101–167. Washington, D.C., 1991.

U.S. Department of the Interior. Bureau of Land Management. *Vegetation Diversity Project: A Research and Demonstration Program Plan. Restoration and Management of Native Plant Diversity on Deteriorated Rangelands. Great Basin and Columbia Plateau.* Portland, Oreg.: BLM, 1990.

U.S. Fish and Wildlife Service. *A Summary of the Northern Rocky Mountain*

Wolf Recovery Plan. Rockville, Md.: Fish and Wildlife Reference Service, 1987.

_____. *Endangered Species Act of 1973, As Amended Through the 100th Congress.* Washington, D.C.: GPO, 1988.

_____. *Endangered and Threatened Wildlife and Plants. August 23, 1993.* Washington, D.C.: GPO, 1993.

U.S. Forest Service. *Highlights in the History of Forest Conservation.* Washington, D.C.: GPO, 1976.

_____. Intermountain Research Station. *Fire's Effects on Wildlife Habitat. Symposium proceedings: Missoula, Montana, March 21, 1984.* Compiled by James E. Lotan and James K. Brown. Ogden, Utah: USFS, 1985.

_____. *The Role of Fire in Wilderness: A State-of-Knowledge Review,* by B. M. Kilgore. General Technical Report INT-82. Ogden, Utah: USFS, 1985.

Usher, Michael B. "Biological Invasions of Nature Reserves: A Search for Generalisations." *Biological Conservation* 44 (1988): 119–35.

Van Ballenberghe, V. *Effects of Predation on Moose Numbers: A Review of Recent North American Studies.* Swedish Wildlife Research Supplement 1. Stockholm: Swedish National Environmental Protection Board, 1987.

VanDruff, L. W. "Urban Wildlife—Neglected Resource." In *Wildlife Conservation: Principles and Practice,* edited by R. Teague and E. Decker. Washington, D.C.: Wilderness Society, 1979.

Veblen, Thomas T. "Stand Dynamics in Chilean *Nothofagus* Forests." In *The Ecology of Natural Disturbance and Patch Dynamics,* edited by S. T. A. Pickett and P. S. White. Orlando, Fla.: Academic Press, 1985.

Vogl, Richard J. "Effects of Fire on Grasslands." In *Fire and Ecosystems,* edited by T. T. Kozlowski and C. E. Ahlgren. New York: Academic Press, 1974.

Wagner, Frederic G., and Charles E. Kay. " 'Natural' or 'Healthy' Ecosystems: Are U.S. National Parks Providing Them?" In *Humans as Components of Ecosystems,* edited by Mark J. McDonnell and Stewart T. A. Pickett. New York: Springer-Verlag, 1993.

Wali, Mohan K., ed. *Ecosystem Rehabilitation.* 2 vols. The Hague: SPB, 1992.

Watts, May Theilgaard. *Reading the Landscape.* New York: Macmillan, 1957.

Weatherford, Jack. *Native Roots: How the Indians Enriched America.* New York: Crown, 1991.

Webb, Thompson, III. "The Past 11,000 Years of Vegetational Change in Eastern North America." *BioScience* 31 (1981): 501–6.

Westman, Walter E. "Managing for Biodiversity." *BioScience* 40 (1990): 26–33.

Wheeler, William Morton. *Essays in Philosophical Biology.* New York: Russell & Russell, 1967.

White, Lynn, Jr. "The Historical Roots of Our Ecologic Crisis." *Science* 155 (1967): 1203–7.

White, Peter S., and Susan P. Bratton. "After Preservation: Philosophical and Practical Problems of Change." *Biological Conservation* 18 (1980): 241–55.

Whittaker, Robert H. "Gradient Analysis of Vegetation." *Biological Reviews* 42 (1967): 207–64.

_____. *Communities and Ecosystems.* New York: Macmillan, 1970.

Wiens, John A. "Vertebrate Responses to Environmental Patchiness in Arid and Semiarid Systems." In *The Ecology of Natural Disturbance and Patch Dynamics,* edited by S. T. A. Pickett and P. S. White. Orlando, Fla.: Academic Press, 1985.

Williams, Ted. "Waiting for Wolves to Howl in Yellowstone." *Audubon,* November 1990, pp. 32–41.

Williamson, Lonnie. "Balancing Act." *Outdoor Life,* October 1993, pp. 26–28.

Wilson, Edward O. *The Diversity of Life.* Cambridge: Harvard University Press, 1991.

_____. "Toward Renewed Reverence for Life." *Technology Review,* November-December 1992, pp. 72–73.

Wilson, Edward O., and William H. Bossert. *A Primer of Population Biology.* Stamford, Conn.: Sinauer, 1971.

Wilson, Paul S. "What Chief Seattle Said." *Environmental Law* 22 (1992): 1451–68.

Worster, Donald. *Nature's Economy: A History of Ecological Ideas.* New York: Cambridge University Press, 1977.

_____. *The Ends of the Earth: Perspectives on Modern Environmental History.* New York: Cambridge University Press, 1988.

_____. *The Wealth of Nature: Environmental History and Ecological Imagination.* New York: Oxford University Press, 1993.

Worster, Donald, ed. *American Environmentalism: The Formative Period, 1860–1915.* New York: Wiley, 1973.

Wright, Henry A., and Arthur W. Bailey. *Fire Ecology, United States and Southern Canada.* New York: John Wiley & Sons, 1982.

Wright, H. E., Jr. "Landscape Development, Forest Fires, and Wilderness Management." *Science* 186 (1974): 487–95.

Wright, R. Gerald. *Wildlife Research and Management in the National Parks.* Urbana: University of Illinois Press, 1992.

Yellowstone National Park. *Wolves for Yellowstone: A Report to the United States Congress.* Vols. II and IV, *Research & Analysis.* Yellowstone National Park, Wyo., 1990, 1992.

_____. "Yellowstone Wolf Answers—a Second Digest." Yellowstone National Park, Wyo., 1992.

ACKNOWLEDGMENTS

As always, I am indebted to the many scientists who have provided me with articles, books, leads, patient answers to questions, and the occasional much-needed admonition. A science writer tries to be the perfect parasite, diverting just enough sustenance from its host to survive without doing any lasting damage in the process; but in the end a leech is still a leech. Uglier parasitical metaphors come to mind, too.

I would especially like to thank Peter Hudson and his family for their very kind hospitality during my visit to the Game Conservancy's Upland Research Group in the Highlands of Scotland.

John Blodgett, Martha Polkey, and Kenneth Rosenbaum read the manuscript and offered many helpful comments. I am grateful to John Walcott, Michael Ruby, and Merrill McLoughlin of *U.S. News & World Report* for their support and indulgence of this project and to the Library of Congress for the use of its research facilities.

INDEX